# Beyond Diversity Day

## A Q&A on Gay and Lesbian Issues in Schools

ARTHUR LIPKIN

ROWMAN AND LITTLEFIELD PUBLISHERS, INC.

*Lanham • Boulder • New York • Toronto • Oxford*

ROWMAN & LITTLEFIELD PUBLISHERS, INC.

Published in the United States of America
by Rowman & Littlefield Publishers, Inc.
A wholly owned subsidary of The Rowman & Littlefield Publishing Group
4501 Forbes Boulevard, Suite 200, Lanham, Maryland 20706
www.rowmanlittlefield.com

P.O. Box 317, Oxford OX2 9RU, United Kingdom

British Library Cataloguing in Publication Information Available

**Library of Congress Cataloging-in-Publication Data**

Lipkin, Arthur.
Beyond diversity day : a Q & A on gay and lesbian issues in schools /
    Arthur Lipkin.
        p.   cm. — (Curriculum, cultures, and (homo) sexualities)
      ISBN 0-7425-2033-1 (Cloth : alk. paper) – ISBN 0-7425-2034-X
(Paper : alk. paper)
      1. Homosexuality and education—Miscellanea.   2. Education—Social
aspects—Miscellanea.   3. Gays—Identity—Miscellanea.
4. Lesbians—Identity—Miscellanea.   I. Title.   II. Series.

    LC192.6 .L56   2004
    371.826'64—dc21

                                                                          2003007672

Printed in the United States of America

♾™ The paper used in this publication meets the minimum requirements of American
National Standard for Information Sciences—Permanence of Paper for Printed Library
Materials, ANSI/NISO Z39.48–1992.

# Beyond Diversity Day

# Curriculum, Cultures, and (Homo) Sexualities

Edited by James T. Sears

Muriel, Bill, and Patty,
Thank you
for Bob.

# Contents

# Series Editor's Foreword

As a homosexual citizen living in the Deep South, I have just been emancipated from the onerous sodomy statute on the eve of the twenty-fourth anniversary of the Stonewall Riots by an enlightened U.S. Supreme Court (Justices Scalia, Rehnquist, and Thomas, notwithstanding). Yet, today—just like yesterday and again tomorrow—Carolina students from kindergarten through college will be socialized through the standard heteronormative school curriculum: stories full of animal families with mothers and fathers dressing their children in gender-appropriate colors and clothing (where is HBO's Queer Duck when you need him?); homophobic taunts, playground torments, and other bullying are overlooked; celebrations of black and women's history month censoring out the non-heterosexuality which contoured the Harlem Renaissance or influenced Virginia Woolf, Susan B. Anthony, Bessie Smith, and Willa Cather. This is the curriculum fare served daily to impressionable students, sustained by a complacent citizenry, propped up by Bible-toting straight-and-proud legislators and school board members, and supported on a foundation of ignorance, fear, and bigotry. Sexual freedom has yet to translate into academic freedom.

Diversity—racial, gender, religious, sexual, physical—remains a dirty word in many American classrooms, where teachers of diversity are pedagogical outlaws. In more liberal-minded communities, diversity is celebrated on Cinco de Mayo or National Coming Out Day but seldom incorporated into a formal curriculum tied to state and national tests. Questions about democratic citizenship, social responsibility, or diversity (of any kind) are not commonly found on these paper-and-pencil instruments. Thus, for educators anywhere in the United States, doing the right thing requires vision, courage, practicality, and resources. *Beyond Diversity Day* encompasses each of these.

Arthur Lipkin uses a question-and-answer format to explore questions raised by educators (and parents) who wish to do the right thing for queer kids: What should be the areas of concern in counseling gay students? Do sexual minority youth do better with gay or lesbian counselors? What kinds of protection do LGBT teachers have? How can we change individuals' attitudes toward gay issues in schools? How should the school respond to parents and staff who object to these goals?

But, as Lipkin rightly points out, schools—like other institutions of the state—are influenced (indeed regulated) by culture and politics. What about readers who live in communities (or entire states) that have yet to celebrate a single diversity day? Providing the most authoritative research coupled with vignettes from every region of the world, Lipkin equips citizens for questions that will most likely be voiced by the guardians of the sexual status quo: Why should the topic of homosexuality be included in the curriculum? Isn't teaching about homosexuality only about sex? Can studying about homosexuality make a student gay? Why isn't it enough just to mention sexual orientation in the context of diversity without going into details that could bring controversy? Is this not more propaganda than education?

*Beyond Diversity Day* is a readable book and should be read by every citizen truly concerned about the woefully inadequate social education that our children receive. Two questions, however, remain: Will you read this book? Will you do the right thing?

James T. Sears
Series Editor

# Acknowledgments

Deep appreciation to Jim Sears for his confidence, advice, friendship, and editing.

Thank you to Dean Birkenkamp, editor at Rowman & Littlefield, for his professional skill and kind responses both to my work and my jokes. And to his assistant, Alison Sullenberger, for her patience and efficiency.

I salute the policy makers, educators, parents, students, and community allies whose valiant campaigns for education reform are documented in this volume. They all deserve recognition, but I thank especially those who sacrifice comfort and safety for our cause.

My gratitude also to the researchers who advance scholarship in glbt youth-related studies. You do so much with so few resources.

Lastly, this book would have been impossible without Aleta Fenceroy and Jean Mayberry, who keep me regularly informed about school-related news.

# Introduction

This book is based on the belief that homophobic bigotry and the heterosexist system will vanish in large part because the attitudes, values, and behaviors of young people in schools will change and that schools themselves must play a role in both encouraging and informing that transformation. First, however, a critical mass of educators must accept the principle that people of all sexualities have equal worth and deserve equal status in safety, voice, affirmation, and curricular representation.

Current prospects for school-based antihomophobia education vary widely around the world and even from locality to locality within nations and states. The larger cultural environment of course influences educator, student, and parent attitudes, as well as a school's institutional character. How are gay, lesbian, bisexual, and transgender (glbt) people generally regarded? What political support do they have? What are their legal rights? How safe are they personally?

Undertaking a gay-related school project without considering these contextual factors is unthinkable. That is not to say that school reformers should take every cue from the public, only that, with reasonable courage, they employ sensibly informed tactics.

## PUBLIC OPINION

Alan Wolfe's 1998 study *One Nation, After All* characterizes middle-class Americans as a "moderate majority" on issues of diversity. He discovered only one exception to their moral pragmatism and tolerance: homosexuality. About that

## BOX I.1   AND THE SURVEY SAYS

- Half of Americans say society should accept homosexuality.
- Younger, highly educated and higher-income Americans are more likely to say that homosexual relations between consenting adults should be legal.
- A majority of Americans say:
  - there is more discrimination against gays and lesbians than any other group
  - violence against gays and lesbians is a serious problem and that homosexuals should be covered under hate crime laws
  - the government should treat homosexuals and heterosexuals equally
  - school boards should not have the right to fire homosexual teachers

"A Nation Divided?" *Public Agenda* <www.publicagenda.org> (February 5, 2002).

- The percentage of people who say they have a gay friend or acquaintance rose from 24% in 1983 to 62% in 2000.

*Gallup Poll,* 1983, and *Kaiser Family Foundation Poll,* 2000.

single human difference they did not hesitate to use words like "sinful," "hateful," "wrong," and "immoral."

On the other hand, there is evidence that increasing gay visibility, besides provoking attacks from social conservatives, is having a positive effect on public opinion. In 2000, 73 percent of Americans said they knew someone gay, compared to just 30 percent in 1983. Visibility, albeit no cure-all for homophobia, renders homosexuality less remarkable and therefore less easily demonized in many instances.

Improvement is clearly demonstrated in some public opinion research. (See box I.1.) Even people with children are more accepting than right-wing spokespeople regularly claim. (See box I.2.) These general statistics do not speak to attitudinal differences among regions, faith traditions, races, and so on. Still, even among Alan Wolfe's judgmental survey subjects, nearly 75 percent felt gays should be left alone in their personal lives. Although primitive and limited, the right to be left alone is a start for a gay rights argument.

## BOX I.2    THE REAL SCOOP ON PARENTS

Of parents nationwide:

- 67% believe in teaching their children that gay people are just like other people.
- 56% believe that prejudice and discrimination against gays are morally wrong.
- 56% favor allowing school groups to promote tolerance and prevent discrimination against gay and lesbian students.

*Horizons Foundation and Lake Snell Perry & Associates Poll*, February 2001.

## POPULAR CULTURE

The trend toward normalization of homosexuality is apparent as well in popular culture. Albeit the mass media do not take great risks in reforming public opinion, they do mirror social changes among segments of the consumer public and spread them more broadly. Someone has surely "changed the channel" since implicitly gay television figures like next-door neighbor "Monroe" on *Too Close for Comfort* or comic Paul Lynde on *Hollywood Squares* winked and "walked the walk" but dared not utter the word *gay*. Although the number of gay characters rises and falls with each season, and cable programming is more representative than network television, the progress of the last few years is remarkable. (See box I.3.)[1] News and public affairs programming is also rife with gay topics, often contentious like "gay marriage" or "gays in the Boy Scouts," but sometimes matter-of-fact.

Other gay and lesbian markers (and marketing) are unmistakable in: comic book heroes (move over, Batman!), rock stars (heavy metal, no less), advice columns (Dear Ann Landers she was), Hallmark cards (e-mail only), automobile, beer, and home furniture ads (covert and overt), politicians (a few), and athletes (clearly fewer).

Still, the positive representation of gays in popular culture is constrained by majority sensibilities. For example, although films like *Get Real, Better than Chocolate,* or *Boys Don't Cry* appear confident in their glbt characters and themes, mainstream cinema has yet to reach their level. The de-gaying of Paul Nash, the protagonist of *A Beautiful Mind,* epitomizes the attitude of studio executives who feel most Americans would accept Russell Crowe as a delusional, abusive, eccentric genius, but not as a bisexual. They have not progressed much in the decade since *Philadelphia,* when Tom Hanks, playing a gay lawyer dying of AIDS, was virtually

## BOX I.3  GAYS ON TV: THE RANGE

- From wannabes on *Who Wants to Be a Millionaire* to competitors on *Survivor*
- From the Lifetime network's *What Makes a Family* to Nickelodeon's *Nick News Special Edition: My Family Is Different*
- From Bert and Ernie Muppets to SpongeBob Squarepants
- From kisses on *Dawson's Creek* to double entendres on *Will and Grace*
- From Ellen Degeneres to Rosie O'Donnell
- From a mayoral assistant on *Spin City* to an undertaker on *Six Feet Under*
- From a black lesbian cop on *The Wire* to a gay white cop on *The Shield*
- From vampire-slaying Willow to law-making Charlie Lawrence
- From *Queer as Folk* to *Queer Eye for the Straight Guy*

de-sexed in scenes with his lover. A gay male kiss in a mainstream film has been virtually taboo, unless it is comic (e.g., *In and Out*) or the actors' heterosexual credentials are impeccable (e.g., *Far from Heaven*). By contrast, Hollywood is not the least restrained about portraying stereotypical drag queens for general consumption (e.g., *The Birdcage, To Wong Foo*).

Popular news media often show both a disturbing lack of openness and a homophobic prurience. After the September 11 terrorist attacks, for instance, they shrouded the homosexuality of gay and lesbian victims—even celebrated figures like Mark Bingham, one of the heroes of United Flight 93 that crashed in Pennsylvania, and Father Mikyl Judge, the martyred New York Fire Department chaplain. On the other hand, the tabloids openly speculated that the trigger for American Taliban Frank Lindh's treason was his father's homosexuality, that terrorist Mohamed Atta and his accomplices led secret gay lives, and that D.C. snipers Muhammed and Malvo were lovers.

Such contradictory representations of homosexuality in American popular culture and its maintenance of the "closet" are a signal that public acceptance of glbt people is still qualified. Autonomy and self-presentation are limited. One is permitted today more than ever before in modern history to be gay, but often not too explicitly so, and always not too proudly so. A gay person is still discouraged from claiming or acting as if he or she shares wholly equal status with heterosexuals. (See box I.4.)

## LEGAL RIGHTS

In 2003, fourteen states and approximately 225 localities had gay inclusive antidiscrimination laws on the books. Yet nearly every year gay rights opponents,

**BOX I.4   A QUESTION OF UNION**

- A gay significant other's picture on the desk? Okay.
- Gay domestic partner's benefits? Well, okay, at least in private companies.
- A gay civil union? Maybe. (Hart/American Viewpoint Poll, July 2003: 53 percent of registered voters supportive or accepting; Gallup Poll, July 2003: 57 percent opposed)
- A gay marriage? Doubtful. (3/4 opposed nationwide in 2000)

both elected and not, move for their repeal. Most of these efforts fail, leaving bitterness in their wake. There are no federal laws prohibiting workplace discrimination or hate crimes against gay people. They are still prohibited from serving openly in the military or the Boy Scouts. Title IX protections against gender-based harassment in schools are only rarely and narrowly applied to glbt students. (See chapter 5.) President Clinton signed the Defense of Marriage Act in 1996, allowing states to refuse to recognize gay marriages that might be valid elsewhere. (It had passed the House 342–67 and Senate 85–14.) Many states have passed identical antigay marriage laws.[2]

A ban against the promotion of homosexuality in schools was defeated in the Congress in 1994, but restrictions on schools' presentation of homosexuality are common today at the state and local levels. These "no promo homo" regulations forbid any instruction or program that encourages or supports homosexuality as a positive lifestyle alternative. (See chapter 6.)

## POLITICAL SUPPORT

Politicians, like the media, more often lag than lead on social issues. The homophobic disparagement expressed by conservative elected officials and their acolytes is ubiquitous and historical. (See box I.5.)

Liberals, by contrast, sometimes come through. The moderate Vice President Gore, for example, observed (to his predecessor Dan Quayle's dismay) that when "Ellen" came out on her TV sitcom, "millions of Americans were forced to look at sexual orientation in a more open light." In another example, Senator Paul Wellstone (Minn.) demanded a 2001 school compliance study on the Department of Education Office for Civil Rights' guidelines on the harassment of gay students (see chapter 6).

## BOX I.5   AN OLD STORY...REPEATS ITSELF

"The point that I make is that, goddamn it, I do not think that you glorify on public television homosexuality. You don't glorify it, John, anymore than you glorify, uh, whores.... I don't want to see this country to go that way. You know what happened to the Greeks. Homosexuality destroyed them. Sure, Aristotle was a homo, we all know that, so was Socrates.... Do you know what happened to the Romans? The last six Roman emperors were fags.... when the popes, when the Catholic Church went to hell in, I don't know, three or four centuries ago, it was homosexual.... Now, that's what happened to Britain, it happened earlier to France. And let's look at the strong societies. The Russians. Goddamn it, they root them out, they don't let 'em hang around at all. You know what I mean? I don't know what they do with them.... You see, homosexuality, dope, uh, immorality in general: These are the enemies of strong societies. That's why the Communists and the left-wingers are pushing it. They're trying to destroy us."

Richard Nixon, excerpts from the White House tapes, in Gene Weingarten, "Below the Beltway: Just What Was He Smoking?" *Washington Post*, March 21, 2002.

"I really believe that the pagans, and the abortionists, and the feminists, and the gays and the lesbians who are actively trying to make that an alternative lifestyle, the ACLU, People for the American Way—all of them who have tried to secularize America—I point the finger in their face and say, 'You helped this happen.'"

Reverend Jerry Falwell on the September 11 terrorist attacks, in John F. Harris, "God Gave U.S. 'What We Deserve,' Falwell Says," *Washington Post*, September 14, 2001.

But often they disappoint, as when the same Senator Wellstone voted for the Defense of Marriage Act. Or when Bill Clinton danced around school issues after meeting with gay activists in 1997. The president said, "I don't believe that anyone should teach school children that they should hate or discriminate against or be afraid of people who are homosexuals" but then was compelled to add that homosexuality should not be "advocated" or be a "part of the public school curriculum." The school taboo continues to infect liberals—even the governor of the only state in the United States to allow gay civil unions. (See box I.6.)

---

**BOX I.6   THE LIMITS OF LIBERALISM?**

[Tim Russert, moderator]: Do you think homosexuality should be taught as an alternative lifestyle in schools?
  [Governor Howard Dean (Vt.)]: No, and I don't think it is. I don't think it should be and I don't think it is, for a moment.

"Meet The Press" <NBC.com> (July 21, 2002).

---

## PERSONAL SAFETY

Besides a slight, 11 percent decrease in reported incidents of antigay violence in the United States in 2001, there is little to celebrate on the subject of safety. First, many victims around the world fail to report attacks for fear of revictimization—namely, public exposure and an unsympathetic, if not hostile, law enforcement system. Second, antigay assaults, perpetrated mostly by groups of young men, are likely to be unusually brutal. (See box I.7.) An increasing percentage of such attacks are committed by youths under eighteen and more victims than before are transgender people and heterosexuals assumed to be gay.

In schools, the teasing, vicious harassment, and physical assault of glbt students and those thought to be gay (see box I.8) are documented in a 2001 Human Rights Watch study, "Hatred in the Hallways." The HRW report found that as many as two million school-age youth may be affected by antigay bullying in American schools. (See chapter 3.) Such incidents are rarely included in the national hate crimes statistics cited above.

The motivation for such assaults arises from individual ignorance, fear, and sexual insecurity. But it is also the product of homophobic cultural messages. Often, when apprehended, these thugs express an assumption that police share their disdain for gays and a belief that society would thank them for performing a public service.

## WHY FOCUS ON SCHOOLS?

A school-based antihomophobia campaign beginning in the early grades could have a preventive effect on some would-be gay bashers directly. It could also positively affect the majority of other students whose peer influence in schools is crucial in the short term and whose values will also set cultural standards of acceptance over time.

## BOX I.7  DELIBERATE, DEHUMANIZING, AND DEADLY

[F]ive youths...lay in wait in Alma Park, a well-known gay meeting place.... They had no one particular in mind: any "faggot" would do. Shortly after midnight their first victim appeared, riding a bicycle. He was pulled to the ground, kicked and punched again and again, and stripped of most of his clothes. As his mates waded in with fists and boots, 19-year-old Clint Teariki brandished his 70cm machete and yelled: "Let me chop him...let me kill him."..."I could see how much force he put into the swing," fellow gang member Nathan Hill, 18, later told police. "It was like he was opening up a coconut."..."I just don't like faggots," Hill [said].

Greg Ansley, "Vicious Attacks on Gays in Australia Like a 'Sport,'" *New Zealand Herald*, August 14, 2002.

Three men attacked a 17-year-old female in a west Denver alley Tuesday, held her down and carved derogatory words in her flesh with a razor....After carving out the word "dyke" in inch-high blocky letters, the man slashed her on the arms and face and then lifted her shirt and began carving the letters "RIP" across her stomach in big letters as he laughed.

Brian D. Crecente, "17-Year-Old Female Reports Mutilation As Anti-Gay Crime," *Rocky Mountain News*, March 28, 2002.

Nigerian police have arrested 14 high school pupils who allegedly beat a schoolmate to death because they suspected he was gay.

Segun Aribike, Birnin Kudu, "Pupils Arrested for Killing Suspected Gay Schoolmate," *African Eye News Service* (Nelspruit), April 15, 2002.

Research has already shown that higher levels of education are correlated with diminishing homophobia. In fact, a 1998 Harris poll found that an individual's amount of education is a better predictor of support for gay rights than having a gay friend or relative. That discovery alone should spur schools to take the initiative in antigay prejudice reduction.

But they rarely do. Although schools regularly challenge other forms of bigotry out of concern for school peace if not respect for multiculturalism, the majority declines to be proactive in reducing homophobia. When reformed neo-Nazi skinhead T. J. Leyden and Judy Shepard, gay murder victim Matthew Shepard's mother, proposed joint high school forums on hate, Leyden acknowledges it is far

## BOX I.8  HOMOPHOBIA HURTS ALL

[Other fifth grade students] said that figure skating is "for girls" and "stupid" and called me a "mama's boy." Then they called me "gay.". . . When I got to middle school. . . the cool guys and their friends started hitting me and ganging up on me. . . . They threatened to kill me if I told my parents. . . . [The] teachers said, "Our hands are tied; we can't do anything.". . . I was transferred to a different school.

Aaron Vays in Dana Shapiro, "On Edge," *New York Times Magazine*, August 4, 2002.

"Dereck called the other boy gay because the other boy is a cheerleader," [Hurricane High School Principle Rob Goulding] said Tuesday. "They called each other gay. You know how kids will make a comment and say, 'That's gay' or 'That's lame.' There was never the intention on either kid's part to say that the other one was homosexual. It clearly wasn't a homosexual situation."

Ashley Estes, "Name-Calling Escalates," *Salt Lake Tribune*, January 19, 2001.

Two Richland High School seniors are charged with severely beating. . . Cody Haines, 17, a senior at L. D. Bell High School. . . . Sgt. Steve Moore. . . said, "There is a scratching on the car. Someone. . . basically put the word fag on it. And this looks to be a hate crime.". . . Cody's mother said, "I think sexual orientation is an issue. But Cody is not gay, but he's not real masculine either. He's not the football type. . . he's in choir and he's a lot of fun and stuff."

Susan Risdon, "Arrest Made in Hate Crime against N. Texas Boy," MSNBC, October 27, 2000.

The stabbing by teenage gang members of a 10-year-old Nigerian boy, who was then left by passers-by to die in an open stairwell of a rundown London housing project, has caused widespread alarm in Britain. . . . Damilola was slight and studious and became a target of bullying at his school by other youths, who beat him and called him "gay." He was so innocent that he had to ask his mother what the word meant.

Warren Hoge, "A Boy's Death Shocks the British and Touches Off Soul-Searching," *New York Times*, December 5, 2000.

The complaint...accuses the two girls and another classmate of threats, intimidation and physical attacks on three Moroccan teen-age girls.... The alleged victims were the targets of anti-gay insults.... [T]hey had moved to the United States six months ago from Morocco, where schoolgirls often hold hands.

"Three Girls Accused of Harassing Moroccan Students Face Civil Complaint," *Associated Press*, April 24, 2000.

A former Averill Park High School student [is suing] for damages...suffered when he was beaten, taunted and otherwise harassed...because his classmates mistakenly thought he was gay.... [C]lassmates told the youth "he wears an earring 'in the wrong ear,' indicating he is homosexual."

"$5M Asked in Student Bias Claim," *Albany Times Union*, April 8, 2000.

easier for him to get in to speak against racism than it is for her to speak against homophobia. Educators either fail to see the relevance of sexual orientation to their mission or they lack the courage or means to act on the conviction that homophobia is a key element in the academic failure, violence, and other harmful behaviors of students of every sexuality. (See chapter 7.)

Granted, the K–12 challenge is formidable. Despite the good news about changing social attitudes and the efficacy of education, homophobia remains a problem even among student leaders. Nearly 40 percent of teens polled in the "Y2K Who's Who Among American High School Students" survey reported being prejudiced against homosexuals, significantly outnumbering those who admit racial, ethnic, or religious bias.

Still, there are reasons for optimism. Antihomophobia efforts are relatively new, compared to other antibias programs. One must also take heart that some 60 percent of "Who's Who" students claimed to be accepting of gays. And there are encouraging signs as well among U.S. adolescents in general. (See box I.9.)

Despite setbacks and exhaustion, reformers must not lose our resolve. We can help turn the schools in a more inclusive and democratic direction. Signs of their transformation are already palpable here and there. (See box I.10.) Yet we must never forget that broad fundamental reforms demand more than token responses. Diversity Day is a good overture but can never be enough.

## BOX I.9   THE NEXT GENERATION

- In 1999, 19% of teens felt that gays had something wrong with them, compared to 27% in 1991.
- In 1999, 54% of teens said they were comfortable with homosexuality, compared to 17% in 1991.

*Seventeen Magazine and Kaiser Family Foundation Poll, 1999.*

Of U.S. High School Seniors:

- 60% report that they have openly gay classmates
- over 85% say that gays and lesbians "should be accepted by society"
- over 77% agree that "gay people contribute in unique and positive ways to society"
- 88% favor laws to protect gays against hate crimes
- 79% favor laws to protect gays against job discrimination
- 66% say marriages between homosexuals should be recognized by law as valid with the same rights as traditional marriage (only one-third of adults hold this position)

*Zogby International and Hamilton College Poll* on gay issues, August 27, 2001.

- 57.9 percent of first-year college students in 2001 said they believe same-gender couples should have the right to marry, compared with 50.9 percent in 1997.

*UCLA and the American Council on Education Polls, 1997–2001.*

## BOX I.10   A NEW DAY

West Shore High journalism teacher Mark Schledorn remembers a lack of reaction to gay couples attending a formal dance. "It didn't seem to faze the other students at all.... I have heard people say, 'She's cute, he's cute, but I can't go out with him because he's gay' [used in the same tone as if saying because] they had a boyfriend."

Lemuel H. Thornton III, sophomore, Satellite High, "Gay Brevard Teens Open Up," *Florida Today*, February 3, 2002.

# NOTES

1. Televised gay representation is still often stereotypical. "Queer eyes" are shown as predisposed to grooming, dress, and home décor. Some programming is demeaning. Half the suitors on the *Boy Meets Boy* dating game are secretly heterosexual—allegedly to show that the gay bachelor and the audience can't tell who's gay or straight. Yet it plays on the assumed discomfort, if not panic, of a straight man wooed by a homosexual.

2. When, in 2003, the Supreme Court decriminalized and dignified gay relationships in the *Lawrence v. Texas* sodomy decision and Canada legalized gay marriage, many in the United States were startled and confused about the implications for public policy and religious prerogatives. Conservatives demanded a constitutional amendment to "defend" marriage and some polls revealed a sudden backlash against homosexuality itself.

# 1

# Homophobia and Heterosexism

*Question 1: What is homophobia? Is it really a phobia?*

Homophobia is the fear and hatred of homosexuality and homosexual people. It is bigotry aimed at gays, lesbians, and bisexuals for who they are and what they represent.

Homophobes target people they assume to be homosexual, but they also fear and despise any character trait or behavior that deviates from their idea of the heterosexual standard. One doesn't have to be gay to be a target of homophobia.

A real phobia is an irrational fear that leads to avoidance; but homophobia is not always irrational, and neither does a homophobe always go away. On the contrary, these haters sometimes pursue and physically attack those whose very existence upsets them. (See box 1.1.)

*Question 2: Why isn't homophobia always irrational?*

Sometimes homophobia is a psychological-emotional response without formal reasoning. At other times homophobia emerges as a response to a perceived problem. That doesn't mean that there are necessarily two kinds of homophobes, the emotional ones and the cerebral ones. Human attitudes and behaviors are products of both feeling and thinking.

A common notion—applied particularly to men—is that homophobia is prompted by a fear of one's own repressed homosexuality. (One provocative study found that over half the men in a homophobic group were aroused by gay erotic videos, some perhaps as a result of anxiety rather than desire.) Although it may be true occasionally that a vocal homophobe is indeed a "closet case," that explanation is simplistic and should not be generalized. (See box 1.2.)

## BOX 1.1   HOMOPHOBIA PERVASIVE AND LETHAL

[T]he badly decomposed body of 16-year-old Fred Martinez Jr. was found near the sewer ponds south of Cortez. . . . "It appeared to be some sort of blunt trauma to the head. . . ," [Sheriff Joey] Chavez said. . . . Martinez often curled his hair, plucked his eyebrows, wore make-up and toted a purse at school. "People talked behind his back, but I'm sure he knew" [sophomore Jessica] Wilson said.

Aspen C. Emmett, "Suspects Questioned in Boy's Murder," *Cortez* [Colo.] *Journal*, June 28, 2001.

In October, a young man who was gay and deaf was lured from a tavern, taken to a remote area of northwestern Wisconsin and savagely beaten to death, authorities say. The murder. . . took place in a community that had just weathered a federal lawsuit over the banning of books about gays from the local high school library. One of the books, "The Drowning of Stephan Jones," is a fictionalized account of the killing of a young gay man by a group of small-town thugs. . . . [Defendant] Reed told police, [Defendant] Kralewski and [Defendant] Walton beat Hatch to death with a tire iron. . . . [T]he three shouted that they hated gay people during the beating.

Susan Lampert Smith, "Gay Man's Murder Seems to Fit Pattern," *Wisconsin State Journal*, August 6, 2000.

## BOX 1.2   SOMETIMES THE HOMOPHOBE *DOES* PROTEST TOO MUCH

Specialist Justin Fisher goaded Private Calvin Glover into beating Fisher's sleeping roommate [Private First Class Barry Winchell] to death with a baseball bat. . . . What he didn't make at all clear was that he [Fisher] had gone to [a] gay club. . . with Winchell and that he had been there before. He never mentioned that. . . he himself had once made out with a transsexual on a downtown street corner in Nashville. He didn't mention that he liked to dress in women's lingerie. And as one witness told investigators, he certainly didn't mention that he had once started stroking Winchell's feet in the middle of the night when Winchell was sleeping.

Buzz Bissinger, "Don't Ask, Don't Kill," *Vanity Fair*, May 2000.

## BOX 1.3  REVEALING EXPERIMENT

In a completely random fashion, [researcher Dr. Richard H. Gramzow of Northeastern University] told half of the students that their Personality Profiles had tested high on "masculine" traits, while the other half were told they scored higher in "feminine" traits. The result? "Male respondents who received feminine personality feedback subsequently reported extremely negative attitudes toward gay men."

E. J. Mundell, "Threat to Masculinity Pits Straight Men against Gay," *Reuters Health*, February 7, 2002.

More commonly, homophobes are distressed by those who remind them of their own insecurities about their gender role. It's not that they are worried they might be gay, but that they might not be man or woman enough. (See box 1.3.) Our culture's requirements for membership in a gender category can be quite rigid and unforgiving, particularly for men and boys. The maintenance of one's masculine "credentials" can be difficult and sometimes dangerous. So it is no surprise that males engage in a homophobic examination of themselves and other males, rejecting any qualities seen as "feminine."

The issues for women and girls, on the other hand, typically center on their physical bodies. For example, their weight, breast size, and sexual appetite are tyrannically scrutinized and self-monitored, but they are generally allowed more latitude in gender expression, dress, and same-gender intimacy than males are. Even so, girls can become suspect if they excel in traditionally male pursuits like competitive sports or if they aspire to power. Female athletes have been forced to compensate for their skills by "femming up" their appearance off the field.

Some think that both male and female heterosexuals are more negative toward homosexuals of their own gender. Being near lesbians has been known to make straight-identified women uncomfortable. If, as some psychologists believe, women are more likely than men to have a bisexual capacity, lesbians could evoke in heterosexual women a fear of what they have repressed.

In the final analysis, however, heterosexual men generally have more negative attitudes toward homosexuality than heterosexual women do.

*Question 3: How is homophobia related to sexism?*

One is uncomfortable with or frightened by homosexuality because it threatens one's understanding of self and society and jeopardizes one's position in the power hierarchy of gender. Since patriarchy—the predominance of men over women—is the prevailing gender system throughout most of the world, homophobia cannot be explained without examining sexism.

Disdain for the feminine and for what is seen as feminine in men is at the root of male homophobia. Homophobic men describe themselves as less feminine and more assertive and independent than do more tolerant men. They also want others to know they conform to male norms of heterosexuality. Masculinity must be demonstrated again and again in a repeated repudiation of effeminacy/homosexuality.

Opinions about gender role are related to attitudes toward homosexuality. Both men and women who show traits that are inconsistent with cultural gender norms are assumed to be homosexual until they demonstrate otherwise. The idea that homosexuality is equivalent to gender inversion has persisted for over one hundred years. People commonly assume that self-identified gays and lesbians really want to *be* the "opposite" gender.

Those who uphold traditional gender roles for men and women are more homophobic than are those who accept flexible gender roles. (See box 1.4.) Victims of this homophobic code can be gay, but they can also be straight. (See box 1.5.)

*Question 4: Why are straight men more homophobic toward gay men than toward lesbians?*

Because gay men appear to have yielded their privilege of male domination over women, straight men see them as gender traitors. The supposedly weak homosexual man engaging in what is perceived as female behavior may feel like a slap.

Because sexist men think all women matter less, lesbians may be less threatening to them. Heterosexual men may also assume they can force homosexual women into their proper roles—hence the notion that a woman is a lesbian only until a real man has sex with her. Those images of lesbian eroticism that some

---

### BOX 1.4   HOMOPHOBIA AS FARCE: THE PURSE DOES IT

[The *National Liberty Journal* claims] Tinky Winky has the voice of a boy but carries a purse. "He is purple—the gay-pride color; and his antenna is shaped like a triangle—the gay-pride symbol."... "As a Christian I feel that role modeling the gay lifestyle is damaging to the moral lives of children," [editor and publisher Jerry Falwell said.]

David Reed, "Falwell Calls 'Teletubby' Gay," *Associated Press*, February 9, 1999.

## BOX 1.5   REAL MEN AREN'T GAY

A Mafia turncoat told a stunned courtroom yesterday how he gunned down his mob boss—because he was gay.... "Nobody's gonna respect us if we have a gay homosexual boss sitting down discussing La Cosa Nostra business," [Anthony] Capo told jurors in Manhattan federal court.

John Lehmann, "Mobster Sleeps with The Swishes," *New York Post*, May 1, 2003.

"A lot of these kids, white and black, want music that reaffirms their masculinity," [pacifist techno music star Moby] told *Spin* magazine [after being assaulted by two young men]. "I'm straight, but I love going to house-music clubs and flirting with women and gay men. This is a leap most of America seems unprepared to make."

Christopher Muther, "Was Attack on Moby Driven by Intolerance?" *Boston Globe*, December 14, 2002.

straight men find attractive include a male voyeur stepping in to put the sexual system back in order. (See box 1.6.)

On the other hand, lesbians, who reject male dominance and claim sexual fulfillment on their own, still pose a challenge to patriarchal authority.

Overall, homophobic stigma is used to discredit both men and women who challenge traditional gender norms.

## BOX 1.6   MALE HOMOPHOBIA'S DOUBLE STANDARD

*Interviewer:* Do you guys feel comfortable showing affection to your boyfriends or girlfriends when you're out in public?
*Heidi:* For us, they can care less.
*Daniel:* The guys whistle at them, it's a big turn-on for them. But if you're a guy and you're holding hands with another guy, they yell at you. Straight guys, they tend to think that they're dominant toward everybody.
*Calisse:* They have to be "macho."
*Daniel:* It's like we're going to give a bad name to them or something.

Theresa Walker, "Out in the Open," [Interview with 4 gay teens] *Orange County Register*, May 13, 2002.

*Question 5: What is heterosexism?*

Heterosexism is the system under which homophobia enforces the supremacy of heterosexuality and the erasure of gay, lesbian, and bisexual experience. Racism, sexism, and anti-Semitism are also systems in which prejudice is elaborated into a social oppression. The phenomenon of heterosexual assumptions rendering non-heterosexual people invisible is called *heteronormativity*.

*Question 6: Why is homophobia so extreme among adolescent males?*

Adolescent boys are generally obsessed by the male role. Nothing is more worrisome to most of them than not measuring up to their peers as men. The consequence of continuous self-inspection, introspection, and comparison is considerable insecurity. And the outlet for this distress, which of course cannot be exhibited or shared, except among the most unconventional men, is to distance oneself from suspicion of "unmanliness" by reckless bravado and homophobic invective. The most powerful, and hence most common, insult among young males is *faggot*, used to police the slightest deviation from the masculine ideal. (See box 1.7.)

## BOX 1.7   HOMOPHOBIA SELLS

"My words are like a dagger with a jagged edge/That'll stab you in the head/Whether you're a fag or lez/Or the homosex, hermaph or a trans-a-ves"; "Hey, it's me, Versace/Whoops, somebody shot me/And I was just checking the mail/Get it? Checking the male?"; "Slim Anus?/You're damn right, slim anus/I don't get f–ked in mine/Like you two little flaming faggots"; "You faggots keep egging me on/Till I have you at knifepoint/Then you beg me to stop."

Eminem lyric, in Anthony DeCurtis, "Eminem's Hate Rhymes," *Rolling Stone*, August 3, 2000.

In 1981, the [DeKalb County, Ga.] school system made [former professional football player Danny Buggs] a "motivational speaker." He earns. . . $74,200 a year. . . . Buggs. . . trains "boys to become men.". . . At a Stone Mountain High School boys-only assembly program in September [2002], Buggs [proclaimed,] "God made Adam and Eve and not Adam and Steve,". . . "I hope that there are not any [epithet deleted] in here."

Cynthia Tucker, "Opinion: Let's Motivate School Board to Fire Buggs," *Atlanta Journal-Constitution*, November 6, 2002.

## BOX 1.8   REAL JOCKS AREN'T GAY

The [Kings and Lakers] regularly trade insults, but the rhetoric heated up before Friday night's game as Lakers star Shaquille O'Neal said, "I'm not worried about the Sacramento Queens."

"Lakers—Kings Game Marred by Fight," *Associated Press*, October 26, 2002.

The yearbook cover photo of... two Millard North students wearing soap on a rope around their necks has sparked a controversy. Some view the soap on a rope as a put-down of homosexuals.... The yearbook picture had been taken at a football game against Creighton Prep... as a taunt to the all-male school's team, apparently insinuating they were gay, [school district spokeswoman] Friedman said.... "Most adults will not understand why this would be controversial, but students know what it symbolizes."

Tanya Eiserer, "Millard North Officials Alter Yearbook Photo," *Omaha World-Herald*, May 13, 2000.

### So What Is This About?

[T]he complaining student was "tea bagged," a term used by members of the football team for an initiation rite. The victim claims he was held down while one of the older team members dragged his genitals across the victim's forehead.

Bruce A. Scruton, "Five Plead Not Guilty in Hazing Incident," [Albany, N.Y.] *Times Union*, December 11, 2001.

Sometimes, the proof of one's heterosexual credentials lies in gay bashing. Often carried out in adolescent packs, these attacks are a rite of group membership and shared values. Such brutality has its origins in schoolhouse and schoolyard bullying.

Homophobia is also manifest in athletics and team sports, which have a long and profound impact on young people—particularly in toughening masculinity and controlling female autonomy. (See box 1.8.) As in the military, young men are goaded with homophobic jibes to perform acts of strength, courage, and sometimes violence.

Military specialists and some athletic coaches believe that open homosexuals damage unit cohesion. They fear the deep male bonding on which they depend could not occur without the assumption that gays have been banished. With

**BOX 1.9  MILITARY HOMOPHOBIA: A FATAL TOOL**

A critical moment in his decision to quit the Army, Mr. [Javier] Torres said...came when his drill sergeant unapologetically bellowed a homophobic cadence in leading his platoon on a five-mile run: "Faggot, faggot down the street/ Shoot him, shoot 'til he retreats."

Francis X. Clines, "For Gay Soldier, a Daily Barrage of Threats and Slurs," *New York Times*, December 12, 1999.

[T]he Associated Press today withdrew a news photograph that showed misspelled graffiti—"high jack this fags"—on an airborne bomb bound for Afghanistan. The photograph, taken on the USS Enterprise, shows a Navy officer scrawling a message on a bomb attached to the wing of an attack plane.

"Navy Photo Shows Antigay Slur on Bomb," *Planet Out* <www.planetout.com> [October 12, 2001].

rampant homophobia, they get both hypermasculine competitors and manly attachments without suspicion. (See box 1.9.)

*Question 7: What about religious proscriptions against homosexuality?*

Over the centuries, powerful people have used the Bible to justify oppression against out-groups, be they blacks, Jews, Catholics, or Protestants. Similarly, fundamentalist interpretations of Jewish and Christian Bibles have been employed to condemn homosexual behavior, if not homosexuals. Some religious conservatives believe that to alter their churches' antigay doctrine would be to destroy the church itself. Others merely use the Bible as a cover for their bigotry—the adulterous three-times-divorced politician, for example, who claims gay marriage would defy God's will.

On the other hand, less homophobic people of faith often belong to liberal denominations that have come to accept and even affirm gays, lesbians, and bisexuals.

*Question 8: Are some racial, ethnic, and class groups more homophobic than others?*

There are prejudiced people in all demographic groups, although the reasons for heterosexism may vary in degree from group to group. Groups tend to be more

> ## BOX 1.10   SCRATCH A LIBERAL...
>
> The gay bogeyman or woman can still be exploited by demagogues with impunity.... And it's not just those on the right who succumb to ignorance and fear on this subject: only a few weeks ago my wife and I were lectured by a prominent figure in Manhattan's liberal literary establishment about a conspiracy to recruit our children into homosexuality at college.
>
> Frank Rich, "JOURNAL: Summer of Matthew Shepard," *New York Times*, July 3, 1999.

homophobic when they are also:

- patriarchal and rigid about gender roles;
- politically conservative;
- religiously orthodox;
- focused on marriage and procreation; and
- less exposed to higher education.

Well-educated agnostics can also be intolerant of homosexuality. Genteel homophobes are often just more skilled at disguising their homophobia under a veneer of civility than less sophisticated folks are. Moreover, it is often easier for self-styled liberals to accept homosexuality in the abstract or in other people's families than in their own. (See box 1.10.) A key to understanding homophobia in all groups and cultures is the degree to which the equality of women is accepted.

## Question 9: Has homophobia always existed?

Before we consider homophobia historically, we need to understand that there have not always been "homosexuals" in the world. As far as we know, there have always been people who are sexually attracted to others of their own gender, but such people were probably not regarded as an identity group until the late nineteenth century.

As far back at least as ancient Greece and the early Roman Empire, men were permitted to have erotic ties with other men without drawing attention to themselves as another type of human being. All adult male citizens were free to penetrate whomever they desired so long as the passive partner was a woman, a slave, or a boy. The issue in this kind of arrangement was power, not gender. That is, the more powerful were expected to dominate the less powerful.

The power system was disrupted if an adult male citizen allowed himself to be sexually dominated. He might be scorned or parodied but not classified by (or investigated for the cause of) his atypical behavior. There is no evidence that he or anyone else thought his erotic proclivities gave him a group identity.

What a woman did with another woman was not very important as long as she obliged her man. The boy, for his part, was assumed to be in a mentored relationship with his older male partner. He was thought to derive power but not pleasure from the receipt of semen. And at a certain age he was expected to end the practice and marry a woman.

Hindu texts, Tantric rituals, and religious statues provide historic examples of same-gender male and female sexual relations in Indian cultures. Descriptions of "fashionable male-with-male sex" can be found in Chinese accounts from the late Ming period. In certain aboriginal cultures, like the Sambia of New Guinea, males engage, even today, in ritualized homosexual activities and initiation rites. A boy is expected to be sexually intimate with other boys until marriage to a woman or women. All these practices and the characterizations of them defy our familiar Western identity categories of gay, straight, and bisexual. (See box 1.11.)

With later Christianity came the notion of sodomitical sin. Even then, however, the sodomite was not classified according to the specific sexual sin he committed, be it with his male servant or his sheep—or his wife or some other woman for that matter. Sodomy, adultery, and fornication were all sinful, but so were avarice and anger.

Eventually, the sodomy that the clergy condemned became the domain of the criminologist and the physician. The inclination toward same-gender intimacy was pathologized and its so-called sufferers were criminalized as a new class of

---

### BOX 1.11   LABELS APPLY... OR DO THEY?

British marines returning from an operation deep in the Afghan mountains spoke last night of an alarming new threat... James Fletcher said: "They were more terrifying than the al-Qaeda. One bloke who had painted toenails was offering to paint ours. They go about hand in hand, mincing around the village."... "We were pretty shocked.... We discovered from the Afghan soldiers we had with us that a lot of men in this country have the same philosophy as ancient Greeks: 'a woman for babies, a man for pleasure.'"

Chris Stephen, "Startled Marines Find Afghan Men All Made Up to See Them," *The Scotsman* [Edinburgh], May 24, 2002.

people, first called *inverts* and later *homosexuals* and *lesbians*. The causes of sexual deviation were investigated and cures were imposed.

Although there is some disagreement among historians about possible earlier examples of homosexual subcultures, all agree that by the middle of the 1800s, many people who were sexually interested in members of their own gender were discovering one another in growing cities.

## Question 10: What caused this change from a kind of sin to a type of person?

The development of these ostensibly scientific categories and the invention of the idea of identities based on sexuality coincided with important economic changes. Industrialization, during which many people left family farms for cities, permitted them to pay more attention to nonprocreative desires and to consider new sexual arrangements in relative anonymity. Thus, a subculture arose as a consequence of sexual tastes.

Still, one has to wonder if these sexual activities would have provoked the level of scrutiny they did, were it not for the rise of the women's movement. The threat that independent women posed to the patriarchal order may have contributed, along with the ascendancy of science over faith, to this sudden fascination with gender/sexual deviance. Indeed, early psychologists like Krafft-Ebbing equated gender role rebellion with lesbianism.

Other ways in which male and female inverts were diagnosed offer clues to the biases of the scientists. Lesbians were described as overly sexed, coarse, and masculine. Women's colleges, a new phenomenon, were suspected of breeding lesbianism. Male inverts were thought to have female souls or to lack male hormones. Freudians later claimed such men were victims of smothering mothers and weak or absent fathers.

To Freud himself homosexual desire, either unconscious or conscious, is inherent in everyone. He did consider exclusive homoeroticism inferior to heterosexuality, yet he felt it was nothing to be ashamed of and objected to jailing homosexuals and keeping them out of the psychiatric profession. Still, some of his successors believe gay men are feminized, retarded at the Oedipal stage, afraid of women, and craving father substitutes as sexual partners.

The cures some professedly compassionate doctors offered, and often imposed, included everything from bicycling and primal screaming to castration, cliterodectomy, and lobotomy. (See box 1.12.)

## Question 11: What does this history prove about homophobia?

Same gender sexual desires and acts have had different meanings over time and in different places. Various cultures have interpreted what we call homosexuality

## BOX 1.12    THE TORTURE CONTINUES

A leading psychiatrist has described how he recently treated a 24-year-old man for "sexual orientation."... [T]he son of an army sergeant sought treatment because he wanted to have a conventional marriage and children.... [Another man] recently revealed his experience of such therapy during the 1960s. More than 700 people have since [said] they had received similar treatment.... "I was locked up alone in a mental institution for 72 hours with supposedly gay pornography, and given drugs to make me vomit and become incontinent," he said.... "There was no lavatory and no water supply in the room. They said the next part...was to apply electrodes to my genitals."

Lois Rogers, ' "Gay Cure' Therapy Offered on NHS," London [U.K.] Times, June 20, 1999.

in many ways and they still do around the world. The way societies give meaning to different aspects of a person's makeup (e.g., race, gender, sexual orientation) is called the social construction of identity. Having a particular skin pigment, for example, has had different identity consequences over the centuries on different continents.

In short, the significance of what we call *homosexuality* is determined by the culture. It is not a universal and timeless given, despite Justice Burger's 1986 opinion in *Bowers v. Hardwick* that it has been condemned through "millennia of moral teaching." The majority opinion in *Lawrence v. Texas* in 2003, explicitly overruling *Bowers*, cites gay studies scholarship as evidence that same-gender sexual relations have been understood and judged differently over centuries.

*Question 12: Does that mean that homosexuality could go back to being a neutral characteristic, without any meaning for one's identity?*

Theoretically, yes. If homophobes stopped fearing and persecuting people because of their homosexuality, then all sexuality categories could lose their significance. We would be no more likely to group ourselves according to the gender of our erotic partners than we would form into groups of redheads or broccoli lovers.

But in the real world, we must concede that gays, lesbians, and bisexuals—at least in Western societies—have already developed a common history and culture, probably as a result of being stigmatized and persecuted, that will not soon become irrelevant to their sense of themselves or others' sense of them. Racism too, even if it were to evaporate tomorrow, has forged ties and identities based on common oppression and cultural survival that would not likely become meaningless in the short term.

## Question 13: Can't these minority identities trap people into "types" at the expense of their individuality?

Yes, labels like gay and lesbian can homogenize individuals. Moreover, stereotyping by straight people is not the only danger. Coming out into a homosexual identity is an act of liberation from debilitating stigma, but it can also produce a culture with stifling "rules" for belonging. Like other minorities, gays and lesbians sometimes enforce their own members' conformity to group norms. It's understandable that solidarity is important to oppressed groups, but it is not acceptable to violate individual autonomy in the name of a united front.

Some cutting edge theorists have even urged their fellow homosexuals to discard gay labels as outdated. Some prefer to form political communities focused on economic injustice, which they see as the overriding oppression worldwide.

There may indeed come a time when sexuality preferences will seem an irrelevant basis for community formation, but we are not there yet. As irksome as it may be to define oneself and organize collectively in reaction to homophobia, there is no alternative except in theory. The relationship between heterosexist patriarchy and many of the world's ills is still quite real.

## Question 14: What is internalized homophobia?

Internalized homophobia is a variety of self-loathing. Nearly all homosexual people are to some degree subject to this deep shame, but it is not inborn—it is instilled through one's relationships and other learning experiences. It takes root or withers, depending on one's psychological needs and capacity to resist. It can also be influenced by external factors such as race, class, ethnicity, religion, geography, family tolerance, and family psychologies.

Internalized homophobia can cause depression and low self-esteem as well as other psychological and cognitive difficulties. (See box 1.13.) On the other hand, coming out is a step toward healthy adjustment. (See chapter 3.)

Even those who appear to accept themselves may harbor an unrecognized sense of inferiority that leads to self-sabotage and acquiescence to second-class status. When stigmatized people blame themselves for their problems, their self-esteem is ultimately diminished.

Because it can be subtle, internalized homophobia requires long-term vigilance. The struggle is between two internal scripts: the shameful "I am bad, wrong, sinful

## BOX 1.13   INTERNALIZED HOMOPHOBIA CAN ALSO BE DEADLY

A teen-ager accused of beating to death his friend told detectives he killed the boy because the two were involved in a homosexual relationship. Jon "Paul" Marsh, 17, is charged with [the] killing of Nathan Mayoral, 14.... Marsh said he considered himself an "abomination." "I didn't want the relationship we had, and I just couldn't, I just couldn't be his friend."... Marsh said the relationship was consensual and that he started hating himself because of it.... He said he beat Mayoral with [a ceramic plant saucer].... Marsh said he also grabbed Mayoral's head and banged it on the ground several times. Then, he said, he stood on Mayoral's neck and beat his head with a hammer.

Lisa Teachey, "Suspect in Killing Tells of Gay Relationship," *Houston Chronicle*, July 3, 2001.

and I must stop being gay," versus the affirming, even defiant, "The solution to my pain is to eradicate heterosexism."

(For further reading, see appendix R.)

# 2

# Homosexualities

*Question 1: How does a gay, lesbian, or bisexual young person come to his or her identity?*

Researchers like Eli Coleman, V. C. Cass, and Richard Troiden propose a number of developmental models to explain how a person reaches a gay, lesbian, or bisexual identification. They represent a blend of psychological stages and outward affiliation. Although the various models differ in minor detail, they all feature initial ambiguity, frequent questioning, imbalance, and information seeking as well as increasing comfort. (See box 2.1)

Because of stigma the process often involves shame, guilt, and avoidance. Sadly, the help that people from other oppressed groups usually have to support their identity development—family love, nearby community, adult role models, and cultural history—are too often absent for sexual minority youth.

*Question 2: Have these models of identity development been proven?*

As helpful as they are for outlining the sequence and nature of homosexual identity acquisition, no one moves along so unambiguously as these models suggest. First, they may be too linear, even if sequences are sometimes clear in individual cases. (See box 2.2.) There are usually fits, starts, and slippage.

Second, these developmental models give the impression that the homosexual orientation is an inner potential, just waiting for the right circumstances to emerge—and that the whole process has a final goal. We might wrongly conclude that an end-stage "mature" identity was uniform within each classification: gay men, lesbians, bisexual males, and bisexual females.

## BOX 2.1  STAGES OF HOMOSEXUAL IDENTITY DEVELOPMENT

1. Pre-Sexuality
   Preadolescent nonsexual feelings of difference and marginality, often, but not always, involving gender role.
2. Identity Questioning
   Ambiguous, repressed, sexualized same-gender feelings and/or activities. Avoidance of stigmatized label.
3. Coming Out
   Tolerance, then acceptance of identity through contact with gay/lesbian individuals and culture. Exploration of sexual possibilities and first erotic relationships. Careful, selective self-disclosure outside gay/lesbian community.
4. Pride
   Integration of sexuality into self. Capacity for love relationships. Wider self-disclosure and better stigma management.
5. Post-Sexuality
   A diminishment of centrality of homosexuality in self-concept and social relations.

Eli Coleman, "Developmental Stages of the Coming Out Process," in William Paul et al., *Homosexuality: Social, Psychological and Biological Issues* (Thousand Oaks, Calif.: Sage, 1982); V. C. Cass, "Homosexual Identity Formation: Testing a Theoretical Model," *Journal of Sex Research* 20 (1984): 143–67; Richard R. Troiden, "The Formation of Homosexual Identities," in Gilbert Herdt, ed., *Gay and Lesbian Youth* (New York: Harrington Park Press, 1989).

*Question 3: Is there a better way to think about homosexual identity development?*

Yes. Sexuality identity development could be a lifelong process without a final stage. The "human development model" proposes that sexual interests are not a simple fixed "status" but are the result of a multidimensional, ongoing, interactive process. Culture, social norms, physical surroundings and interactions, and biology all affect one's sexuality over time. People come to and go from homosexual feelings, behavior, and identity when outer circumstances and inner readiness coincide.

This perspective recognizes that people arrive at their sexualities via their singular constitutions and unique life experiences. It also acknowledges that choice plays a role in recognizing and pursuing one's inclinations, declaring one's sexuality identity, or affiliating with a sexuality community.

**BOX 2.2   DEFINITIVE STAGES 2, 3, 4**

We had to have the courage to say, oh my God, there are people out there who are like that. What if I'm like that? You start questioning it. And then you know for sure—you feel it. It's attraction. Just like how straight people know I like this boy or I like this girl. You know it. You know yourself. . . . Until I dated some girl at school, and that's when they started getting a notion, that's when they started knowing. I started being open with it more. Me and Daniel, we even made a necklace that says "Queer" and we used to wear it at school. Everybody would just laugh about it or look at it like, you know, wow, they're really open with it. That put them in assurance, that you don't have to be scared of us because we're not scared of you.

Calisse, in Theresa Walker, "Out in the Open" [Interview with four gay teens], *Orange County Register*, May 13, 2002.

*Question 4: Isn't this model just theoretical?*

We need to study individuals over a lifetime. Complete sexuality histories across cultures will yield the details about how people travel their affectional and erotic paths and how they make sense of themselves as they do. It is of course impossible to determine the real scope of anyone's sexuality potential as long as homophobia remains a factor in his or her self-admissions, sexual decisions, and public presentation.

*Question 5: If sexuality is so flexible and if choice plays a role, can people really choose not to be homosexual?*

All sexualities are chosen and fluidity can go both ways. Everyone should be freed from the restraints that impede their full sexual expression. The answer to the question, "Why did you decide to be gay?" could be "When did you decide to be *inflexibly* heterosexual?" (See box 2.3.)

*Question 6: How important are biology and environment in determining sexual orientation?*

Although this question could mean, "What makes some people gay and others straight?" most folks are only interested in why some people are gay. The heterosexual norm usually remains an unexamined given.

## BOX 2.3   I AM WHAT I AM—FOR NOW

[I]t seems that something different is emerging on the street these days.... It is composed of... ordinary women and men of all varieties who sleep with, fall in love with, live with and break up with both women and men over the courses of their lives.... This is not a movement, certainly not an identity;... If pushed, some of these people, sighing, will call themselves bisexual or queer, but only as a political convenience, shorthand for "not straight."

Stacey D'Erasmo, "Has Sexual Identity Outlived Its Usefulness?" *New York Times*, October 14, 2001.

[I]t's more common for today's young GLBT people to express and accept fluid gender and sexual identities.... On one hand, there's a push for GLBT young people to come out at earlier ages, [Esther D. Rothblum, Ph.D.] notes; on the other, more young people are pausing indefinitely in what she calls the "lingering" category.

Tori DeAngelis, "A New Generation of Issues for GLBT Clients," *Monitor On Psychology* 33, no. 2, www.apa.org/monitor/feb02/generation.htm (February 2002).

Some search for a cause in order to change or prevent homosexuality. Others claim there will be less homophobia if homosexuality is proven to be biological, that is, not a choice, but a fate. Of course bigots who think homosexuality *is* biological could still want to suppress it. Nor is it clear why same-gender behavior in other animal species (e.g., swans, Japanese macaques, and fruit flies) should be relevant to the discussion.

So-called scientific reports on homosexual causation have a large audience today because of the mass media's fascination with the question. (See box 2.4.) Yet there is little questioning of the heterosexist bias that may influence this research.

We can probably safely conclude from recent studies that a variety of factors, both biological and environmental—nature and nurture—contribute to one's sexual orientation at a given time in one's life. It is also possible that male homosexuality entails different combinations of factors than lesbianism does.

*Question 7: Do gender nonconforming boys and girls become gay adults?*

Some retrospective studies have tried to "prove" that childhood effeminacy precedes male homosexuality. But when answering researchers' questions, adult

**BOX 2.4   IS IT GENETIC?...A SHOW OF HANDS AND OTHER PARTS**

Homosexual men and women are more likely to be left-handed than their heterosexual counterparts...Canadian researchers said....

"Homosexuals More Likely to Be Left-Handed, Study," *Reuters*, July 6, 2000.

Researchers...say the relative lengths of the forefinger and the fourth finger can provide a pointer to sexual orientation.

AFP, "Fingers Point to Sexuality," *The Age* [Australia], March 29, 2000.

[Two professors] have documented differences in brain response of homosexuals and heterosexuals to sound.

Ben Wear, "UT Research Backs the Nature Theory of Homosexuality," *Austin American-Statesman*, July 14, 2000.

Stiff homosexual organs are one-third of an inch longer, claims an article titled "The Relation between Sexual Orientation and Penile Size...."

Hank Hyena, "Research Claims Erect Gay Penises Are Bigger," *Salon.com*, www.salon.com (November 4, 1999).

gay men may merely be more open to recalling their early gender nonconformity than heterosexuals are. And although nearly half of gay men remember not fitting in with other boys, most "sissies" do not become gay men. The most reliable predictor for boys seems to be the intensity and persistence of their nonconformity. (See box 2.5.)

**BOX 2.5   SISSIES**

For the cross-dressing toddler in Toronto and other boys who show "pervasive and persistently" effeminate behavior, the odds of being gay lie at about 75%, according to [psychologist] J. Michael Bailey.... That is a probability of homosexuality 20 times as high as that in the broad population of boys.... Among girls, this so-called gender-atypical behavior also is a good predictor of later lesbianism, though the pattern is weaker.

Melissa Healy, " Pieces of the Puzzle," *Los Angeles Times*, May 21, 2001.

Tomboy violations of gender norms do not correlate well with adult lesbian identity.

## Question 8: What is transgendered?

Usually by age three, people have a sense of what their gender is. Their gender identity is probably a product of both biology and socialization. Occasionally individuals develop gender identities that do not match their biological sex in a conventional sense. (Some were hermaphroditic, now called "intersexed," at birth and were surgically assigned a sex.) A "transgendered" person often considers himself or herself as a male or female trapped in the body of the "opposite" gender. Sometimes they feel as if they are differently gendered, yet neither male nor female.

Transgendered people may choose to express their gender through verbal self-representation, dress, and deportment alone. Or they might pursue drug therapies or gender reassignment surgery to become transsexual.

## Question 9: What is "coming out"?

Coming out consists of affirming one's own homosexuality, making contact with the gay/lesbian community, and acknowledging oneself as gay/lesbian/bisexual to others. Coming out publicly increases personal integrity, decreases feelings of isolation, helps identity integration, and increases intimacy in relationships. Because people are usually assumed to be heterosexual, coming out to others can be a life-long task.

Coming out completely defies the notion that only heterosexuality is natural and good. Still, ridding oneself of internalized guilt and shame can go on into adulthood.

## Question 10: At what age do people come out?

Many boys and girls experience same-gender desire and fantasy between the ages of seven and twelve and come out, at least to themselves, in their mid-teens. A drop in the mean age of "self-awareness" from nearly twenty in 1979 to about thirteen in 1998 may have been caused by the increased public visibility of homosexuality. (See box 2.6.) Years ago, young people had less opportunity and positive incentive to give a name to and make sense of their same-gender feelings.

Those who are identifiably gender nonconforming and have no heterosexual experience may come out earlier and go through the process faster. Those who

> ## BOX 2.6  UP AND OUT EARLY
>
> On the last day of seventh grade, Dave Grossman mounted some cardboard boxes down the street from his junior high school and held a one-boy rally. "I'm sick of pretending," he announced into a cheap loudspeaker. "I'm gay." ... In fourth grade, he says, "I came to my senses. I was just staring benignly at the boy across from me." At 11, Dave found online chat rooms and located the gay bulletin board in short order. At 12, he told his parents. ... [His mother responded], "Wow, I didn't even know you had a sexuality."
>
> Libby Copeland, "Out of the Closet, But Not Out of Middle School," *Washington Post*, June 29, 1999.

are able to pass as heterosexual might begin the process later and proceed more slowly. Opposite-gender sexual experience can prolong confusion or aid denial.

## Question 11: What are the stumbling blocks in homosexual identity development?

In the beginning of the process some people try to rationalize the significance of their feelings or acts. "It was only a physical thing. I was just horny," is typical for boys. "It was loving and beautiful, and therefore not lesbian" may be a girl's mode of denial. "It only happened this once," "it's just a phase," "it was the liquor that made me do it," or "it isn't gay because neither male partner plays the woman" are also heard.

Some look for a cure through religion or medicine. Some flee from people of the opposite gender, whereas others have sex with them to hide the truth from themselves or others. Heterosexual promiscuity and pregnancy are common covers. Some grasp at a bisexual identity to mitigate the stigma.

Some avoid facing their own psychological needs by immersion in hobbies, schoolwork, or giving care to others. They may use these activities as a screen against personal questions from others and strive for perfection to prove to themselves that they are not worthless.

Another form of denial is to shun information about gays and lesbians or even to attack them.

Even after coming out, there may be setbacks. Rejection may send one scurrying back into hiding in the "closet" or force one into "passing" as heterosexual. On the other hand, one may give in to societal expectations and adopt stereotypical appearance and gestures, becoming a caricature because of internalized homophobia

## BOX 2.7    WHAT A DEFENSE!

[I]n this macho, male-dominated culture [in Turkey], the only option for an openly gay person is to live on society's fringes in the most outlandish and outrageous manner possible. "If you are homosexual, society pushes you toward this feminine behavior. Society says if I feel a little bit womanish, I have to be a woman."

Tom Hundley, "Pushed to the Edge in Turkey," *Chicago Tribune*, December 19, 2000.

or as a self-defense. "Minstrelizing" as the "opposite gender" is one strategy, particularly for gay males in patriarchal cultures—the "act like the woman we think you really want to be and we'll cut you some slack"syndrome. (See box 2.7.)

### Question 12: What is bisexuality?

The bisexual orientation spans the realm of erotic preferences and behaviors be-tween exclusively homosexual and exclusively heterosexual. Since sexual orien-tation is complex and can be fluid over time, these divisions may seem arbitrary when applied to an individual.

There is a difference between transitional and mature bisexuality. The former is a way station on the path to a homosexual identity, a refuge until internalized homophobia is overcome. The latter is an authentic and lasting identity.

Some people mistakenly expect mature bisexuals to "get off the fence"and affil-iate with one or the other side. Outright homophobes don't see much difference between bisexuality and homosexuality. And some gays and lesbians wrongly as-sume all bisexuality is a form of repression.

### Question 13: What does a young person need to get through the identity process successfully?

Support and good information are vital. At the start, one can feel liberated yet also at a loss. Even if one's prior heterosexual identity did not feel genuine, its roles and expectations were at least clear. A gay future is usually less familiar. Moreover, one might encounter devaluation, rejection, and hostility from family members and peers.

Because media images of homosexuality are often distorted and negative, those who are questioning or just coming out need accurate school curricula.

## BOX 2.8  NAVIGATION AIDS

- Language (to understand oneself and to tell one's story)
- Humor (to put oneself, one's community, and even one's oppression into human context)
- Traditions and rituals (to bring people together and tie them to those who preceded them)
- Norms of conduct (to signal membership and, when rejected, non-conformity)
- Professional and personal roles (to suggest possibilities for sustenance and fulfillment)
- Political options (to offer agency)
- Strategies for stigma management (to thrive despite heterosexism)
- Opportunities for friendship, sexual experimentation, and love relationships (to develop capacities for sustaining interpersonal connections)

Adapted from L. D. Garnets and D. C. Kimmel, *Psychological Perspectives on Lesbian & Gay Male Experiences* (New York: Columbia University Press, 1993), introduction, p. 14.

(See chapter 7.) Furthermore, they require direct contact with other gay people and access to the subculture for affirmation, safety, and a sense of belonging. Finding their places in an open, confident, gay and lesbian community is nurturing on many levels. (See box 2.8.)

*Question 14: Are there differences between male and female homosexual development?*

Males tend to self-define following homosexual activity and generally equate being gay with erotic attraction rather than romantic connection. Of course, all young men are socialized to put sex before relationship. Gay men often resemble straight men in sexual assertiveness, roaming, valuing physical attributes, and finding love, if at all, after sexual conquest.

Because girls used to be conditioned to do the opposite, research on lesbians often found them self-defining after falling in love. Their erotic feelings evolved from prior emotional attachment. (See box 2.9.) Perhaps homosexual subculture has reinforced these gender differences. Until recently urban gay males were acculturated mostly in bars and other places where sex was the object. Lesbians

## BOX 2.9  LATE-BLOOMING

More than a decade ago, [Nancy] Walsh and [Carol] Flyzik met as nurses at Hale Hospital in Haverhill and became fast friends. Then they fell in love. No one was more surprised than Nancy Walsh that the object of her affection was a woman. "Totally, totally shocked," she said. She had been married for 19 years, then divorced, and had never before been involved with a woman. "You fall in love with a person, you don't fall in love with a sex," Walsh said.

Kathleen Burge, "Sept. 11 Leaves Same-Sex Partners Adrift," *Boston Globe Online*, www.bostonglobe.com (March 18, 2002).

socialized in friendship circles and the women's community, where personal ties and mutual support were stressed. Because many women seem capable of intense connections to other women there were opportunities for their attachments to become homosexual relationships.

Women's sexual autonomy, partly a product of their economic advancement, has only enhanced those opportunities. (See box 2.10.) Moreover, as women in general grow less ashamed of their erotic appetites, lesbians, too, are freer for libidinous romps.

Lastly, since sexual identity and behavior can be more nuanced and fluid for women than for men, stage models may be less helpful for categorizing female development.

## BOX 2.10  IMAGES AND EARNINGS

[The percentage of women who said they had recently had gay sex] climbed from 0.2% in 1988 to nearly 3% [in 1998]. . . . [Amy C. Butler of the University of Iowa] suggests . . . that positive images of gay people in the media and declining legal and economic barriers "may have made it easier for people to recognize their same-gender sexual interest and to act on it. . . . Equalizing the earning potential of men and women may enable women to consider family structures and sexual partnerships that do not include men."

"More Americans Having Gay Sex, Study Shows," *Reuters Health*, March 14, 2001.

*Question 15: Isn't being homosexual generally the same for all homosexual people?*

It is not a uniform identity. There are many ways to experience and express one's same-gender attractions. Thus, there are numbers of homosexual identities or "homosexualities."

Some folks think that homosexuality must overpower and displace all other aspects of a person's identity, that being gay or lesbian would make one have more in common with other homosexual people than with anyone else. A better analysis is that sexuality affects the other aspects of one's identity but is also likely affected by them.

The factors that influence one's sense of self and determine how one presents oneself to the world are an interdependent matrix. Gender, race, and ethnicity, for example, can affect one's sense of being gay. Conversely, one's homosexuality is likely to have an impact on one's gendered, racial, and ethnic "selves."

Cultural forces influence whether and how same-gender desire affects one's identity. Mass media and mobility have spread the idea of a monolithic Western "gay" identity around the world and have had an impact both in places where sexual behaviors are interpreted differently than in the West (see box 2.11.) and also in repressive states. The Internet is having a demonstrable effect in Eastern Europe and Asia. (See boxes 2.12 and 2.25.)

In the West, individuals with same-gender desires from different racial, ethnic, religious, class, and immigrant groups may reject the "gay" identity for themselves. And if they accept it, they face the challenge of forging their multiple identities into a new self in which sexuality does not harmfully diminish the other components.

---

### BOX 2.11   EAST MEETS WEST: STRUGGLE AND PROGRESS

In a major reversal of previous policy, psychiatrists in this country of 1.3 billion people have decided to stop classifying homosexuality as a mental disease.... [T]he American Psychiatric Association... [had] urged the Chinese group to change its stance.... In December, a popular TV talk show originating in Hunan province and broadcast nationwide invited gay people on to the set to talk about their experiences—a first for Chinese television.

Henry Chu, "Chinese Psychiatrists Decide Homosexuality Isn't Abnormal," *Los Angeles Times*, March 6, 2001.

**BOX 2.12   WIRED FOR CHANGE**

Seislak, the software engineer, said he believes the Internet revolution, more than anything else, helped accelerate the gay revolution in Poland. "... The access to information, to literature, to other gays—this is our real revolution," he said.... "Gays from my generation still feel this shame, and we are still afraid to talk openly, but not the new generation."

Tom Hundley, "Gay Life Gains Steam in Warsaw," *Chicago Tribune*, August 2, 2002.

*Question 16: Can people integrate their homosexuality into their other minority identities?*

The process can be difficult. Since racial, ethnic, class, and religious affiliations are usually well established by the time an individual begins to come out as gay, the homosexual component may appear to threaten one's other minority identities.

The pervasive image of the homosexual as white, Anglo, secular, and middle-class sends a message to immigrant, minority, working-class, and religious youth that to be gay they would have to abandon their neighborhoods, friends, cultures, faiths, and families. That would mean losing a dependable refuge from racial, ethnic, class, and religious intolerance. Yet homophobia in their culture of origin is also alienating.

Antigay/lesbian bias is no worse in any single minority group than it is in another or in the majority culture. Each group has its own homophobic ideas and behaviors. Some may be more subtle or polite than others, but they are no less damaging, particularly to the young.

Lastly, although we might generalize, no minority group is uniform. There are always individuals and sometimes subcultures within them that offer shelter and encouragement to gays and lesbians.

*Question 17: How does class relate to homosexual identity development?*

Compared to race and religion, little attention has been paid to the intersection of class and homosexuality. Rigid gender role expectations among working-class people may lead to the belief that homosexuals want to *be* the opposite gender. In fact, working-class gay and lesbian youth often engage in minstrelizing gender behavior, either because they agree that gay means gender inversion or because they suffer less hostility if they go along with the expectation. Since conservative views of gender and sexuality are related to less schooling, working-class gays and lesbians might suffer as a result of their family's lack of educational opportunity.

## BOX 2.13   POOR RELATIONS

See how hard you have to search for media images of queers who are part of the vast working poor in this country. Find the homeless transgendered folks. Find stories of gay immigrants, lesbian moms working three jobs, bisexual truckers falling asleep from too many hours on the road, gay men in the unemployment line.... The myth of our wealth goes deep, so deep that even other gay people seem to believe it.... We treat the poverty that exists among us—as well as the differences of class—as a dirty secret to be hidden, denied, repelled.

Amber Hollibaugh, "Queers without Money," *Village Voice*, June 20, 2001.

Poverty also limits access to counseling services, particularly in times of government cutbacks, so poor youth who need professional coming out support are at a disadvantage. In addition, low-income students in poor schools also have less chance of being exposed to up-to-date gay positive curricula and library holdings.

Poor people can also feel unwelcome in a mainstream gay movement that emphasizes middle-class proprieties and assimilation. (See box 2.13.)

*Question 18: How does being African American relate to homosexual identity development?*

For black gay youth in the United States (or in the West Indies, U.K., et al.) the three pillars of racial pride and solidarity—community, church, and family—can also be the sources of destructive homophobia.

The young black male peer group, like those of other races, often bonds through hypermasculinity and antigay harassment. Homophobia, in rap and reggae lyrics, for example, enforces the code of the "street." A male who listens to the wrong kind of music, does well in school, or avoids gangs, promiscuity, or violence can be gay-baited.

African American homophobia is linked to historical concerns about emasculation. Black manhood has been battered by the humiliations of slavery and the law enforcement, education, health, and welfare systems. Since male homosexuality is seen as feminizing and weakening, it is anathema in this context.

Gayness is also seen as a "white thing." This perception goes beyond media images. A black homosexual, it is thought, *learns* to be gay by associating with whites. It is an outside contagion. Because same-gender sex has traditionally had different meanings in Africa than in the West, gayness can be labeled a New World phenomenon to which black people, as colonized Africans or involuntary African American immigrants, have been exposed. (See box 2.14.)

---

**BOX 2.14   IN AFRICA: HOMOPHOBIA, DESPITE OLD TRADITIONS**

Kenya's president, Daniel Arap Moi, derided homosexuality as a "scourge."..."It is against African tradition and biblical teachings."... "Homosexuality is against all the norms of African society and culture," [Zimbabwe's President] Mugabe once said. "Let them be gay in the United States, Europe and elsewhere. They shall be sad people here."

Chris McGreal, "Debt? War? Gays Are the Real Evil, Say African Leaders," *The Guardian* [U.K.], October 2, 1999.

"In some cultures in the northern part of Nigeria," [the president of Alliance Rights Nigeria says] "there are people called dan daudu.... It means 'men who are wives of men.' In olden days, to show your immense wealth, it was easy to have a harem of wives. But to show that you were truly rich, you had to keep a stable of men."

"Gays of Nation Unite!" *The News* [Lagos, Nigeria], April 22, 2002.

---

One hopes that the pro-gay stances of prominent African Americans like Coretta King and John Lewis and of Desmond Tutu and the South African constitution will change some of these homophobic ideas and behaviors.

*Question 19: What role does the black church play in this identity struggle?*

The black Christian church, a major force in community cohesion, has often been a source of estrangement for gays, lesbians, and bisexuals. African American ministers regularly condemn homosexuality from the pulpit as an abomination worse than other sins because it goes against the divine plan for the family. (See box 2.15.) The gay black man is sometimes depicted as a threat to racial survival. Gay black Muslims, scorned as "degenerate," don't fare any better in their mosques.

*Question 20: Is there no accommodation made to homosexuality in the black community?*

Homosexual African Americans have a long history, from humble church choir directors to luminaries like Bayard Rustin, Lorraine Hansberry, and Ralph Bunche. But it seems toleration has often hinged on keeping sexuality under cover, even if that meant marrying and leading a secret gay life on the side. Coming out publicly is not allowed and may even be frowned upon as a white practice.

## BOX 2.15   FEW SANCTUARIES

[R]umors of [Chris Coleman's] homosexuality had spread around the church, and rather than being welcomed back, he was mocked.... "As soon as I sat down, all of a sudden, the sermon got turned around to homosexuality.... It was about damnation. You heard how wrong it was.... There were times I would just leave, because it was too much."

Laura Putre, "Hell to Pay: Reviled as the Worst Sinners, Gay Black Men Find Refuge in the Closet," *Cleveland* [Ohio] *Scene*, October 4, 2001.

[T]he Rev. Kenneth Samuel is trying to lead his 6,000-strong congregation on a path few black churches have trod: wholehearted acceptance of lesbians and gays. After convincing himself that homophobia should be combated as zealously as racism, Samuel severed his Victory Church's links with black- and white-led Baptist organizations.

"Religion Today," *Associated Press*, May 16, 2002.

Open African American gays and lesbians have created a vibrant rich subculture in many places, including in the conservative South, yet they often struggle to find acceptance within the larger black community. The result can be social schizophrenia and denial. (See box 2.16.)

Gays and lesbians of color also face the dilemma of competing loyalties, the question: which are you first—black or gay? The relative significance of race versus sexual orientation to a person's identity may be related to the stigma he or she suffers because of either factor. Although race is usually more conspicuous than sexuality, it is not always so.

Greater social stigma, moreover, does not always result in greater self-identification, particularly when one's identifying features can be hidden. It might in fact drive an individual who can "pass" toward denial and repression.

Racist and homophobic oppressions are different, yet linked. Both are driven by an appropriation of power to demean and control. Although *which are you first?* can lead to an interesting social and psychological case history, the question is in the end unfair to put to any individual.

*Question 21: Do black lesbians have an easier time?*

All black women face strong pressure to have families. Although demeaned, lesbians are still expected to marry, but without the same sexual freedoms afforded to gay and bisexual men. Less income allows even fewer options. Their invisibility

## BOX 2.16  DOUBLE LIVES

[B]eing on the DL [down-low] means they may have sex with men but don't see themselves as gay. It means they may maintain relationships with women while secretly engaging in sex with men, but they're not going to label themselves bisexual either. For this generation, spoon-fed on hip-hop's hypermasculine culture, those labels just don't fit, are too politicized. . . . And in socially conservative black communities, where being gay is generally tolerated—so long as it's not too pronounced—that works just fine.

Steven Gray, "Brothers in Arms: By Day, They're the Guys on the Block. But Come Friday Night, It's Time to Head Out and Hook Up at Jenny's," *Washington Post*, August 31, 2001.

If you're a man and you're influenced by hip-hop and you're intimate with another man, you're a homo thug. . . . Whether the homo thugs want to identify themselves as gay is a different story. Alot have issues—you know, self hatred and all that. Some of these men deal with full-on, 24/7 drag queens, and they do not believe that they are gay. They still consider themselves straight. Every homo thug has your hard side and then you have your softer side, that you might be comfortable with behind closed doors.

Rapper Caushun, in Jane Spencer, "Is Hip-Hop Ready for a Gay Rapper?" *Newsweek*, www.msnbc.com/news (June 29, 2001).

may be an even greater burden. Denied prominence in cultural and intellectual affairs, black lesbians are also nearly invisible in the popular mass media. Still, the hate crime murder of fifteen-year-old black lesbian, Sakia Gunn, in Newark in 2003 sparked a public display of grief and pride among her African American lesbian high school peers that is evidence of new attitudes and a promising emergence.

*Question 22: Can black gays and lesbians find safety in the gay community?*

In the larger gay community, gay and lesbian African Americans face racism, tokenism, and sexual objectification. Outright racism may be the easiest to combat. Most have good role models, strategies, and ready allies for fighting racism. Liberal tokenism is also being effectively challenged.

Avoiding becoming a fetish is perhaps more complicated. Of course, not everyone who finds excitement in the body of the "other" is exploitive, yet the potential

**BOX 2.17   COMING HOME**

I ask you brother: Does your mama really know about you? Does she really know what I am? Does she know I want to love her son, care for him, nurture and celebrate him? Do you think she'll understand? I hope so, because I am coming home. There will be no place else to go that will be worth so much effort and love.

Essex Hemphill, "Introduction," in *Brother to Brother: New Writings by Black Gay Men*, ed. Essex Hemphill (Boston: Alyson Publications, 1991), xx.

for objectification is real. It takes honest communication to tease out the power issues when partners of color are exoticized in interracial relationships.

Because the antiracism struggle is familiar to them, it may be more comfortable for homosexual black people to fight racism in the gay community than to seek affirmation in a homophobic black community. Still, many gay and lesbian African Americans have called on their peers to return home to engage proudly in that effort. (See box 2.17.)

*Question 23: Do lesbians and gays of Latin descent face the same identity issues?*

Gay Latinas and Latinos also wrestle with gender, family, cultural survival, and religion. Like their African American counterparts, they find the price of remaining in their community is often silence. (See box 2.18.)

Latinas who value their traditional honored roles as daughters, wives, and mothers do not easily give them up. They understand that coming out as lesbian

**BOX 2.18   A SILENT PRESENCE...OR AN ODD ABSENCE**

The Hispanic cultural stance on homosexuality can be reduced to a popular saying: 'ojos que no ven, corazón que no siente' [What the eyes don't see, the heart doesn't feel], says Martin Ornelas-Quintero.... "All of our families knew that hairdresser who would do all the women's hair.... Everyone has that tía or tio who's no longer part of the family. That's diferente. Es asi"—or that way—"No one ever deepens the conversation of what asi is."

Andrea Elliott, "Living a Dual Life," *Miami Herald*, June 11, 2002.

could be viewed as a threat to the strict Latin gender and religious systems and, indeed, to cultural survival. They also fear losing a special bond with their mothers, who are often role models in the struggle against racism, poverty, and sexism.

A Latina lesbian's sexuality violates the cultural norm that women do not discuss sex or expect sexual gratification. She may be viewed as an insult both to women who accept sexual conventions and to the men who thrive on them. She may appear to have adopted Anglo values. The Catholic Church's attitude compounds her condemnation.

*Question 24: Do Latino men face the same pressures?*

Latino men are allowed greater sexual freedom, but they still risk everything by coming out. (See box 2.19.)

Not all Latino men who have sex with other men are stigmatized. The critical factor is the role one assumes in the sexual act. Only the man who takes the passive role is thought to be homosexual (*passivo, cochón, joto,* or *puto*). Because he chooses the presumably inferior female position he can be degraded, bashed, or even killed, sometimes by the very man who has slept with him. The *activo* (also *mayate* or *machisto*), on the other hand, suffers no stigma because he is seen as merely taking advantage of the universal male privilege of dominance.

---

### BOX 2.19  NO SAFETY

More than 100 gays, lesbians and transsexuals were killed in Brazil last year as a result of hate crimes, the largest number recorded of any nation....

"Report: Brazil a Leader in Gay Hate Crimes," *United Press International,* April 23, 2002.

"There is no location in the country where you can be openly gay without being harassed,"...a Mexico City human rights activist said.... The Pasadena court granted asylum to a gay cross-dresser named Giovanni Hernandez...after he had been repeatedly beaten and raped by Mexican police.... Just last month, most newspapers covered the story of a privately operated swimming pool in the city of Aguascalientes that displayed an entry sign that read: "No Dogs, No Homosexuals."

Wendy Patterson, "A Life of Fear for Gays," *San Francisco Chronicle,* October 12, 2000.

## BOX 2.20    PRESSURE POINTS: GOD, COMMUNITY, AND THE RELATIVES

It took Leivas-Andino . . . seven years to overcome her religious and cultural prejudices and to accept the fact that her son, Paolo Andino, was gay. . . . "It was such a horrendous, horrific, incredibly impossible idea, that I wouldn't even entertain it. . . . We were quite 'normal,' you know, your typical upper-middle class Catholic Cuban-American family in Miami," she says.

Magaly Morales, "She Fights Bias for Gay Son's Sake," *Tallahassee Democrat*, July 23, 2002.

["Francisco"] turned to prostitution at the age of 16, after his parents and aunts . . . threw him out of their home for being gay. . . . When [Alex Sánchez] finally came out to his family, they threw him out of the house and called him "a curse," and a shame to the family to say the least. . . . "My mom was crying and disappointed. When she found out, she called my girlfriend's parents to tell on us in order to separate us," says [Joette] Carrillo, a 15-year-old Alhambra resident.

Gabriela Hasbun, "Under Our Wings," *Tentaciones Magazine*, April 2002.

An older Mexicano/Chicano generally dominates a younger effeminate male. The majority of these young men (*maricóns*) begin these practices before puberty, usually with relatives, but they do not always remain passive as they get older.

Effeminacy may be tolerated as comic and macho homosexual behavior can be condoned as long as it is not advertised. When a Latino comes out, however, his identity, like lesbianism, is seen as an assault on family, church, and community. Whether or not a man having sex with other men voluntarily takes on a "gay" identity depends on a number of factors, including: outward virility, social class/mobility, exposure to white gay culture, and capacity for survival as a cultural outcast.

The burdens of conforming to community norms are intense. Many Latina lesbians and gay Latinos maintain their status only by staying in the closet, often marrying and having children as a lifeline. (See box 2.20.)

*Question 25: How does being Asian American relate to homosexual identity development?*

Because Asian American cultures represent a range of Asian traditions, it is difficult to generalize. We can say, however, that many gay and lesbian Asians

## BOX 2.21  FAMILY FIRST

I would have no daughter-in-law or grandchildren to visit. . . . I was ashamed. I thought of my son as being one of those gay people who do unnatural things. My family and friends would find out. They would think that I raised a Bakla or Binabae—a man who acts like a female. In the Philippines, homosexuals are looked upon as bad people. They don't belong anywhere. There isn't even a word for "gay" in Tagalog. The words are all derogatory.

Belinda Rayos Del Sol Dronkers-Laureta, "Out, Coming Together," *Asian Week* [San Francisco, Calif.], November 23, 2001.

Discrimination at the workplace is the norm. . . . But the most painful rejection occurs at home. The typical Korean family won't think twice before summarily disowning its gay members.

Glen Choi, "Church Offers Special Haven for Korea's Gay Community," *Korea Herald*, February 12, 2001.

feel estranged from native communities that regard homosexuality as white and Western. Among Chinese Americans, for example, a person's actions may be limited by reverence for ancestors and strict ideas of role and duty, particularly to family. Self-exploration of any kind is considered too individualistic. Sexuality of any kind is not discussed publicly.

Unless one is Christian or Islamic, Asian negativity toward homosexuality has nothing to do with sin. Rather gayness is frowned upon because it appears to put individual needs before gender role and family duties. Women are expected to be deferential daughters, wives, and mothers; men are supposed to further their lineage and provide for the family. To reject these obligations is shameful. Having gay or lesbian children indicates a failure of parenting, especially for women, who are held responsible for child rearing. (See box 2.21.)

In Thailand men must marry, have children, and not be effeminate in public, yet they can have gay relationships on the side. In Vietnam, male homosexuals, *lai cai* (half man–half woman) are seen mostly as transvestites. Nevertheless, in late 2002, thirty gay men found having sex in a massage parlor were sent to an "education centre." In Japan, male-centered heterosexuality abounds in ubiquitous unembarrassed pornographic display. Homosexuality is acknowledged, sometimes depicted, but not understood or accepted. (See box 2.22.) Even the family of deceased writer Yukio Mishima, known to the world as homosexual, successfully sued to block publication of his gay letters.

## BOX 2.22   JAPAN: NO WAY OUT

[F]ew Japanese truly understand what homosexuality is, even though the media is at times awash in gay topics.... All titillation and little information, and popular.... To come out is considered by the vast majority of homosexuals to be suicidal.... Society demands that men be married by a certain age.... [F]or most male homosexuals, their orientation must remain a closely guarded secret, or society...will crush them.

Scott Gordon, "Examining the Marginalization of Male Homosexuality" [book review], *Daily Yomiuri* [Tokyo, Japan], March 18, 2001.

In large cities on mainland China, some gay men gather in bars and discos, but most lead double lives, meeting for clandestine sex in parks and bathhouses. The gay rights movement, whose members call themselves *tongzhi*, or "comrades," is led from abroad. Although the old "mental illness" diagnosis has been officially revoked and the Internet (where gay sites aren't banned as they are in South Korea, for example) is enhancing communication, traditional pressures still make life difficult. (See box 2.23.)

In India Hindu fundamentalism, harsh laws, prying police, and dangerous hoodlums add to the familiar Asian burdens of mandatory marriage. Most urban

## BOX 2.23   OLD CHINA YIELDS...SLOWLY

"I thought I was mentally sick.... I took a lot of herbs, and even followed some traditional prescriptions by eating baked scorpions, lizards, and toads. Apparently it didn't work," [Hua Zhen] added. "I met a lot of gay people [in Beijing]. It made me feel good and normal because I was not alone." ... "For many years, ordinary folks treat people of the same sex having a sexual relationship as a social disease, like gambling or prostitution or syphilis," [gay activist Yanhai Wan] says.... Gays are still constantly subject to harassment, blackmail, and arrest by the police.... "After I got home, my mother knelt in front of me and cried. She said I brought disgrace to the family and she would kill herself if I do this again," [Jason Li] said. "I hated myself, but I couldn't change. If I come out to my wife, she will leave me and take my son away."

Wen Huang, "China's Gay Community in Half Fight," *Boston Globe*, April 29, 2001.

## BOX 2.24  INDIA: CHARADES AND SHACKLES

[F]ew of the hundreds of men who turn out for the weekly parties in Delhi, Bombay, and Calcutta are openly gay. Even though they have sex with men, a majority would probably not identify themselves as homosexuals—a charade that is bolstered by Indian culture's emphasis on conformity.... "If you are a woman and gay, you are really at the bottom of the totem pole," [Angeli Gopalan] said. While men are generally given free rein in India, women's movements are restricted—particularly in rural areas.

Marion Lloyd, "Out of India's Antigay Closet," *Boston Globe*, October 24, 1999.

gay men prefer to lead a double life, while in remote villages, both identity-informing gay concepts and social opportunities are scarce. Indian lesbians are subject to even greater cultural restrictions. (See box 2.24.) The Indian term for gay male sex is *musti* (mischief), boyish fooling around that may continue into adulthood but cannot be deeply romantic or take the place of marriage. Pakistani men also may have quiet gay affairs as long as they do not detract from their family obligations.

In sum, across Asia and the Mideast the experiences of gays and lesbians are not uniform and are in flux. Where there have been advances, the influence of the West and the Internet and the importance of income are undeniable. (See box 2.25.)

*Question 26: How can gay and lesbian Asians answer the charge that homosexuality comes from being exposed to the West?*

Some have tried to find homosexual precedents in their own cultural histories. They have researched gay male relationships in the Chinese tradition of the "shared peach" (fourth century B.C.) and the "cut sleeve" (sixth through first centuries B.C.). Others have uncovered homosexuality in Hindu erotic texts and sculpture, and lesbians in the *Mahabharata* and before the Aryan invasion.

Many point to the male-to-female transsexuality of the Indian *hijra*, some of whom are hermaphrodites and others deliberately castrated. Alternately feared, mocked, or respected, *hijras* dance and bestow blessings at village births and weddings.

There is little comfort for most of today's gays and lesbians in the apparently mandatory fusion of gender identity and sexuality in such traditions, whether in India or elsewhere. (In Roman Britain, for example, transsexual priests of the Greek goddess Cybele castrated themselves and wore jewelry, colorful female robes, and turbans or tiaras.)

**BOX 2.25   PAN ASIA AND MIDEAST**

[I]t is true that the Internet has opened things up considerably for many gays and lesbians in Asia. "Most of the growth [in the gay community in Asia] has been within the middle classes because there has been a lot of overseas travel and it has become quite an international network," says [Dr. Alison Murray].

Helen Signey, "Homosexuality: That Unspeakable Western Disease," *Sydney* [Australia] *Morning Herald*, February 18, 2001.

"It was the only free space to express our ideas," says [Maher] Sabry, who got online in 1997 and immediately became a cyber activist. "The Egyptian media likes to say homosexuality came through the Internet from the West, but the forums and discussion groups were all Egyptians."

Mubarak Dahir, "Courage in Adversity Personified," *Bay Windows* [Mass.], May 9, 2002.

*Question 27: Don't homosexual Native Americans point to the "two-spirit" people as their predecessors?*

Some tribes do have "two-spirit" (or *berdache*) traditions. Not all were identical, but the general pattern was one in which males (and more rarely females) were permitted from childhood to adopt the dress and role of another gender. Many homosexual Native Americans who suffer the condemnation of their tribes' adopted Christianity are eager to find validation in the earlier two-spirit practice. (A similar pattern of missionary-induced homophobia has been noted in the indigenous Hawaiian experience, where the transgendered sacred healers, *mahu*, were once revered.) One must ask, however, whether the two-spirits were actually homosexual and how their tribes regarded them.

Two-spiritedness was rooted in gender presentation, primarily in labor and clothing, rather than in erotic desire. The tradition was demonstrated chiefly in men dressing like women, doing women's work, and occasionally "marrying" men. On the other hand, men who now and then had sex with other men, but did not prefer women's social role, were not deemed two-spirits. And without two-spiritedness, homosexual conduct was thought ridiculous or evil. So, like the *hijras*, two-spirits were more about gender than sexuality. Also, like the *hijras*, they acted as shamans, particularly regarding rites of marriage.

Native American women who acted like men were seldom called two-spirit. Girls were generally discouraged from complete gender crossing. In those rare cases when they did, the pattern was similar to the male one: childhood visions, unconventional work preference, cross-dressing, and cross-marriage. It was also believed that such women did not menstruate.

Some anthropologists object to the term *cross-gendered*, that is, adopting the role of their "opposite." Claiming that gender roles were not so rigid, they prefer *third gender*, neither male nor female.

As to treatment, tribal reaction varied. Sometimes objects of ambivalence or approval, two-spirits could also be stigmatized and tormented. In the intertribal warfare of the far-flung cultures of the Americas, East Asia, and Islamic Africa, vanquished men were compelled to adopt women's dress and work and to submit to the sexual advances of the victors. And within the tribe, certain men underwent initiation and lost status, wife, and children, if they had them. They might be treated like village whores, providing an outlet for young and unmarried males. By the late nineteenth century, perhaps provoked by Christian missionaries, families were ashamed to have their men become two-spirits and spurned those who persisted.

It is understandable that multiple minority gays and lesbians would look for sexuality roots in their own people's histories. However, both Asian and Native American gay rights claims that depend on ambiguous precedents are ultimately weaker than those based on human rights arguments. Because past practices are so often used to deny rights, no liberation movement should depend on them.

*Question 28: How do Arab/Muslim people negotiate these issues?*

As is the case in other groups, rigid gender roles, family expectations, and conservative patriarchal culture and religion usually complicate gay identity acquisition. If they don't want to be disowned, young people have to stay in the closet and engage in a straight charade. Women particularly have little physical freedom, whereas men may fool around discretely. (See box 2.26.)

---

**BOX 2.26   OVERLOOKED ACTS**

There is a conditional permission for [male-on-male] erotic games or even rape as an exercise of male power. Pretend it is a joke, or a put-down and you can get by. But call it true love or honest and real sexual desire and you are in trouble. If you . . . fail to prove that your ultimate desire is dominating a woman, you would be considered a suspect.

Saviz Shafaie, in Jack Nichols, "Saviz Shafaie: Iran's Gay Pioneer" [interview], *Greenwich Village Gazette*, September 16, 1999.

## BOX 2.27   BEATEN: IN BODY AND SPIRIT

Last year [an American] and his Palestinian boyfriend [Ahmad], moved into Ahmad's West Bank village.... "[T]hen one day we found a letter under our door from the Islamic court. It listed the five forms of death prescribed by Islam for homosexuality, including stoning and burning. We fled to Israel that same day." Now they live in hiding—mostly from Ahmad's brothers, who have searched for the couple in Tel Aviv and threatened to kill Ahmad.... A 17-year-old refugee from Nablus named Salah [a pseudonym]...spent months in a [Palestinian] prison where interrogators cut him with glass and poured toilet cleaner into his wounds.... "I've tried to kill myself six times already," says Salah.

· Yossi Klein Halevi, "Refugee Status," *The New Republic*, August 19, 2002.

[Muna Hawatmeh] testified [her] family members hit her, kicked her and verbally abused her until she kissed her father's feet and promised to change her sexual orientation.... [Her brother] held a large knife toward her: "And he said, 'You going to die tonight.'"

Michael Janofsky, "Family, Culture and Law Meet in a Utah Court Case," *New York Times*, April 21, 2001.

Nobody knows how many gays are languishing in Egyptian jails.... But because of the strict societal taboos against homosexuality, Egyptian human-rights groups have shunned such cases, leaving it to a handful of local gay activists to raise legal fees and provide other support.

Josh Hammer, "One Man's Tale," *Newsweek International*, www.msnbc .com/news (February 16, 2002).

Because the "traditional family" is seen as the cornerstone of a moral society (even in a more sexually liberal country like Lebanon), openly homosexual people are often appallingly treated in their native countries and their adoptive ones. (See box 2.27.)

*Question 29: Isn't religion a central issue for people coming out?*

Orthodox Jewish, Christian, Muslim, and Mormon creeds do not accept homosexuality. Hindus are encouraged to have only procreative sex. (In 1998, Hindu

## BOX 2.28  DON'T ASK...

"Mother, Dad and family. I have committed suicide," [the suicide] note began.... "As I believed I was Christian, I believed I could never be gay." ... The people who dressed him for burial were struck by the sight of his knees, deeply callused from praying for an answer that never came.

Mark Miller, "To Be Gay—and Mormon," *Newsweek,* www.msnbc.com/news (May 8, 2000).

The plight of gay students at right-wing religious schools is a painful one.... Suicide is not infrequent.... [The students] are also told at a lot of these schools that they can find change if they draw close to God.... [They] are regularly forced to reveal the identities of other students they believe may be gay and are coerced into ex-gay programs, where "treatments" can include electroshock therapy.

Erin O'Briant, "The Right 'Spot,'" [book review] *Southern Voice* [Atlanta], August 16, 2001.

[Shalom] tried behavioral therapy, wearing a rubber band around his wrist and flicking it every time he felt attracted to a man. He went to Israel, where a rabbi told him to eat dates and recite a psalm every day. When that failed, he entered Aesthetic Realism, a New York-based group that works with gay people to change their sexual orientation.... "I felt emotionally raped," he says. "I couldn't keep acting. I decided to accept it. At 31, I came out to myself."

Naomi Grossman, "The Gay Orthodox Underground," *MOMENT,* www.momentmag.com (April/May 2001).

fundamentalist mobs ransacked theaters in India that showed *Fire,* a film about two Indian housewives who have an affair.) The Chinese Falun Gong, struggling against their own oppression, still believes God will eliminate homosexuality in the Earth's final days. The Catholic and Mormon churches make some distinction between homosexual persons and sinful homosexual acts. Jewish orthodoxy deems desire irrelevant.

Rome still classifies homosexuality as a "disorder" and advises repentance and cure, despite the revolution at its very front door. Mormons, who cannot get into the highest level of heaven unless married, are offered deprogramming or excommunication. Orthodox Jews and Protestants are presented with the "cures"

**BOX 2.29   THIS IS EUROPE TOO**

[Croatia's first Gay Pride parade], that gathered amid tight security some 200 people, rather supporters than homosexuals themselves, also showed that opposition to homosexuality is still strong here as at least 15 persons supporting the event were beaten up. . . .

"Croatian Homosexuals Step Out from Shadow to Demand Equal Civil Rights," *Agence France-Presse*, July 18, 2002.

Gays have been the targets of threats by right-wing groups. Only a small proportion of people who are gay dare to tell family, friends and colleagues.

Carlotta Gall, "BUCHAREST JOURNAL: It's Still No Breeze for Gays," *New York Times*, October 17, 2001.

Slovak employees fire homosexuals with impunity, especially homosexual teachers who are thought to be unsuitable to work with children.

Matthew J. Reynolds, "Slovak Gay Leaders Take Case to Deputies," *Slovak Spectator* [Bratislava], March 20, 2001.

of prayer, aversive conditioning, and psychological counseling. "Jews Offering New Alternatives to Homosexuality" ("JONAH") and "Nefesh" are the new Jewish "ex-gay" ministry. Being gay and staying in these churches, synagogues, or mosques means being ignored or alternatively being pathologized or demonized. (See box 2.28.)

In Eastern Europe gay people suffer the condemnation of Catholicism, Eastern Orthodoxy, and the historic antipathy of once-communist states. (See box 2.29.)

Such hostility from fundamentalist churches can evoke a defensive antireligious response from the gay community. Thus, gays and lesbians may find little peer support for remaining in their denominations.

Welcoming congregations and gay religious organizations make it easier to reconcile one's sexuality and one's spiritual roots. (See appendix A.)

*Question 30: What other pressures make it hard for multiple minority people to integrate their sexualities with the rest of their identities?*

Prejudice in the gay community and homophobia in their native cultures are the most obvious obstacles, but multiple minority people also must grapple with the monolithic notion of homosexuality in the West. They are often expected to adopt an identity label, a psychological profile, and even a set of behaviors, any of which may seem alien to them. Pressure to conform to this preconceived "lifestyle" can come from both straight and gay "identity police." Usually safe from outright persecution, they are still encumbered in self-invention and self-definition.

Multiple minority people must be free to reject these strictures and to forge their own authentic integrated identities. Sexual expression must be affirmed along with other vital elements of the "self." If some component in the realm of "homosexualities" contributes to this self-definition, it should be able to be named as freely and respected as much as any other feature of their humanity.

(For further reading, see appendix R.)

# 3

# Counseling GLBT Students and Their Families

*Question 1: How are gay youth different in their counseling needs from their heterosexual peers?*

Exploring one's sexuality, forming one's sexual identity and sexual values, and finding significant others preoccupy nearly all adolescents. This critical endeavor coincides with the challenges of honing competencies and vocational interests, moral and spiritual values, and the skills needed for friendship and family relations. Adolescence is often a period of disequilibrium, stress, and confusion.

Because their sexuality is stigmatized, lesbian, gay, and bisexual youth have even more to contend with. Usually struggling along their developmental path in secret, they have less help overcoming obstacles. The shame of internalized stigma is just one impediment to their healthy development.

*Question 2: Does that mean that gay youth are more likely to suffer from mental illness than straight youth?*

The complete answer to that question is still unknown. Because so many gay and questioning youth have not come out publicly, most studies of this population have been based on the experiences of teens receiving social services as gay clients. A convenient interview sample, they don't necessarily represent gay youth as a whole.

Some new studies using broader samples still point to increased health risk for gay youth compared with their straight-identified peers. Since much of this research is conducted in schools, it does not include most habitually absent students or any dropouts. As a result, the risks to gay kids may still be underreported.

## BOX 3.1   RESILIENCE IN IOWA

- Scott Spilger of Iowa City: National Merit scholar, debate team star, National Forensics League's top 10 students, and hopes to study environmental law. Students threw objects and epithets at Spilger and his boyfriend at a Valentine's Day dance.
- Michael Bowser of Waterloo: editor of the school paper at East High School, on the honor roll, and recognized by the art department for outstanding achievement. Bowser was punched out at school while walking down the hall with his boyfriend.
- Jonathan Darby: editor of the "all-state honors" Washington High School yearbook for two years, National Honor Society, and Quill and Scroll. Darby transferred out of biology class rather than take more abuse.
- Jerryn Johnston of Gilbert: honor roll, band, chorus, speech, drama. Enrolled in classes at Iowa State University. Endured subtle and egregious acts of discrimination and violence from teachers and classmates since coming out in 1999.
- Iowa's First Friday Breakfast Club 2002 Matthew Shepard Scholarship winners for outstanding openly gay and lesbian high school seniors— four years' tuition, books and fees at a state university.

Marc Hansen, "Four Openly Gay Teens in Iowa Earn Scholarships," *Des Moines Register*, June 8, 2002.

One aspect of these discouraging statistics, however, is often overlooked. Although the numbers indicate that sexual minority youth are disproportionately endangered compared to heterosexual youth, they also show that the *majority* of gay youth are *not* at risk. In fact, they suggest that despite the obstacles they face most glbt youth are resilient. (See box 3.1.) Thus, instead of a "deficit model" of gay youth development that stresses pathology, researchers are beginning to produce an "asset-based" model, focusing on the strengths that keep most sexual minority youth healthy and stable.

Coming out of the closet and family acceptance seem to be prime generators of resilience. Coming out is often an act of desperation; not proof of established resilience, but an entry point to it. The consequences of self-disclosure, especially positive response from others, facilitate recovery from stigmatization. Pride, better relationships, and social activism frequently replace depression and low self-esteem. Being out, especially at school, does bring its own stresses and some find respite in hiding again for a time. But, notwithstanding the retreat, they eventually thrive in the open. (See box 3.2.)

**BOX 3.2   COMING OUT IS HEALTHY**

[R]esearchers found that the more "out" lesbians and bisexual women were—as measured by self-identification as a gay or lesbian, number of years out and level of involvement in the lesbian or bisexual community— the less psychological distress they reported. These findings held true for a range of racial and ethnic subsamples ... [and] support the idea that therapy that facilitates the coming-out process is good for lesbians' mental health.

Tori DeAngelis, "New Data on Lesbian, Gay and Bisexual Mental Health," *Monitor on Psychology*, www.apa.org/monitor/feb02/newdata.html (February 2002).

*Question 3: Is there a way to predict which gay youth are more at risk?*

There is evidence that those who have been victimized are at greater risk of harm, both self-inflicted and imposed. Physical attack, harassment, and other kinds of abuse increase the likelihood of suicide, substance use, truancy, and other negative outcomes. (See box 3.3.)

**BOX 3.3   VICTIMIZATION = RISK**

[Researchers] explored whether ongoing discrimination fuels anxiety, depression and other stress-related mental health problems among LGB people. The authors found strong evidence of a relationship between the two.

Tori DeAngelis, "New Data on Lesbian, Gay and Bisexual Mental Health," *Monitor on Psychology*, www.apa.org/monitor/feb02/newdata.html (February 2002).

Half of [lesbian, gay and bisexual pupils who are bullied] contemplate killing or harming themselves, and four in 10 actually harm themselves at least once ... [a]lmost a third ... on more than one occasion. [N]early one in five ... display[s] symptoms associated with post-traumatic stress disorder later in life. As adults ... those who had been bullied ... were found to show symptoms of depression, anxiety and internalised hostility.

" 'Suicide Wish' of Gay Bullying Victims," *BBC ONLINE*, www.bbc.co.uk (July 18, 2000).

Clearly, students who feel unsafe, isolated, and cut off from the support of other people and institutions are most in peril. One matter, however, is certain: there is nothing inherent in homosexuality itself that puts gay youth at risk. Except for the few with underlying mental illness, their predicament stems from homophobia, heterosexism, and persecution.

Depending on their individual coping skills, gay youth may respond to heterosexist stigma in either healthy or self-destructive ways. To be resilient, they need good interpersonal skills and self-esteem, positive family relations, and extrafamilial reinforcements. Affirmative counseling and gay-positive school environments and curricula can make an enormous difference. There is evidence that merely having gay-sensitive HIV/AIDS instruction leads sexual minority students to feeling safer and displaying fewer risk behaviors.

Preliminary analysis of Vermont and Massachusetts student data indicates greater risk (i.e., being harassed, violent, and suicidal; using alcohol, drugs, and unhealthy weight control practices) for youth who have sex with both same-gender and opposite-gender partners. It finds little difference, on the other hand, between strictly heterosexual and homosexual students. Although the region under study and the numbers of nonheterosexual students are small, these discoveries are provocative. One explanation could be that the source of the statistical difference is not to be found among genuinely bisexual youth, but rather among troubled homosexual youth struggling to be straight by having relations with opposite-gender partners. This hypothesis is strengthened by the finding that the suicide rate is higher among youth who identify as straight yet engage in same-gender sex.

## Question 4: What should be the areas of concern in counseling gay students?

First, we should understand that not every counseling need of sexual minority students is about sexuality. They have other issues to attend to in academics, family life, and peer relations that are unrelated to their being gay.

Still, when we look at the environment and supports that all adolescents require for good psychosocial development (see box 3.4.), we cannot ignore that each can represent a significant challenge for glbt youth.

## Question 5: How is safety a concern for gay youth?

Appalling national statistics on antigay violence, from name-calling to murder, make clear why safety is a critical concern for all gay people. Homophobic assaults are likely underreported because victims fear both exposure and a lack of sympathy from the authorities. Indeed, most police departments and schools lack protocols to protect privacy and provide follow-up support. A "blame the victim" attitude is not unusual. (See box 3.5.) Since many localities require parental notification after such incidents, it is no wonder young people hesitate to bring complaints.

## BOX 3.4   REQUIREMENTS FOR HEALTHY ADOLESCENT DEVELOPMENT

- safety and structure;
- belonging and membership;
- self-worth and an ability to contribute;
- independence and control over one's life;
- closeness and several good relationships;
- competence and mastery;
- self-awareness.

From Karen J. Pittman and Michele Cahill, "A New Vision: Promoting Youth Development," Testimony before the House Select Committee on Children, Youth, and Families, Commissioned Paper #3, (Washington, D.C.: Academy for Educational Development, September 1991).

## BOX 3.5   INHERENTLY PROVOCATIVE

Liz Skaggs is only 17. But she has already spent four years shouldering insults from Gilbert High schoolmates, who yelled "lesbo" and obscene slurs while hurling drinks and garbage at her from school buses and cars.... As a freshman, Skaggs was banned from the school lunchroom "for her protection" after another girl attacked her.... The other student was not reprimanded....

Mel Meléndez, "Gays Being Heard," *The Arizona Republic*, February 6, 2002.

"I was pushed in the hallways. [M]y things would get stolen and come back a week later with anti-gay graffiti written all over it. I couldn't attend school dances because I would get beaten up afterwards.... [The principal told me]... I could either transfer to another school or hurry up and graduate early.... There was one teacher who actually said to me that I was setting myself up to be made fun of and treated like that... by the way that I talk and the way that I dress and the way that I act."

Dominick Halse, in Nancy Guerin, "The Kicks in the Hall," *Metroland* [Albany, N.Y.], July 5, 2001.

## BOX 3.6   SCHOOL AS NIGHTMARE

Four Hillsborough High School students were charged yesterday with attacking a bisexual student in the school cafeteria.... [T]hey had allegedly been harassing [the victim] for several weeks before the April 30 assault, in which his nose was broken and a tooth was chipped.

Bev McCarron, "2 Face Bias Charges in School Attack," The [Newark, N.J.] *Star Ledger*, May 14, 2002.

An anti-gay epithet in bold, red letters was written in lipstick across a sign on [the classroom] door.... The same disparaging word was written, much larger, on [the] classroom wall.... [A] girl said she found a slang term for lesbian written in black ink on the taillight of her car in the school parking lot this week.

Roxanne Stites, "Gay Slurs Spur Saratoga High to Discuss Insults, Hate Crimes," *San Jose Mercury News*, April 5, 2001.

When he heard that a gay teenager at his summer school thought he was cute, Thomas Rivers quickly lashed out. He shouldered the boy in the... school's hallway and shouted slurs. He spit on him in a school bus. [Later he] saw the 15-year-old boy walking in an Aquia Harbor park, became incensed and bashed the gay youth over the head with a metal pole, almost killing him.

Josh White, "Guilty Plea in Attack on Gay Teen," *Washington Post*, December 8, 2000.

One unidentified girl threatened to jump the victim because she is gay, while another threw a lapel pin from the school's Gay/Straight Alliance at [her].... [O]n the bus ride home, the juvenile defendant taunted the victim in Spanish, allegedly threatening to do her physical harm.... Two days later... Defendant Luis Campos... kicked the victim about her face and body.... [She] was treated at the hospital for internal bleeding and injury to her left eye.

Laura Kiritsy, "Reilly Gets an Injunction against Lesbian's Alleged Attackers in Western Mass. High School," *Bay Windows* [Mass.], August 17, 2000.

Two former prep school roommates have been sentenced to probation after admitting they cut the word "homo" into the back of another student.

The Associated Press, "Pair Sentenced for 'Humiliating' Attack on Rutlander," *Rutland* [Vt.] *Herald*, April 20, 2000.

Despite these reporting obstacles, Human Rights Watch, the Gay Lesbian Straight Education Network, American Association of University Women, the Safe Schools Coalition, and other organizations have been able to document enough incidents of harassment and violence against gay youth to make a strong case for how pervasive they are. (See chapter 6.)

Harassment and attack, either experienced or anticipated, cause great pain and anxiety for gay youth. Schools are often no refuge. (See box 3.6.) Local and national surveys confirm that nearly all students hear antigay comments in high schools as many as twenty-five times per day. Adults, however, often appear oblivious to these insults. Sadly, some educators have been known to participate in the put-downs. (See box 3.7.)

---

### BOX 3.7  ET TU?

[George] turned to teachers and administrators for help, but he said they did little to stop the abuse.... [Spanish teacher Juan Garcia] stood behind George's desk and said first in Spanish then in English: "There are only two kinds of men who wear earrings. Pirates and faggots, and there is no water around here.".... "His thing was to bother me, to torment me," George said. "I got so upset once that I walked out of his class.... I stopped wearing my earring, but he kept calling me pirate."

   Valerie Avalos-Lavimodiere, "Gay High School Student Speaks Out for His Rights," *Fresno Bee*, May 22, 2000.

[O]n Valentine's Day, [Middle School history teacher Donald E. Miller] is said to have replaced the inoffensive message on a heart-shaped sweet with the word 'Fag' [and given it to a boy] who suffers from Tourette's Syndrome.... Miller bullied other students, pointing a television remote control at them and calling it a 'fagometer.'

   "Teacher Sued over Homophobic Taunts," *Rainbow Network* [U.K.],www .rainbownetwork.com (March 16, 2001).

When someone recently whistled in class, the teacher told the student to stop, and then said that only "queers and shipmates" whistle....

   Paige Hewitt, "Seeking Tolerance," *Houston Chronicle*, April 4, 2002.

A principal finally took his locker away because she feared some type of explosive might be put [there].... [A] male student...yelled "Faggot!" and threw shoes at him in a classroom. "I went to the school security guards and told them about the incident. . . . They then told me that they don't tolerate faggots at Santa Fe High and if anything happened with me again, they would personally beat the (expletive) out of me." When the matter was brought to the attention of an assistant principal, he said she advised him to leave the school because she couldn't assure his safety.

Jeannie Johnson, "Sexual Tolerance Sought for Curriculum," *Albuquerque Journal*, November 18, 1999.

## BOX 3.8   BULLYING

Who gets bullied "all of the time"
  Latino kids - 2%
  Asian kids - 3%
  White kids - 3%
  Black kids - 4%
  Disabled kids - 6%
  Fat kids - 11%
  Kids who dress differently - 12%
  Kids who are gay or thought to be gay - 24%

*Source:* 2002 National Mental Health Association survey of 760 12- to 17-year-olds.

Human Rights Watch . . . concluded as many as 2 million school-age youths may be affected by bullying related to sexual orientation.

Darcia Harris Bowman, "Report Says Schools Often Ignore Harassment of Gay Students," *Education Week*, June 6, 2001.

"They call me like fag, gay, because I'm a figure skater, and things like that," [12-year-old Aaron Vays] said. . . . One bully beat and kicked Aaron while another student held him down. . . . The boy suffered internal injuries in that incident, his parents said.

"Cold Shoulder," *ABC News.Com*, abcnews.go.com, May 6, 2002.

## BOX 3.9   NO PLACE AT HOME

A 14-year-old... teen bludgeoned his only sibling to death with a claw hammer... because he thought his brother was a homosexual, witnesses testified Tuesday during a preliminary hearing.

Paul Peirce, "Bishop Thought Brother Was Gay," *Pittsburgh Tribune-Review*, June 5, 2002.

Police say that [the parents] repeatedly smashed their [17-year-old] son with a lead pipe at a relative's home as they yelled anti-gay slurs. "God will punish you for your lifestyle!... You can't be gay!"

Richard Weir and Dave Saltonstall, "Parents Charged in Beating of Gay Son," *New York Daily News*, August 13, 2000.

Bullying based on sexuality begins in lower grades, then escalates in aggressiveness through high school and is particularly directed at boys. (See box 3.8.)

The Massachusetts Department of Education's Youth Risk Behavior Survey (YRBS), along with YRBSs in Minnesota and Vermont, are school-based research tools that contrast the incidence and impact of violence on gay youth as compared to their heterosexual peers. According to the 2001 Massachusetts YRBS (4,204 grade 9–12 respondents in 64 high schools), glb students were: more than twice as likely to have skipped school because of feeling unsafe; over one and a half times more likely to report being in a school fight, and more than three times as likely to need medical attention afterward; more than twice as likely to have been threatened or injured with a weapon at school; and one and a half times more likely to have carried a weapon at school.

Sometimes homes are unsafe as well. Many families are demeaning and some are dangerously hostile. Family violence against gay children may be even less often reported than other types of attack. (See box 3.9.)

It has also been suggested that gay youth are more likely to perpetrate violence, perhaps as a result of witnessing it, being objects of it, and anticipating it. Being threatened or injured with a weapon at school, for example, put them at greater risk for gun possession—as well as substance abuse and suicidality. (See box 3.10.)

*Question 6: How is belonging an issue for gay youth?*

The question is really: where do sexual minority youth feel welcome? Family estrangement, invisibility in school activities, and lack of curricula and adult role

## BOX 3.10  VIOLENCE BEGOTTEN

A gossip column in the [middle school] newspaper implying that Michael Carneal was gay fueled constant teasing and had a profound effect on the mental state of the teen charged with the Dec. 1 shooting at Heath High School, according to Carneal's psychological evaluations.... [M]onths after the column was published—and even when he entered high school last fall—students continued to harass him and call him gay.

Bill Bartleman, "Gay Implication Spurred Teasing: Carneal," *The Paducah* [Ky.] *Sun*, June 24, 1998.

A [high school] student...lashed out at a classmate who had been teasing him, slashing his tormenter in the head with a box cutter before school....McCottry was teasing Swanson about his sexual orientation. Swanson had complained to school officials about being teased....

John Chambliss, "G. Jenkins Student Slashed with Box Cutter," *The Ledger* [Lakeland, Fla.], August 29, 2000.

[A] senior point guard on Columbine's state championship basketball team [said] jocks taunted the pair by calling them gay.... [A]nother student [said] the Trench Coat Mafia was widely viewed as gay. "Boys would hold hands in the halls sometimes," [a] sophomore...told the paper. "They were called freaks, homos and everything in between."

Dave Cullen, "The Rumor That Won't Go Away," *Salon.com*, www.salon .com (April 24, 1999).

models persuade them they are alone. Diminished status in civic life and humiliation in popular culture tells them they have no valued place in society. Religious condemnation deprives them of a spiritual home. And homophobia among their peers severely limits friendship, the primary adolescent consolation.

It is not surprising that many gay youth assume the price of belonging is silence. Many families, even liberal ones, send few warm signals on the possibility of one of their own being gay. Unlike young people from other minority groups, whose families commonly share their stigmatized identity, gay youth are not statistically likely to have gay parents. There is not the same sense of a united home fortress against an old enemy. Their peers' homophobia is an omen of ostracism if they come out or are discovered. Most communities are unsafe and many churches offer more guilt than hospitality. Because they rarely acknowledge their presence—and then mostly negatively—schools seldom feel comfortable.

As many as 28 percent of glbt youth drop out of school and about 25 percent leave home. Although boys are more likely to be evicted by their families, girls are often kept home and mistreated.

Gay homeless youth, estimated to constitute nearly half of the street kid population, may turn to prostitution and other criminal activities to survive. When they and other glbt youth in trouble enter the juvenile justice system, they face misunderstanding and mistreatment from police, judges, lawyers, agency employees, and peers. Juvenile justice workers have even resisted identifying sexual minority offenders for targeted support, fearing they would only be further endangered. Placed in foster care or group homes, they may encounter the same or worse treatment as they had before. Foster parents and community service providers may be hostile toward gay youth or lack knowledge to protect and counsel them. Few states have policies to protect glbt youth in the foster care system. In a promising but unique move, the California legislature mandated glbt sensitivity training for foster parents in 2002.

Isolated gay youth lack contact with people like themselves to provide company, share feelings, and learn about the culture. The number of school and community groups for sexual minority youth is growing, but they are still scarce, especially in rural and conservative areas. Some young people might shrink from attending a group meeting in their school or neighborhood and not be able to get to one further away. Rural youth are particularly cut off.

Some community and school groups hold events like movie nights, performances, skating parties, and dances, including proms for those who might feel unwelcome at (or are illegally barred from) their official ones. (See box 3.11.) Some of these activities are organized with the help of the adult gay and lesbian community and thus foster ties between generations.

Many youth explore the community through books and magazines, some aimed at adolescents. They also find confidential connections through telephone information lines, radio programs, and the Internet. (See box 3.12 and appendix B.) These resources are especially vital for young people who are geographically isolated or otherwise hindered from personal contact with the gay community. The Internet can be a tool for abusers, but monitoring, censorship, and filtering must be exercised appropriately. Those who would block all homosexual Internet content with a blunt instrument like the Children's Internet Protection Act of 2000 are a danger to glbt youth who need both peer support and the information provided to them by responsible adults. It is alarming that a 2002 Kaiser Family Foundation study found many schools and libraries blocking all sites using the words *gay* or *lesbian*.

For several generations glbt youth have been finding their way into adult clubs and bars as a rite of passage. But noisy, smoky, alcohol-soaked nightlife is not the best long-term venue for healthy socialization and rational sexual

## BOX 3.11   HAVE A GAY PROM

"Being [at London, Ontario's first Pride Prom] tonight... words can't describe it," said John Duval... who was barred from his high school prom when he arrived with another gay youth.

Nicole MacIntyre, "First Pride Prom Lets Gay Youth Celebrate in Safety," *London* [Ontario] *Free Press*, June 9, 2002.

Little doubt, the queen was the most conventionally beautiful boy in the room. And he showed little interest in dancing any kind of state dance with the king, a short girl with short hair and short pants and a long backpack... as the near-1,600 teenagers who attended this year's Boston Alliance for Gay and Lesbian Youth prom teemed onto the second landing of Boston City Hall's lobby.

Tara H. Arden-Smith, "They Could Have Danced All Night," *Boston Globe*, May 27, 2001.

## BOX 3.12   LIFELINES

[Jeffrey] called a crisis line for gay teenagers, where a counselor suggested he attend a gay support group in a city an hour and a half away. But being 15, he was too young to drive and afraid to enlist his parents' help.... It was around this time that Jeffrey first typed the words "gay" and "teen" into a search engine on the computer... and was staggered to find himself aswirl in a teeming online gay world... [with] thousands of closeted and anxious kids like himself.... "The Internet... has kept me sane," he [says].

Jennifer Egan, "Lonely Gay Teen Seeking Same," *New York Times Magazine*, December 10, 2000.

Without unfettered access to the Internet at [the public library], 16-year-old Emmalyn Rood testified... she might not have found courage to tell her mother she was gay.... Rood told a special three-judge panel weighing the constitutionality of the Children's Internet Protection Act [,] "...I didn't have anybody I could talk to in real life."

Jim Barnett, "Gay Teen Testifies Against Law on Internet," *The Oregonian*, March 27, 2002.

decision making. Alcohol- and drug-free, youth-only club nights are a better option, as are other gay youth–oriented outings organized by community-based agencies.

Adult mentors can provide gay role models and help youth feel connected to the larger gay community. Adults may be hard to find, however. Some avoid troubled youth who could remind them of their own past struggles or well-adjusted youth whose ease with their sexuality stirs resentment. But the greatest barrier seems to be the fear that their outreach will be misconstrued as predatory. Young folks themselves may be wary because of persistent stereotypes. Structured intergenerational contact and honest dialogue help dispel fear, envy, and mistrust.

Gay youth can even feel lonely in tolerant cities with crowds of lively gay adults because they think themselves different from those who have accepting families, friends, and churches. They have heard enough from those they care about to make them certain of it. It takes time to forge ties in the gay community to make up for the losses felt at home, but once made, those connections lead to better coping strategies and less stress, a positive sense of well-being, better psychological adjustment, and more intimacy in relationships.

## Question 7: How is self-worth an issue for gay youth?

Some critics think self-esteem is overemphasized in schools—that students are encouraged to think highly of themselves, regardless of their accomplishments or moral character. But such critics ignore the blameless victims of internalized prejudice. Their loneliness, brought on by stigmatization and harassment, may result in a sense of worthlessness, depression, despair, and suicidality.

The most common spurs to all adolescent suicide are interpersonal conflict and rejection by family and peers. The American Psychological Association warns that loss and humiliation are the deadliest harbingers—hence the greater danger to gay and lesbian youth who lose heterosexual identity and privilege, friends and family, and who suffer repeated assaults to their egos. (See box 3.13.) The American Medical Association recognized these hazards in its 2001 resolution urging the Boy Scouts not to exclude gay members.

Studies linking suicide risk to sexual orientation have generated some controversy. Critics ask how suicidal behaviors are defined (thoughts or actions), how sexual orientation is categorized (by self-definition, behavior, affiliation, or some other indicator), and how subjects are found. Samples of runaways or service agency clients are not typical. Adult recollections are unreliable and, perhaps, not relevant to current youth experience. Young people driven to suicide by the shame of being gay are unlikely to have come out to a counselor or to leave explicit notes or other "incriminating" evidence.

Particular criticism has been directed at a 1989 study claiming that gay youth are two to three times more likely to attempt suicide than their heterosexual peers.

## BOX 3.13  FRIGHTENED TO DEATH

The mother of a Minersville teenager who committed suicide after a borough police officer allegedly threatened to tell his family he was gay has won the right to take her wrongful death lawsuit to trial.... [Officer F. Scott] Wilinsky arrested the boys for underage drinking and took them to the police station. There... he lectured them about biblical warnings against homosexuality and demanded [one boy] tell his grandfather he was gay. If he failed to, Wilinsky threatened to "do it for him."

Chris Parker, "Mother's Suit over Suicide to Continue," *Allentown* [Penn.] *Morning Call*, November 9, 2000.

In fact, the research on which that study was based, although providing some good descriptive information, depended too much on convenience sampling in social service settings and was flawed in other ways as well.

More recent and dependable studies of representative samples of high school students still show far greater risk for sexual minority youth. (See box 3.14.) In light of these findings, the schools' lack of attention to gay youth suicide prevention is alarming.

## BOX 3.14  SUICIDE: GAY VERSUS HETEROSEXUAL YOUTH

- Over three times more likely to have attempted suicide in year (8.4% vs. 30.6%)
- Over five times more likely to have had an injurious suicide attempt in year (2.8% vs. 15.5%)

*Source:* 2001 Massachusetts Youth Risk Behavior Survey (YRBS). 4,204 grade 9–12 respondents in 64 high schools.

- Over two times more likely than heterosexual peers of the same gender to attempt suicide

*Source:* Stephen T. Russell and Kara Joyner, "Adolescent Sexual Orientation and Suicide Risk: Evidence from a National Study," *American Journal of Public Health* 91, no. 8 (2001): 1276–80.

*Question 8: Aren't some gay and lesbian youth high achievers?*

Yes, but we should not always equate achievement with self-esteem. Some sexual minority youth throw themselves into schoolwork, sports, or hobbies, seeking perfection in parts of their lives they feel they can control. Such overachievers try to distract themselves and others from their dark secret and to reassure themselves that they are not worthless. They also often lose themselves in assiduously caring for family members and friends. Yet their personal and interpersonal successes still leave them feeling inauthentic, shameful, disconnected, and depressed.

*Question 9: Are some gay youth more at risk for suicide than others?*

Victimization is a key factor in suicide risk. (See box 3.15.) Effeminate early- and middle-adolescent boys are vulnerable because they are targets of bullying. The trauma of harassment may be alleviated by family support, yet school persecution and peer rejection are sometimes overwhelming factors.

Boys who resist thinking themselves homosexual, despite homosexual thoughts or behavior, seem to be at less risk than those who identify as gay early. Because gender-nonconforming boys are more likely to be labeled, they are also more likely to self-label. Although linking homosexual acts to homosexual identity is less apparent among racial and ethnic minorities, several studies have found more suicide attempts among minority gay and lesbian adolescents than among their white peers, perhaps due to psychological isolation.

There is evidence, on the other hand, that girls who self-identify may be less at risk than those who don't. The support that girls get when they come out might be greater or more effective than that afforded to boys. Open lesbian and bisexual girls are not harassed to the degree that boys are. Still, girls who are victimized are also at risk for substance use and suicide.

---

### BOX 3.15   NO EXIT

Someone had loosened all the lug nuts on [Jerryn Johnston's] left front tire. "That was the week I broke down," Johnston said quietly. Two days after the lug nut incident, Johnston was spotted by a friend of the family walking down the center line of U.S. Highway 69…between the cars…and traffic was heavy. Johnston was crying. "I knew I didn't want to die; I just felt trapped," Johnston said. "I felt powerless…."

Mary Challender, "The Student Who Wouldn't Be Silent," *Des Moines Register*, May 6, 2002.

## BOX 3.16   TEEN SELF-MEDICATION

"It was four years of hell.... From the moment I came out to a friend when I was 14, I was subjected to beating taunts and punches from the entire rugby team.... I was a straight-A student before my troubles began.... I began to drink to escape my troubles, often waking up with a need to have at least half a bottle of vodka before it was time for me to go to school. I considered suicide many times."

Graeme Ross, in Ryan Levitt, "Beating the Bullies," *Pink Paper* [U.K.], September 28, 2001.

Finally, gay youth are disproportionately subject to the factors that contribute to suicidality among all youth: depression, hopelessness, and alcohol and drug abuse.

### Question 10: Why do gay youth use alcohol and drugs?

Some use alcohol and drugs to cope with the emotional pain of interpersonal conflict and the stresses of concealment and self-monitoring. (See box 3.16.) Substance use may also provide an excuse for homosexual behavior and cushion the blow of being discovered to be gay or lesbian. (See box 3.17.) The importance of bars in homosexual socialization and the use of drugs and alcohol to deal with stress constitute a double threat.

### Question 11: Are there other ways in which sexual minority youth show a lack of self-acceptance?

Piercing, body cutting, anorexia, bulimia, and overeating might be signals. Body dissatisfaction and eating disorders affect gay males as they do straight women and appear related to low self-esteem. Bulimia, for example, is found among gay boys at ten times the rate of heterosexual boys. Lesbians, however, are thought to be happier with their bodies, but somewhat more at risk for obesity, smoking, and drinking than straight women are. (See box 3.18.)

### Question 12: How are closeness and good relationships issues for gay youth?

All adolescents search for personal identity and meaningful connections with others. In coming out, gay and lesbian youth often struggle with the former.

**BOX 3.17   SUBSTANCE USE: GAY VERSUS HETEROSEXUAL YOUTH**

- Over twice as likely to have consumed alcohol on school property in the past month (12.6% vs. 5.1%)
- Over twice as likely to have used marijuana on school property in the past month (14.6% vs. 6.6%)
- Over four times more likely to have used cocaine in their lives (31.2% vs. 7%)

*Source:* 2001 Massachusetts Youth Risk Behavior Survey (YRBS). 4,204 grade 9–12 respondents in 64 high schools.

Use before age 13:

- alcohol (59.1% vs. 30.4%)
- cigarettes (47.9% vs. 23.4%)
- cocaine (17.3% vs. 1.2%)

*Source:* Robert Garofalo, R. Cameron Wolf, Shari Kessel, Judith Palfrey, and Robert H. DuRant, "The Association between Health Risk Behaviors and Sexual Orientation among a School-Based Sample or Adolescents," *Pediatrics* 101, no. 5 (1998): 900–901.

They can also be hampered in finding the latter. If having a relationship with family members and peers requires concealment and dishonesty, those relationships cannot offer meaningful support. Some gay youth immerse themselves in academics or hobbies to avoid closeness and questions about relationships.

**BOX 3.18   BODY IMAGE**

"Twenty years ago, your body image was about what you wore, how you wore your hair and so on. Now, it's about the transformation of the body itself. These [young gay] guys want to reshape their bodies to make them look [muscled and perfectly toned]. A lot of times that's achieved with chemicals, hormones and even surgery."

Alex Carballo-Dieguez, Ph.D., in Tori DeAngelis, "A New Generation of Issues for GLBT Clients," *Monitor on Psychology* 33, no. 2 (2002), www.apa.org/monitor/feb02/generation.htm.

## BOX 3.19    SEXUAL ACTIVITY: GAY VERSUS HETEROSEXUAL YOUTH

Of all adolescents who report having had sex, gay youth are:

- twice as likely to have had four or more sexual partners in their lives (50% vs. 25.2%)
- two and a half times more likely to have been or gotten someone pregnant (26.5% vs. 10.5%)

*Source:* 2001 Massachusetts Youth Risk Behavior Survey (YRBS). 4,204 grade 9–12 respondents in 64 high schools.

There are also differences in sexual behavior that are cause for concern. First, gay youth are over three times more likely than their peers to have had sexual intercourse before age thirteen. Comparisons with sexually experienced heterosexual peers are also alarming. (See box 3.19.) Some seek clandestine sexual intimacy and one-night stands. Boys slip off to rest stops and other cruising places. Girls and boys go to bars to "hook up" for an evening. Meeting through the Internet for sex is increasingly common. Such short-term sexual relationships are not necessarily harmful. They are often part of their first forays into gay life. But when internalized homophobia, secrecy, and shame dictate the terms, there is little chance for developing the capacity for deeper connection and the skills for relationship maintenance.

Sexual minority youth might become sexually compulsive because they lack opportunity and freedom to develop their courting skills. Besides being inhibited by shame and having no role models, they also don't know who is approachable. All teens fret over rejection, but gay boys especially might fear a violent response rather than a polite "no thanks."

Some gay males choose sex without affectionate displays like kissing to keep a gay identity at bay. Some use drugs and alcohol to summon the nerve for sexual pursuit and soften the guilt. Furtive sex under those conditions puts them at greater risk for STDs and HIV.

Lastly, dating violence and abuse can be problems for sexual minority youth. Although rarely mentioned in health education, power, control, and manipulation on the one hand and lack of agency and self-esteem on the other should be red flags for gay and lesbian couples as they are for others.

Any student who has had sex unwillingly is at much greater risk for substance use, multiple partners, and suicide. Because sexual minority youth are three times more likely to have had forced contact (not necessarily with same-gender perpetrators), they are in greater peril.

## BOX 3.20  AIDS/STDS

[Male high school students] who self-identified as bisexual were more likely to have four or more sexual partners and were more likely to have used alcohol or drugs before their most recent sexual encounter than were other survey respondents. Bisexual teenagers also were the least likely to use condoms.

"Survey: Bisexual Male Youths Most Likely to Have Risky Sex," *Advocate Online News* (www.advocate.com), February 7, 2002.

*Question 13: Is AIDS really a danger for school-age youth?*

The HIV problem is severe, particularly among young men of color. And because the HIV virus takes a long time to produce symptoms, the number of people becoming ill in their twenties points to an alarming rate of infection among teenagers. (See box 3.20.)

Some HIV incidence among young gay men is related to prostitution, substance abuse, isolation, and low self-esteem. The last two can be related to the level of homophobia in the community. In a 2002 CDC report on HIV-positive men, 90 percent of blacks said they did not know their HIV status (versus 70 percent for Latinos and 60 percent for whites). These alarming disparities might be attributed to poverty and lack of access to health information and care. But the results of a 2000 CDC study of HIV-positive men points in another direction as well: 25 percent of black men who said they'd been infected through sex with another man still identified as heterosexual (as opposed to 6 percent of white men). Men of color in identity conflict may equate the necessity for HIV testing with a virtual admission of homosexuality. Their denial and repression of stigmatized labels prevents them from getting life-saving information.

HIV among young lesbians is related to drug use, prostitution, and engaging in sex with multiple male partners to get pregnant. It has also been related to sexual involvement with bisexual and gay males. Half of gay male teens have sex with girls and are less likely to use condoms with them than with other males. Some lesbians have also not been informed about safer sex with other women.

Young gay and bisexual males may think that risk-taking and HIV are part of the culture and that AIDS is no longer very threatening. (See box 3.21.) They lack experience at negotiating sex and fear rejection or being thought weak if they insist on a condom. For some, the exchange of bodily fluids is a sign of commitment. Love is a protection. And monogamy, even short-term, seems safe. Finally, we cannot ignore the possibility that unsafe sex may be a form of deliberate self-destruction.

## BOX 3.2I    DENIAL AND SHORTSIGHTEDNESS

For younger men...a preference for unprotected sex has arisen largely as the result of new drug therapies....Younger men assume that if they contract the disease at 30,...it will take 10 years before they become symptomatic, and another 15 until the drug therapies stop working. They might be 55 or 60 before they get really sick, they figure.

Yvonne Abraham, "Unsafe Sex on Rise," *Boston Globe,* June 18, 2000.

*Question 14: Is pregnancy really an issue for gay youth?*

Sexual minority youth are two to three times more likely to become pregnant or get someone pregnant than straight youth are. Some gay boys and girls engage in "opposite gender sex" as a disguise from others and denial to themselves. As noted above, many gay and bisexual boys do not use condoms when having sex with girls. Lastly, those gay girls who are depressed and lonely may, like their similarly afflicted heterosexual peers, want a child to give them a purpose and unconditional love.

*Question 15: Why is it difficult for gay youth to learn relationship skills?*

From their early years at home, in school, at play, and through the media they are conditioned for heterosexual dating and marriage. Few have gay adult role models in their families. Health, sex education, and family life classes give scant attention at best to their issues. According to the Sexuality Information and Education Council of the United States, only twenty states mandate sexuality education (thirty-seven require instruction on HIV and STDs). None demands that teachers address homosexuality. (See box 3.22.) Mass media treatment is mostly superficial, distorted, or sensationalized.

Besides the common challenges experienced by all couples, gay relationships can be harder to maintain because of heterosexism and homophobia. These disadvantages may not affect adolescents as they begin gay relationships, but they are still important for imagining their future and preparing for it. (See box 3.23.)

*Question 16: Are friendships as problematic for gay youth as sexual*
*relationships can be?*

They can be difficult, both within the gay community and outside it. Regrettably, a history of low self-esteem can inhibit formation of deep friendships among

**BOX 3.22   OUT OF SIGHT**

"It was like three days. The first day we covered the male sex organs. The second day we covered the female sex organs. The third day, 'This is what happens when you have sexual intercourse.' "... [Daniel Farrish, 16,] says he believes the school district undermines respect among students for gay peers because its sex education curriculum doesn't acknowledge homosexuality.

Joan Whitely, "Homosexual Students Say Curriculum Shortchanges Them," *Las Vegas Review-Journal*, January 13, 2002.

gay men in particular. Years of victimization and internalized homophobia can lead to depression, bitterness, and overcompetitiveness for partners, attention, or praise. Although the AIDS epidemic has often elicited the best in gay friendship, gay men still have work to do. Lesbians, on the other hand, appear to have more success, perhaps because of a feminist ethos of caring and cooperation.

Relations between lesbians and gay men have sometimes been rocky as well. A gay man can be as misogynistic as a straight man or at least unconcerned with

**BOX 3.23   HOW HETEROSEXISM CAN HURT GAY RELATIONSHIPS**

- Parents and teachers discourage and punish same-gender affectional play, causing a developmental lag in gay children.
- Closeted couples and partners at different stages of coming out experience conflict. Hiding diminishes spontaneity, inhibits bonding, and creates stress.
- Rejection of partners by families and friends deprives the relationship of support. Both hiding a relationship and losing loved ones make partners resentful.
- The absence of religious and civil sanctions as well as material privileges deprives relationships of common supports.
- Anger about homophobia diminishes the ability to be loving and lovable.
- Internalized homophobia makes the relationship feel illegitimate.
- Internalized beliefs about masculine and feminine roles lead to inflexibility and discord.
- Safe sex can be stressful especially when one partner is HIV positive. Grief over AIDS deaths can decrease intimacy.

women's issues. For their part, some lesbians have favored separatism. The AIDS crisis has mended relations somewhat, primarily because women have advocated and cared for the sick. Whatever the problems of the past, the younger generation seems drawn to friendship and mutual activities, especially in school and community groups. Their coed socialization into the gay community encourages a relaxed mutual affection. Even the club scene seems less rigidly gender-segregated than it was a decade ago.

Friendships with heterosexuals are sometimes set back during the coming out period. Sexual minority youth often need a respite from old friends and old haunts. They retreat from the straight world to avoid negative judgments and conflicts and find safe spaces to find and express their new selves and to explore gay relationships.

It can be annoying to keep straight friends when they are oblivious to heterosexual privilege and assumptions. Habitually referring to their sexual partners and children, attractions, and tastes, many straight people seem to think everyone shares their orientation and the freedom to express it. When gay friends declare their love interests they can be criticized for exhibitionism, hypersexuality, and callousness toward majority sensitivities. Sometimes they have to escape from this humiliating or simply tiresome double standard.

## Question 17: How is having a sense of competence an issue for sexual minority youth?

Gays and lesbians may have difficulty developing confidence in their own agency and abilities and as a consequence lack hope, goals, and resiliency. Failure can be a self-fulfilling expectation, whether they see their own sexuality or someone else's homophobia as the cause.

Some gay and lesbian youth feel powerless because they have tried so hard to be straight—and failed. Some young men abandon safe sex practices, which require a sense of competence and control. Lesbians may feel even more powerless and purposeless because they are females.

Repeated denial of their sexual feelings can also leave them numb to other emotions and lead to inertia. Family disappointment and rejection can make them give up on themselves. Their lack of confidence is only compounded by peer harassment. When attendance and schoolwork suffer, their sense of incompetence grows.

Gay youths' feelings of ineptitude also relate to gender and sex-role stereotyping. Gay has become synonymous with male incompetence, immaturity, and weakness. Conversely, when girls exhibit physical prowess, competitiveness, and other traditionally "male" competencies, they may be called lesbian because their skills cast doubt on their adequacy as women. Many young gays and lesbians are dismayed by these doubts about their gender identity. Some may come to believe they can never master traditional male or female roles or skills.

When they do achieve competencies they may still expect to be unmasked as frauds. These attitudes detract from career ambitions, which require feelings of proficiency and expectations of success.

## Question 18: How is self-awareness an issue for sexual minority youth?

Self-awareness is a keystone counseling issue for these young people. Sexual minority youth are blocked in acknowledging their identities by cultural stigma and internalized homophobia. Stifling their true nature, they may be fooled into thinking they can choose to be someone else. They fear that coming out will be a dire irreversible step that could obliterate both their old selves and prior relationships.

Those who have already passed through adolescence as heterosexual or asexual get a second round as a gay person. The experience can be both liberating and frightening, both prudent and excessive.

GLBT youth might also chafe against the limitations of conventional sexuality categories in defining who they are. They may reject "homo," "bi," and "hetero" labels entirely. (See chapter 1.) They don't want mandatory scripts—either gay or straight—to dictate their lives. For the short term, acknowledging they are homosexual probably helps settle some troublesome uncertainties, but that new self-awareness is just one aspect of self-discovery. Imagination, self-expression, spirituality, morality, lovingness, and lovability are also important. Sexuality informs these other personal dimensions, but it does not totally determine them.

## Question 19: Who should counsel sexual minority youth?

Ignorance and institutional policy often limit the provision of counseling. Schools and communities may not acknowledge the presence of gay youth or provide services for them. Officials might be blind to the need or fear the political fallout. Educators and social service workers may be deterred by their own prejudice, fear of controversy, or thoughts of having their own sexuality scrutinized. Moreover, the youth themselves might shun services to avoid exposure or they might undermine their counseling by not divulging their sexual orientation.

Thinking the subject is outside their realm or that parents might disapprove, many physicians do not discuss homosexuality with adolescent patients. Some just assume that everyone is heterosexual unless they present otherwise. Others are homophobic and misinformed. There are still instances of youth being forced by parents and doctors into abusive therapies to change their sexual orientations and of gender nonconforming children being diagnosed with Gender Identity Disorder (GID).

Admired and trusted teachers are often counselors of first resort. Yet, few teachers receive training about gay or lesbian teens. Many depend on professional journals, mass media, and professional conferences for information on homosexuality. Although some understand that gay students are often harassed and isolated and some teachers may want to help, few feel competent to do so.

Most school counselors are also untrained in these matters. Some are uncomfortable with homosexuality or have religious objections. (See box 3.24.) Those who might offer direct help or refer a student to an outside counselor sometimes fear parent and administrator disapproval.

According to the American Psychological Association, school nurses' and counselors' conversations with glbt youth, when they have them, often center on coming out, family relations, harassment, and safety. Such interventions are usually short-term and may end in referral. Risky behaviors, STDs, and AIDS are rarely broached. Few school health professionals feel equipped to deal with gay and lesbian sexuality matters, identity development, or the special concerns of multiple minority youth.

There is scant research on the best practices to promote healthy development and prevent self-destructive behaviors of sexual minority youth. GLBT inclusion in teacher and counselor education is mostly a superficial token. School professionals who want to support sexual minority youth generally rely on the experience and common sense advice of those who have been working with glbt youth in community settings.

---

### BOX 3.24  INAPPROPRIATE COUNSEL

[Tina] Ransom was facing lewd pictures left on her desk, pointed slurs and joking insults. All because she is gay. [Her public high school] counselor took a "love the sinner, hate the sin" look at her problems, telling Ransom she might not always be gay and to accept Jesus into her life.

Marijke Rowland, "Teen: 'Be Honest and Open,'" *Modesto Bee*, October 8, 2001.

As Thomas McLaughlin tells it, the trouble began when his eighth-grade science teacher overheard him refusing to deny to another boy that he was gay. It got worse that afternoon, when his guidance counselor called his mother at work to tell her he was homosexual.

Tamar Lewin, "Arkansas School Is Accused of Harassing a Gay Student," *New York Times*, March 25, 2003.

*Question 20: Where should the counselor or teacher begin?*

First, they should not assume that all gay students are in crisis. As we have seen above, the majority of glbt youth are well adjusted and resilient. One reason the public might think otherwise is that proponents of gay youth programs have emphasized grim statistics to win political and financial support. Sexual minority youth themselves may have the impression that such ills are unavoidable. (See box 3.25.)

But victimhood is not empowering or attractive in the long term. It is more prudent and accurate to affirm the strengths of gay youth at the same time we acknowledge their possible vulnerabilities. Even the outwardly stable ones retain damaging bits of negativity about homosexuality, learned early on. We can safely assume that they all need support as we focus treatment on those with emotional and psychological problems. And even those can recover quickly when sexuality is their chief concern. In a nurturing environment, they can learn to resist shame and develop their own voice. With this "assets" emphasis in mind, the Massachusetts Department of Public Health has renamed its counterpart to the Department of Education's Safe Schools Program for Gay and Lesbian Youth. It is now called Supportive and Healthy Communities for Gay and Lesbian Youth.

*Question 21: How exactly should teachers and counselors raise the issue of homosexuality?*

Because many young people fear broaching the topic in the school setting, the teacher or counselor should initially project an accepting attitude and invite

---

### BOX 3.25   SELF-FULFILLING WOE?

Ritch C. Savin-Williams, Ph.D., reports . . . that even though sexual-minority teens are more likely than heterosexual youth to report suicide attempts, half of those reports are false—that is, the young people had thought about suicide but hadn't acted on it. . . . "The heterosexual youth had hardly any false attempts, while those with same-sex attractions had a lot of them." . . . The findings suggest that gay youth are vulnerable to the media's and researchers' well-meaning but negative depictions of gay youth as highly troubled people heading on a collision course with life. . . .

Tori DeAngelis, "New Data on Lesbian, Gay and Bisexual Mental Health," *Monitor on Psychology* 33, no. 2 (2002), www.apa.org/monitor/feb02/newdata .html.

## BOX 3.26   INDIRECT AND GENTLE AS A FIRST COURSE

- Put up gay-positive posters, "Safe Zone" stickers, or event announce-ments. Leave support service literature on information carrels, books and articles in the office or classroom. (Note: These strategies are vital in schools, like Lubbock High in Texas, where community-based sup-port group postings on general school bulletin boards are prohibited.)
- Take opportunities to show you do not assume everyone is hetero-sexual.
- Use inclusive language and refer specifically to gay/lesbian people in conversation with students and parents.
- Use nongendered pronouns when referring to student relationships and parents.
- Use the same terms that the student uses to denote his or her feelings and orientation.
- Assure confidentiality. (This assurance may not be possible in the con-text of suicidality or substance abuse, where reporting is mandated. Discretion is needed in deciding which underlying details of the prob-lem should be divulged.)

Note: To avoid both assumptions and labels, counselors and health care providers might ask, "Are you sexual with men, women, or both?"

disclosure indirectly. (See box 3.26.) Students have been known to come out first to a teacher who is not their own, just because they have heard that he or she is "cool about gay stuff."

Frequently students themselves are indirect. (See box 3.27.) Counselors can ask about relationships or start a conversation about the constraints of conven-tional gender roles. Or they can be more forthright by asking "Are you want-ing to talk to me about sexuality?" Or, "Are you concerned that you might be gay/lesbian/bisexual?"

*Question 22: When teachers or counselors ask such questions, aren't they putting the idea of being gay in a student's head?*

It depends on how teachers and counselors ask the questions. Even when strug-gling students appear to want an authority figure to tell them what they are, the adult shouldn't do it. The answer might seem obvious and still be inaccurate. And

## BOX 3.27   HINTING AT HOMOSEXUALITY

- dressing or behaving in a gender-defiant manner;
- lingering in the nurse's office with no apparent medical problems;
- referring to a gay "friend";
- wanting to talk about sex repeatedly;
- relating a distant homosexual event in their own lives;
- showing no interest in dating, while being otherwise gregarious and/or involved in academics or extracurriculars.

even getting at the truth requires strategic thinking. Trying to relieve a student's distress with, "Don't worry. You're gay. That's wonderful! Let's talk about what your life will be from now on," could panic him or her back to the closet.

Working sensitively with each student, counselors need to balance two approaches: support and encouragement to come out versus restraint that could be interpreted as fear or negativity. (See box 3.28.) The goals are: to help struggling adolescents rid themselves of internalized homophobia and deal with social stigma, family reactions, and other responses to their sexuality; to encourage them to celebrate and cultivate their homosexual potential; and to advise them that sexual orientation is not static nor is identity fixed.

*Question 23: Will adolescents really accept the idea that they don't need to label themselves?*

Some earnestly take the stance, "I'm not gay, straight, bi, or queer—I'm just me." But others find it hard to adopt that position, even if they understand the theory behind it. After all, students live in a real world that puts stock in such categories. Because sexuality labels have consequences, most young people scrutinize themselves and others for signs of their position on the spectrum of sexuality.

Then, there are those who already "know" they are gay or bisexual and want affirmation from a counselor. A student who is looking for self-love, confidence, and a glbt community does not necessarily want to hear restrained advice about meaningless labels and sexual fluidity.

As much as educators may want to protect young people from the stifling aspects of all identity constructs and to free them to their own individuality, they should not discourage the positive consequences of group affiliation: solidarity and pride. There's plenty of time for identity deconstruction later on and for finding the right balance between unique individual and group identities.

## BOX 3.28    RESPONSES TO THE PERPLEXED

POOR:

- Gosh, let's not jump to conclusions.
- No one's sexuality is certain in adolescence.
- It's probably just a phase you're going through.
- If you pay too much attention to these feelings you might make yourself gay.
- Bisexuality is just the latest teen fad, right?
- What will your parents think?
- This will totally change your life.

IN SHORT: It isn't real; it will pass; and don't, for heaven's sake, act on it.

BETTER:

- I like you a lot—gay, straight, bi, queer, or undefined.
- Your life holds joyful possibilities whatever your orientation.
- Sexuality can be fluid over time, but it's also important to understand your feelings now.
- Since you seem uncertain about how to characterize your feelings, let's look at each possibility.
- Sexuality labels seem important, but they are less important than the quality of your love relationships.

IN SHORT: It may be real for you now; it could be right for you for a long time, perhaps all your life. Live the experience, but don't foreclose on any others.

*Question 24: How should counselors support homosexual young people who adamantly reject labeling?*

They should try to determine the source of the rejection. Is it the perceived inadequacy of narrow categories or is it homophobia? Are students wisely avoiding a trap that limits their self-definition and relationship potentialities? Or are they merely finding a sophisticated defense from stigma? In a homophobic culture, it would be a stretch to believe that shame has nothing to do with it. Therefore the main thrust of a counselor's response to adolescents who are just coming out should be congratulatory and enabling. These teens need release from internalized homophobia and defenses against prejudice. They need consolation over their losses and help seeing a future. Their gayness shouldn't be a straitjacket any more than another's heterosexuality should be. Every aspect of identity can be acknowledged as subject to further development and yes—fluidity.

Openly gay, lesbian, and bisexual educators are happy when students come out successfully. But when some young people judge homosexual identities as rigid and irrelevant, some of us cringe. Part of our purpose has been to make sexual orientation a nonissue, but we don't expect to hear that "gay, out, and proud" is passé. Like many women and people of color, we continue to be partly self-defined by our oppression. Still, we don't have to abandon our politics in accepting with understanding and good humor our students' right to call themselves "queer" or whatever else they prefer.

And we must still direct them toward positive information and role models (including career role models). They should be helped with family and peer ties. They should be encouraged to make the most of their gay, lesbian, or bisexual potential, to explore the gay world, tend to new relationships, and stay healthy.

*Question 25: How should counselors respond to students who want to change their sexuality?*

Gentle, cautious skepticism is demanded. The American Psychiatric Association maintains there is no evidence that sexuality "conversion therapies" work and some indication that they are harmful. Although some highly motivated individuals can change their behavior for short periods of time and deny their attractions, they often suffer great anxiety and depression as a result. A far better counseling approach is to reduce internalized homophobia and stress self-acceptance.

Still, some therapists tout cures for homosexuality, often religiously based, and aimed tellingly at men more than women. These "cures" get a lot of press attention. (See box 3.29.) Even less rabidly homophobic therapists think conversion therapies should be offered to patients who are unhappy with their sexualities.

### BOX 3.29  CURES?

"I wanted this [exorcism] to work so bad. . . . I grunted and squeezed and tried to shove this homosexuality out of me. I remember afterwards, going out for fast food and trying to coach myself, 'It's gone. Yeah, it's gone.' But it wasn't. . . . When people say they're happy being married, they're really saying, 'I am acceptable to myself and to the people around me.' I don't think they'll feel that way in the long run."

Jallen Rix, in Barry Yeoman, "Gay No More?" *Psychology Today*, March 1999.

They do not seem to understand that the source of their patient's problem is shame, not homosexuality itself.

Teens who are distressed by their homosexuality could be advised to cultivate their bisexual potential, if they have one. But that course requires an honest exploration of the range of their desires, not the purging of its gay elements. Those who want to be bisexual as a way to cling to some shred of "normalcy" need to get a grip on internalized stigma.

*Question 26: Are there topics that teachers and counselors should be sure to cover?*

One can easily imagine a starting list of topics for discussion. (See box 3.30.)

## BOX 3.30  COUNSELING TOPICS: A CHECKLIST

- Express gratitude for the confidence.
- Assure confidentiality. (Perhaps not possible where reporting of suicidality or substance abuse is mandated.)
- Assess whether the student needs immediate extended counseling or if disclosure is enough for the time being.
- Make sure to see the student again, but do not assume that sexuality must be the focus of every subsequent interaction.
- Refer to the positive aspects of being gay/lesbian (solidarity, loving relationships, perseverance, diversity of the community, rich history, and culture).
- Guide the student to sources of information and confirmation regarding these happy prospects.
- Discover the extent of disclosure to others and explore the consequences of coming out in various settings, including safety and shelter issues, reporting of harassment, stigma management, and possibilities for further support like referral to school or community-based groups.
- Ask about relations with family, teachers, and peers.
- Explore feelings about lost heterosexual identity and expectations.
- Discuss relationships, including courtship and breakup.
- Discuss alcohol and drug use.
- Discuss safe sex practices and the motivation to engage in them.
- Discuss resources for researching gay-supportive colleges, e.g., "Finding an GLBT-Friendly Campus: A Guide for Counselors Advising GLBT Students Pursuing Higher Education" (www.glsen.org), *The Princeton Review* (www.review.com).

Because there is so little depth in the media about same-gender relationships, it's helpful for adolescents to think about their past, current, and potential partnerships. How have they been or might they be different in their dynamics from heterosexual ones? Because many teens still think being gay means giving up the idea of having children, they need to know about possibilities for creating families of choice.

Young people should have access to good books and media treatments of glbt relationships. Gay publishing now offers serious magazines, fine fiction, sociological and psychological studies, and a stream of self-help books, some for adolescent readers. (See appendix B.)

Substance abuse counseling must include the role of bars in the gay/lesbian community. It must also probe the underlying psychological needs that drive gay teens to alcohol, drugs, and tobacco use. Although some elements of substance counseling are common to people of all orientations, some strategies have been developed for gay young folks in particular. (See appendix B.)

AIDS counseling and education must be consistent, detailed, clear, and frank. It should reflect the real practices and interests of adolescents. Fearful or flip, teens need adults who are seriously concerned for them, yet relaxed and good humored. The curriculum cannot be limited to anatomy, degrees of risk, condom use, or abstinence. Like effective pregnancy prevention programs, HIV education should be understood in relation to the factors that influence sexual practices: self-esteem, love, communication, oppression, and cultural conditioning. An open, pluralistic, respectful environment must be created for students to take account of their sexual lives and responsibilities.

If any topics lie beyond the counselor's knowledge or comfort level, she or he should refer students to someone better prepared to help, in either the school or the community. Lists of such resources should be available to all personnel. They may include health, counseling, and drop-in centers, advocacy groups, and shelters.

Some community agencies provide targeted services for sexual minority youth, such as: GED preparation, adult mentoring, family counseling, and residential options, including group homes, supervised independent living, and placements with gay and lesbian foster families (e.g., Twin Cities Host Home Program, Minn.; Safe Homes, and the Home for Little Wanderers, Mass.; Green Chimneys, N.Y.; L.A. Gay and Lesbian Center, Calif.).

*Question 27: Why do some gay and lesbian youth seem to go overboard expressing their sexuality?*

Of course there are issues of propriety regarding any expression of sexuality, but let the judges consider the following: gay people are regularly accused of flaunting their sexuality by merely correcting the assumption that they are straight.

Those who are squeamish about public displays of homosexual affection may be charmed by similar shows of heterosexual puppy love. This double standard is not only inherently discriminatory; it also ignores the genuine needs of sexual minority youth to be open. Coming out is a key element in healthy identity development. Even well-intentioned teachers wanting to shield students from homophobia may hurt them by overemphasizing caution.

Advising these young people how to navigate coming out without neglecting other emotional, intellectual, and practical needs requires delicacy. These are adolescents in the throes of first love—love for themselves and perhaps another—and little else may matter for the moment.

Some also throw themselves full throttle into the movement for glbt social justice. That is both morally admirable and self-enabling. Of course, when their social life or activism interferes with other important tasks, like academic achievement, counselors can help them recenter and prioritize.

*Question 28: What kinds of behaviors can teachers expect of students in the "pride stage" of gay identity development?*

These adolescents are exhilarated to be out of hiding and are revved up for cultural exploration. They want to try out different styles, join affinity groups, and be around colorful people. Like their straight peers, they often identify by means of dress, comportment, musical tastes, and other interests. Lesbian identity signifiers include butch, femme, earth mother, jock, lipstick lesbian, baby dyke, bad girl, and vanilla. Boys might label themselves clone, jock, prep, raver, club kid, or drama queen. Many are not wedded to any one appearance or affiliation, and are eclectic in their search for costume, demeanor, community involvement, and erotic preferences.

They are looking for intimate friends as well as sexual partners. Sometimes the former become the latter and vice versa. Girls seem better at adapting to such changes. Boys, on the other hand, might have difficulty forging deep nonsexual friendships with other gay males. Those boys who have been taught to equate homosexuality with sex may have trouble sorting their affectional needs from their sexual ones.

Youth without access to social groups of glbt peers may end up going to bars and dating older partners. Age differences are not necessarily problematic but still worth discussing with a counselor. Significant inequalities in power, income, sexual experience, and worldliness are hard for a teen to negotiate.

Gay and lesbian youth need guidance and encouragement in these explorations. They require consolation for mistakes and heartbreaks. Unlike their heterosexual counterparts, who have likely had a head start with sexual roles and relationships, they are just starting. (See box 3.31.)

**BOX 3.31   WHAT TO ADVISE THE NEWLY "OUT"**

- Relax and be patient—this is just the beginning.
- Be proud but prudent. (The closet is okay, when danger threatens.)
- If you are harassed, find allies, report to the authorities, and demand justice.
- Be safe with sex and substances.
- Don't let yourself be exploited. Say "no" to anything that makes you uncomfortable.
- Nightlife is exciting...on weekends.
- Activism is great...and so is doing well in school.
- Remember your family needs you too.
- If you're feeling down, talk to friends and counselors.
- Keep your sense of humor.

*Question 29: Do sexual minority students do better with gay or lesbian counselors?*

Some youth (and adults) prefer a counselor who is more likely to share their perspective and experience. They assume he or she will be more empathetic. Youth especially are wary of negative judgment, but of course heterosexual counselors can earn their trust. When counselors, gay or straight, talk frankly about how they have dealt with their own homophobia, they contribute to two goals: earning the student's confidence and giving him or her permission to work on the vestiges of shame that nearly all sexual minority youth must exorcise. When students want a role model to mentor and advise them, a gay teacher or counselor can be most effective.

Teachers who have not had counselor training require preparation for these tasks. They need not only understand the issues but also be familiar with the techniques. They should be alert for attempted manipulation by emotionally needy, possibly angry adolescents. Sexuality counseling in schools is risky terrain, not only because of conservative opposition, but also because teens can misread intentions and cross boundaries. Teachers must not shrink from this crucial role, but they should be prudent and sensible. (See box 3.32.)

*Question 30: How should gay and lesbian students be counseled about coming out to their families?*

Counselors should discuss with glbt students the extent to which they have already come out to their families and how the latter have responded. (See

## BOX 3.32   MORE CAVEATS

- When a student self-identifies as gay, don't jump to conclusions about his or her experience.
- Alert a colleague or supervisor to what is going on.
- When advisable, do not meet privately with a student unless another adult is within view.
- Be clear about boundaries.
- Allow students to talk about their intimate lives, but don't share details of your own. Discuss sexual behaviors without personal attribution, suggest readings, etc.
- Let the young person have the floor as much as you can.
- If you are gay, don't let yourself be idealized.
- The more identities you have in common with the counselee, the more careful you should be about overidentification in both directions.

## BOX 3.33   COMING OUT TO FAMILY

A Checklist:

- Has the student come out to any or all family members?
- Might some know and pretend not to?
- If they know, are they accepting?
- How does the student think accepting family members really feel?
- Is the family open with extended family, friends, etc.?
- How do unaccepting family members behave toward the student?
- Are there other gay people in the family? How are they treated? Have you spoken with them?
- Why are you coming out to your family right now? If you're coming out in anger or spite, wait. If you're tempted to come out during a family event, choose a quiet time instead.
- How have your relations with family members been until now?
- Are there other conflicts or stresses in the family right now?
- Are you confident enough in your own sexual identity to be self-assured with your family?
- Can you be as loving and patient with your family as you want them to be with you?
- Do you have pamphlets or other resources to give your parents and do you know where they might go for support?

box 3.33.) Hiding from one's family is damaging, but coming out to them, even with a counselor's help, can also have negative results. These consequences can range from shaming and harassment to outright violence and expulsion from the home. The counselor must broach these possibilities. If the family is likely to respond drastically and the student might be left without support, safety, and shelter, it might be better to keep the secret. The student should be counseled and referred confidentially. (See box 3.34.)

Conservative religious families are often less accepting, but liberals might not react as well as counselors expect. They could be less progressive about sexuality than about other social issues, or their attitudes might change where their own children are concerned, or they could fear for their child's well-being. (See box 3.35.)

Even students who don't anticipate dire results might worry about hurting or disappointing their parents. A child could be afraid to come out if another sibling has already done so. They might anticipate another painful scene or be aware of lingering disapproval for a sister or brother that they dare not bring upon themselves.

Learning about successful coming out experiences of others with similar family backgrounds can help both counselors and students anticipate some issues. They could prepare by enacting a family members role-play. When advising discretion and planning, the counselor should also stress the healthy aspects of coming out—reasonable risk-taking, growth promotion, and improved communication—applied in the family context.

### BOX 3.34   THE PARENTAL NOTIFICATION DILEMMA

- President Bush's education reform bill of January 2002 allows gay youth to seek school-provided physical and mental health services without parental notification.
- Referrals to outside services are not covered by this law.
- Prior state and local laws and policies may muddle the issue.
- Counselors should confer with administration in advance of any real case on how to act in the best interest of the child when the risks of parental involvement seem dire.
- Mandates for reporting suicidality or depression need not include the supposed reasons for the problem.
- When an administrator cannot assure student confidentiality, the counselor is left to conscience. He or she might quietly or indirectly provide the student with a list of community services (hotlines, mental health centers, etc.).

## BOX 3.35   THE SHAKEN LIBERAL

When my son told me he was gay at 9 . . . I played baseball with him more. I tried to get him to sign up for sports. I signed him up for karate so he could at least defend himself. I coached him on being more masculine. I called it being more assertive, told him to speak in a gruffer voice, told him not to flail with his hands when he was talking. I hated myself for trying to make him into something he wasn't, shaming him for the things he was, buckling under what society considered "normal" and therefore OK. But I was afraid he might end up beat up someday, maybe even dead. I'm still afraid of those things.

Mary Olson, "Homosexuals Deserve Loving, Sexual Relationships," *Minneapolis Star Tribune*, August 11, 2000.

At the end of this anticipatory process, the decision is always the student's to make. If he or she opts for disclosure and expects ejection, prearranged housing and support must be available. This is no simple matter. When adolescents are thrown out or need to be rescued from abusive homes, counselors may have trouble finding appropriate long-term placements.

### Question 31: Should students come out to all their family members?

They generally start with someone they think will be sympathetic, often a sibling. GLBT youth could welcome the chance to strategize with one relative about coming out to others and to have an ally when the time comes. More mothers are confided in than fathers are, especially by sons. It may indeed be easier to find a toehold of support before taking on the whole family project, but there are still risks in selective disclosure within families. Usually discrete relatives might divulge the confidence for reasons they think are the child's best interests. Even when they don't tell, their well-intentioned advice might be wrong.

When some family members know and others don't or pretend not to, honest relationships are splintered. This avoidance conspiracy requires the student's acquiescence. The family claims to be interested in the child's life, but both family and child are careful not to ask or tell anything too honestly. Lovers are treated and pose as friends, and so on. There is no intentional malice in these deceits—just relatives doing what they think they should to spare feelings and avoid dissension. This path may seem best, but it is disastrous in the long term. Because sexual orientation is not trivial, promoting a charade invites dishonesty in family relationships at many levels. Most importantly, gay adolescents conclude they cannot be loved for who they really are and waste energy in self-monitoring and pretense. Concealment itself ends up being more alienating than the perhaps difficult truth.

Of course, coming out to some family members may be more intimidating than sharing with others. Older people in general are more conservative about sexuality and therefore might be less tolerant. Or, they may be inclined to pity because they think homosexuals must still lead sad and shameful lives as outcasts. On the other hand, some family elders might agree with progressive social developments or just have matured beyond harsh judgments in general.

Young siblings, on the other hand, may lack the understanding and maturity to handle the news well. Even older ones could be baffled or angry over the prospect of losing their friends. They may worry about their own sexuality and what others think they are. These fears are natural and need to be addressed.

If they are welcome, extended family members who have experience with coming out issues or are even gay themselves could be invited into the counseling conversation with the immediate family. On the other hand, counselors should not accede to parents' requests to bring in extended family to pressure their children to give up their so-called lifestyle.

Previous family experience with homosexuality can also make counseling more difficult. For example, great empathy and tact are required in talking with a parent who is divorced from a gay spouse or in including a closeted relative in the conversation.

## Question 32: How should schools counsel families of gay and lesbian students?

Extraordinary discretion and sensitivity are required in broaching sexuality issues with parents or other family members of glbt and questioning students. A family may want to accept their child's homosexuality but may still be uncomfortable with it. They should know that such adjustments take time, like the coming out process itself. If popular misunderstandings and bad psychological theories have influenced them, they may think their child's homosexuality is their fault. They may also fret about negative responses from other family members, friends, neighbors, and church communities.

Parents may go through a grieving period, mourning the child they thought they had and some of their expectations of him or her. Yes, the child is still their child, but with this revelation, he or she may indeed seem to be a stranger. Some who ostensibly take the news well and offer their embrace are still surprised by aftershocks of grief. It may take from six months to some years to process this information. (See box 3.36.)

Yet grief must end, as must denial, guilt, anger, and regret. The family should be helped to learn more about gay and lesbian life, renew their appreciation and

## BOX 3.36   GRIEF AND RECONCILIATION

For a few years after my son Adam came out to me, Father's Day was a day of mourning, the day when I was reminded of what I lost. . . . He was going to be the captain of the football team. . . . the stud that I bragged about . . . the husband . . . the father of the children I would cherish. . . . [T]oday I realize that all those dreams I had weren't really for Adam. They were for me. . . . Father's Day has changed for me. It isn't any longer about what I lost, but what I gained: the ability to love my son unconditionally.

Jeff Ellis, "It Took Years, But Dad Very Proud of Gay Son," *Seattle Post-Intelligencer*, June 16, 2002.

Even 10 years since [Maria Ortiz] came out, [her Cuban refugee parents] sometimes struggle with the idea that Maria won't be marrying a man and having children with him. "It is like a death of a daughter," [her father] Heriberto says. "All your expectations die and you have to learn something new."

Martha Irvine, "Revelation Forever Alters Relationship with Parents," *Associated Press*, October 2, 2002.

revise their expectations of their child, and reaffirm their love. Researchers describe six stages of family adjustment: shock, denial, guilt, expression of feelings, return to rationality with varying degrees of acceptance, and, finally, true acceptance. Adolescents should be advised to be patient with their families. (See box 3.37.)

The goal in counseling family members should be complete and equal inclusion of the gay student in the family. Restrictions on dress, dating, sexual activity, and so on should be no different from what they are, or would be, for straight siblings. Communication should be encouraged. "I accept what you are, but I don't want to hear about it" is not a proper family resolution. Nor should family members be voyeuristic. Like other adolescents, sexual minority youth deserve some privacy. The rest of the family must understand that gays and lesbians want to feel loved as much as other family members are and that they want to have their relationships equally respected. The social customs celebrating heterosexual dating, courtship, and union (Valentine's Day, proms, weddings, anniversaries, et al.) must extend to gays and lesbians too. And when breakups and other disappointments come, they deserve the same consolations.

**BOX 3.37   WHAT TO REMIND SEXUAL MINORITY YOUTH ABOUT THEIR FAMILIES**

- It took you time to adjust to the discovery of your own homosexuality.
- Family members need to express their feelings and be heard before they can move on to better understanding.
- Finding out a loved one is homosexual can shake one's confidence in an entire belief system.
- Family members may feel guilty that they did something wrong or that their child has suffered without their knowledge or comfort.
- Each family member moves at a different pace.
- People sometimes regress in the progress they were making toward acceptance, but usually recover.
- Most gay/lesbian people themselves spend years working out their internalized homophobia.
- They may be having trouble expressing it, but they still love you.

Even though some families and cultures want glbt youth to keep quiet in exchange for tolerance, it is not wise to counsel adolescents to be satisfied with such conditional love or second-class family status. They are a source of pain and resentment over the long term. At the same time counselors must appreciate that racial, religious, and cultural identities are not always easily abandoned in favor of sexual liberation. As the powerful 2000 film *Trembling before God* illustrates, gay Orthodox Jews don't feel any less Jewish than gay or lesbian. So for some, it is not about "quitting the club that won't have you as a member." Many sexual minority people agonize over the "impossible" choice between one piece of their heart and another. (See box 3.38.)

*Question 33: What help can counselors offer to apparently accepting families?*

They need to know how to educate themselves about gay and lesbian life. They may want help examining their own attitudes more deeply or devising strategies for inclusion of their gay child in family affairs. They might need support for disclosing to others—what has been called the "coming out" process of the family. (See box 3.39.) Like parents of glbt children whose adjustment seems more tentative, they would be well advised to join a group like PFLAG. (See appendix C.)

## BOX 3.38   IMPERFECT, BUT HOME

I must admit, many gay friends of mine regard it as peculiar, if not worse, that I would belong to a [Catholic church] that teaches me that my love is no more than a lifestyle. I reply to critics that the church's treasury of the sacraments is a great consolation to me.

Richard Rodriguez, "My Sad Gay Church," *Salon.com*, www.salon.com (June 14, 2002).

A Miami-raised Cuban, [Grisel] Rodriguez, 49, tried living in Allentown, Pa., years ago but missed Miami's Hispanic culture. "They may be homophobic, but they're my homophobes!"

Andrea Elliott, "Living a Dual Life," *Miami Herald*, June 11, 2002.

*Question 34: Do multiple minority students have special counseling needs?*

They have all the concerns of other gay and lesbian adolescents and then additional ones related to their other minority identities. As described in chapter 2, coming out can threaten their established links to the ethnic, racial, class, or religious groups where they have been taught to resist stigma and oppression. The

## BOX 3.39   REMINDERS TO FAMILIES ABOUT THEIR SEXUAL MINORITY CHILDREN

- You may need time to grieve, but not forever.
- Homosexuality is nobody's fault.
- Your child's coming out is not an act of betrayal.
- Don't blame his or her sexuality for any of your child's failings.
- Concern for your child's safety is warranted, but think about whether some of your worry might be about yourself.
- Educate yourself about sexual orientation.
- Your child has not been recruited or forced into homosexuality by anyone.
- Honor and celebrate your gay child's relationships as you would those of any other child.
- There are many gay-affirming religious teachings and accepting churches.
- Look forward to your child's productive and happy future.

## BOX 3.40   DOUBLE JEOPARDY

A. Charlene Leach, [of] the National Youth Advocacy Coalition... says ... that black and Latino families are often less accepting of a teenager's homosexuality than white families. Gay youth of color also face dual hostility from the outside community—for being gay and for being a minority. "What is typically viewed as being in the closet for [white gay kids] doesn't have the same connotation for gay youth of color.... A lot of times they won't come out because of safety and survival.... The impact is definitely greater for youth of color."

Laura Lang, "Below the Gaydar," *Washington* [D.C.] *City Paper*, May 19, 2000.

family, community, church, and sometimes the school as well have provided positive reinforcement for these identities but rarely for a homosexual one.

In the mind of a multiple minority adolescent, coming out as gay means casting oneself into a gay environment that could be as oppressive as the majority world has already been. Where would one's anchor be then? Multiple minority adolescents may be frustrated and angry to find that they cannot feel entirely safe in either community. The risks are great for psychological isolation and its typical consequences: depression, substance abuse, and so on. (See box 3.40.)

The best counseling strategy is to demonstrate that the gay identities are not incompatible with multiple minority ones. If an adolescent is caught up in competing loyalties—the "which are you first?" question—they should be assured that the question is unfair. These young people need role models, affinity groups, readings, films, and other materials to make a convincing case for successful identity integration. (See appendix B.) In some communities these resources are plentiful and accessible. In others it will take perseverance to find them. Sometimes a few books, magazines, or websites are all that can be provided; yet they may still be lifelines.

These students need support dealing with all their oppressions, including heterosexism. They cannot wait to be psychically whole, postponing coming out until racial, ethnic, class, and religious prejudices have been vanquished. The counseling aim is to achieve congruence between sexual identity and the rest of the self. (See box 3.41.)

Immigrant youth may also have particular counseling needs. They may be discovering their homosexual desires for the first time or they may be finding new meanings and words for feelings that were interpreted differently in their native cultures. The sexual repertoire that men particularly are allowed in other parts of the world is replaced here by a rigid labeling system that could estrange them not only from their established sense of themselves but also from their families

## BOX 3.41  MULTIPLE MINORITY GAY
## IDENTITY INTEGRATION

- Denial of Conflict—minimizing both race and sexuality as sources of stress.
- Bisexual versus Gay/Lesbian—using bisexual label to retain affiliation with the ethnic/racial group.
- Conflicts in Allegiances—anxiety over prioritizing memberships.
- Establishing Priorities in Allegiance—during which ethnicity/race prevails and resentment arises from rejection by the homosexual community.
- Integrating the Various Communities—commitment grows toward developing a wholly accommodating identity, even with continuing limitations.

*Source:* Edward S. Morales, "Third World Gays and Lesbians: A Process of Multiple Identities" (paper presented at the 91st Annual Convention of the American Psychological Association, Anaheim, Calif., August 1983).

and other cultural supports. (See box 3.42.) Girls from patriarchal cultures and religions would likely need help in both asserting their sexual autonomy and resolving lesbian identity issues. If these young people feel pressured to come out, they might turn their distress into resentment toward their counselors, as might their families.

On the other hand, those who have dealt successfully with one stigmatized identity may have an advantage in negotiating another. Gay and lesbian minority youth should be counseled in adapting the skills they learned to combat racism and other forms of bigotry to meet the challenges of homophobia.

## BOX 3.42  DIFFERENTLY QUEER

While coming to the States might provide us with the opportunities to come out, that coming out is always compromised by the fact that we are negotiating our queerness in a larger social world which, due to racism and imperialism, does not recognize or speak to our own ways of being queer.

Chandan Reddy and Javid Syed, "I Left My Country for This?" *Asian Week* [San Francisco], January 11, 2002.

*Question 35: How should counselors deal with the families of multiple minority and immigrant gay youth?*

Counselors should talk with the student about his or her family's cultural history, power dynamics, and experience with oppression. What are their ideas about procreation, religious observance, gender, and sexuality? What words do they use to describe sexuality and sexual identity? How do they feel about popular culture, the gender system, and sexual expression in their adopted country? Some parents might consider a homosexual identity to be a Western, North American, white, incomprehensible, inconceivable, or sinful concept. They may accuse their children of betrayal and threaten to disown them if they come out as gay.

Counselors might encounter barriers characteristic of particular minority populations. Chinese families, for example, might not discuss painful issues, even among themselves. Asian youth might use their successes to divert their families' attention away from sexuality and expectations of marriage. In Latin cultures the customs both of face-saving and indirectness in conflict management work against coming out explicitly, and quiet toleration may signal denial more than acceptance. Chicanas' special devotion to their mothers might also keep them silent.

These particulars can be elusive to those who are not members of the culture. Counselors can recruit minority colleagues, parents, or community-based psychologists or social workers who are "culturally competent" to assist in family counseling. (See box 3.43.)

Resources developed for multiple minority families are useful (see appendix C) but sometimes fail. The counselor's reassurances about the integration of homosexuality with other identities may be rejected. Role models may evaporate as students conclude that whatever worked for these paragons would never persuade

---

### BOX 3.43  DIFFERENT ROOTS—NEW HOPE

For Those We Love [is the first support group for parents of glbt youth]...to target African Americans.... "Because of our culture, and the way we're grounded, some of us don't want to share our feelings with [nonblack] people," [founder William] Beale said. ... [Pamela Birchett, of the Sexual Minority Youth Assistance League], who is black, said she has found that socioeconomic status—perhaps more than race—signals whether a family will seek help from a support group. Still, she senses an increasing openness to support groups.

Steven Gray, "Finding Strength in Shared Circumstance: New Group Is Uniting Parents of Black Gays," *Washington Post,* May 28, 1999.

## BOX 3.44   UNACCEPTABLE CONDITIONS?

- coming back to a family or community that offers pity or second-class status;
- accusations that they have been corrupted by American or homosexual culture;
- proffering of cures, including heterosexual match-making or prayer;
- having to lead a double life (silence in the minority community, even in the face of blatant homophobia, and openness in the gay/lesbian community);
- conforming to norms of gender role and gender expression;
- membership in a church that loves you but not who you are.

their parents. And they might be right. Coming out can indeed estrange them from their families, at least for a time. Still, there is no need to lose all connection to their cultural heritage. There are pockets of acceptance all over the world and in all faith traditions. (See appendix A.)

It may be impossible to reintegrate at home without conflict, misery, and unacceptable terms. (See box 3.44.) Families might demand the kinds of compromises that cause sexual minority sons and daughters long-term distress. GLBT people may be unable to let go of expectations for parental and community acceptance that will never come. Counseling can give them the capacity to turn away from repeated disappointment and to find love in new families, faiths, and communities.

*Question 36: What special risks do multiple minority youth encounter in the gay community?*

Regrettably, they face the same twin oppressions of stereotyping and prejudice that they find elsewhere. Offenses range from outright racism or religious bigotry to marginalization in the political, social, and cultural arenas of the gay community.

Not all white Western homosexuals understand or acknowledge multiple minority perspectives on the world. In their zeal to fight heterosexism, they sometimes seem oblivious to the other oppressions that many gays and lesbians face. They act as if they expect multiple minorities to disengage from their matrix of identity issues just to be gay in the gay community, and then deal with other concerns by themselves and on their own time.

Outreach and inclusion must go beyond quotas, tokenism, and good intentions to comprehensive multicultural education and the cultivation of empathy. Teachers and counselors should not rely only on multiple minorities to instruct everyone else on the interconnectedness of oppressions and the indivisibility for each individual of racial, ethnic, gender, class, ability, and religious identities.

Relationship issues between different race/ethnicity couples can also be problematic for people of any sexuality. Being fetishized, that is, loved as an exotic object rather than as a full human being, can be disturbing, particularly in the context of societal oppression. A redhead might not object to a partner's passion for red hair, yet a black person could be troubled by his or her lover's excitement over dark skin. Conversely, some minority people are drawn to their physical "opposites" because of internalized racist standards of beauty.

Sometimes opposites attract and there's the end. Yet the experiences of adults in mixed relationships suggest that these issues do come up. Young people too can be concerned about being objectified or about never being interested in partners like themselves. If they cannot see their own beauty and the beauty of the "other" with equally loving eyes, they are more likely to use and be used.

Multiple minorities' cultural practices could also contribute to relationship difficulties. Young men and women from cultures that promote male dominance and rigid gender roles, for example, might have difficulties with power and role in their same gender relationships. They need to cultivate their capacity to be flexible, compromise, share, and reverse roles comfortably.

## Question 37: Do any of these concerns relate to the experience of young people with disabilities?

Deaf, visually impaired, physically handicapped, and learning disabled adolescents constitute comparatively few of the glbt youth population and are often omitted from consideration. But when they are treated as if their psychosexual and sexual identity development were ancillary considerations compared to their other needs, they are poorly served.

Their experience is indeed analogous to that of other multiple-minority glbt students. They face similar challenges in integrating sexual orientation with the rest of their identity constructs and in finding their place in the different communities of their lives. Although they may encounter no distinctive kind of homophobia in their disability community, it is still likely to be there in its generic form. They also face prejudice, disregard, condescension, and being fetishized in the gay community.

## Question 38: How should counselors support transsexual youth?

Counselors should approach these young people with the same respect and positive attitude they bring to their interactions with glb students. Some "trans" youth are exploring their gender identity and expression the way others try on different sexuality labels. Some are minstrelizing as a defense against harassment or as a consequence of internalized homophobia. Although the vicious murders of transgender teens Fred Martinez in Colorado in 2001 and Gwen Araujo in 2002 in California suggest otherwise, some trans youth feel that they will be less vulnerable to attack or less blameworthy for their desires if they just switch genders. Others are as sure of their internal gender, even at an early age, as anyone can ever be.

Good counseling can help them work through these issues. There should be no objection, if, after thoughtful self-examination, a young person wants to present as his or her nonbiological gender and be treated as such for the long term. When counselors remain skeptical they should examine the origins of their discomfort. Gay or straight, are they too deeply wedded to immutable gender categories?

A more justifiably troubling issue is gender reassignment by medical means. What level of transition is appropriate for a minor? Drug treatments and surgery

## BOX 3.45   CAVEATS AND COMPROMISE

As more young transsexuals push to begin transitioning at a younger age, the social workers and medical providers who work with them are confronting a new frontier in gender ethics. . . . Should we make them wait as long as possible, to be sure their decisions are not simply adolescent rebellion? Or take them at their word and let them begin hormones during puberty? "Every day, I feel torn between wanting to empower my patients and wanting to be sure not to harm them," says Jayne Jordan [of] the Callen-Lorde Center's transgender medicine program.

Maria Russo, "Teen Transsexuals," *Salon.com*, www.salon.com (August 28, 1999).

While one in 30,000 men and one in 100,000 women eventually initiate treatment for sex-change operations, even more say they are just as happy to be neither male nor female. At the University of Minnesota's Program in Human Sexuality . . . administrators now routinely admit patients who take only half the journey from one sex to the other, choosing hormones without surgery, or surgery without hormones. . . . "We see there's a lot more complexity to the world," [the associate director] says.

David France, "An Inconvenient Woman," *New York Times Magazine*, May 28, 2000.

**BOX 3.46   MORE LIKE A HEART TRANSPLANT THAN A NOSE JOB**

"I did not transition because I think one must have a male body to do certain things or behave in certain ways....I did it because I was miserable having a female body, and I'm so much happier having a masculine body....The desire to have a differently sexed body is the essence of being transsexual. It is a very immediate, somatic, physical thing. It is the difference between living with a degree of unhappiness and misery I wouldn't wish on anybody, and feeling good."

Shannon Minter, in E. J. Graff, "My Trans Problem," *Village Voice*, June 20, 2001.

are serious steps, requiring adult permission. Only specially trained psychologists and doctors are qualified to help a trans person of any age with these decisions. One question, however, is salient, even for the layperson: why would trans people feel that in order to be male or female, they must have the external biology of a man or a woman? In their disruption of the "naturalness" of gender, can't they also disrupt the attribution of particular gender qualities to specific biological bodies? When they feel male or female on the inside and want to change their lives, what dictates that they can't be males with vaginas or females with penises?

Transsexuals who undergo reassignment surgery give credence to conventional gender categories based on physical appearance, but so do cross-dressers, for that matter. It's just that surgery and hormone treatments are more hazardous to one's health than fitting into a size 10 pump.

In the end, why should people have to define as either male or female at all? Gender, policed with a vengeance, is ultimately in the mind. Ideally, might it not be better to support trans youth in dismantling gender categories—in mixing and matching accessories—rather than in radically altering their bodies? (See box 3.45.) On the other hand, theory must ultimately defer to individual desire and autonomy. After affirmative counseling and at an age of informed and mature judgment, the trans person's wishes are paramount. (See box 3.46.)

(For further reading, see appendix R.)

# 4

---

# Gay Teachers and Gay Families

## PART 1: TEACHERS

*Question 1: Should glbt teachers come out at school?*

There are powerful reasons for glbt teachers to come out. GLBT students regularly testify that openly glbt teachers are supremely important to them. Out teachers are their dependable indicators of school safety. They are often their allies in school reform, their role models, and their personal counselors as well.

Confidently out gay teachers can be significant participants in the dialogue that makes schools more affirming of glbt people. (See chapter 5.) They can have a positive influence on all students and on the larger community. At the same time, disclosure can endanger teachers both professionally and personally. They may face demotion, termination, poor evaluations, punitive class assignments, unfair extra burdens, or secretarial and janitorial vengeance. They could also anticipate harassment, property damage, or outright violence. GLBT teachers could fear defamation such as accusations of child molestation or the absurd, yet common, lesser charge of recruiting students to homosexuality.

After many years of progress in gay rights, expecting the worst may seem far-fetched. Indeed, some teachers' fears more accurately reflect their internal struggles than outside realities. Yet, there are still many communities where the dangers are significant.

Two horror stories have become legend. The first began in 1995, when Gerry Crane, an honored Byron Center, Michigan, music teacher, confirmed to school administrators the rumors that he was gay and was about to have an out-of-town wedding. An angry former student got a copy of the wedding program and informed the school board, clergy, and other students. Conservatives called for his firing and two school employees secretly helped send antigay videos to the parents of his 140 students. In tape-recorded responses to student questions, Crane acknowledged the rumors, and only asked if his alleged sexuality should matter. Denying to his principal that he was making an issue of his sexuality, he said he would not lie about it either. When he refused their buyout offer for his resignation, the school board issued a statement that homosexuality violates community standards, that gay teachers could not be proper role models, and that they would continue to monitor the situation and take action when justified.

Although he had had strong student support, twenty-six students were withdrawn from his classes, including one girl whose church warned that her boyfriend would become gay if he remained in the school choir. After he assured the girl her boyfriend would be fine, Crane was reprimanded for religious harassment.

Within a year, discouraged by a series of baseless complaints and a poisonous environment, Crane resigned his position. Six months later, at age thirty-two, he suffered a fatal heart attack. It took school board members three years to act on a judgment in a lawsuit on Crane's behalf. They begrudgingly paid a lump sum of $25,800 to a scholarship fund in Crane's name and not to his estate.

A second famous case is that of Utah psychology teacher and coach Wendy Weaver who had led her Spanish Fork High School girls' volleyball team to four state championships. In 1997 Weaver, a divorced mother, was asked directly by a prospective player if she was gay and answered yes. The community exploded, Weaver was dismissed from coaching, and both she and her teacher ex-husband were forbidden to speak of her sexuality with anyone connected with the school— even if asked.

Although Weaver never intended to discuss her sexuality in the classroom, she sued, claiming that many in her small town had school ties. She was herself sued by people who accused her of improprieties with her players, such as overnight trips to a cabin and to her home, all-night hot tub parties at school, leading a football game in which girls wore only bras and shorts, promoting a network of lesbian relationships, witnessing displays of affection between the girls, discouraging them from having boyfriends and benching those who did, and pulling their shirts up to inspect for "hickeys." Twenty-seven hundred parents demanded that their children not have Weaver as a teacher.

In 1998, a federal judge awarded Weaver $1,500 in damages and ordered that she be reinstated as a coach and permitted to speak freely. She declined to resume coaching.

A year later, a judge dismissed parents' charges in state court that Utah law forbids Weaver from speaking about homosexuality in class because teachers are prohibited from supporting criminal conduct, including sodomy, by students. The parents' appeal was denied by the Utah Supreme Court in 2003.

The Crane and Weaver cases made headlines nationwide, but some local outrages proceed with less scrutiny. In just one example, after a nervous breakdown and disability retirement, an openly gay Wisconsin teacher sued his former district in 2002, claiming it had failed to halt five years of harassment by elementary and middle-school students. Incidents included: anonymous phone calls, sexually

**BOX 4.1   DETAILS AT ELEVEN**

WKOW-TV in Madison reported that . . . a Jefferson Middle School teacher, allegedly showed the students a picture of his partner while the eighth-grade class talked about tolerance and harassment.

"Teacher Allegedly Showed Class a Picture of Same-Sex Partner," *Associated Press*, June 6, 2001.

graphic bathroom graffiti, AIDS-related insults, and homophobic catcalls. One student had threatened in front of adult and student witnesses to kill him, but the boy was not disciplined. An assistant principal had advised him to ignore the attacks because middle school students can't be stopped from saying such things. A federal appeals court ruled against the teacher, saying he was experienced enough to withstand insults and intimidation. A majority wrote it would be too difficult to tell children "why it is wrong to mock homosexuals without discussing the underlying lifestyle or sexual behavior."

Flagrant homophobia is easier to spot than the subtle punishments schools inflict on gay teachers for being as open about their identities as their straight peers. Teachers' being gay in the abstract disconcerts critics less than their being gay, fully human beings. A gesture that would be innocuous if performed by a heterosexual can be alarming in a gay context. (See box 4.1.)

A completely safe school for glbt teachers is rare indeed. Therefore, even as we urge teachers to come out, we must ultimately defer to their individual judgments. And we should be especially patient with those just entering the profession. Courage can be tempered by discretion—timing is everything.

### Question 2: When, then, should teachers come out?

Teachers have to intuit the right moment, but as a rule the first days of class are not an opportune time. To shorten the agony of anticipating "the question," a gay teacher might want to get it over with as soon as possible, but he or she should wait.

Some students could take an early declaration as an unwelcome, if not aggressive, challenge. (Indeed some glbt teachers could secretly hope that the worst antagonists would be spurred quickly to transfer out.) On the other hand, when mutual respect, trust, and affection are allowed to develop, the odds favor student acceptance and attitudinal change.

If teachers' reputations or demeanors spur questions before they are prepared to come out, they could scold students or otherwise tell them they are out of

## BOX 4.2   TEACHER IDENTITY MANAGEMENT STRATEGIES

- PASSING—lying explicitly and by pretending, assuming no one knows, and wanting to be known as heterosexual.
- COVERING—lying by omission, censoring oneself, assuming no one knows, and wanting not to be seen as gay/lesbian.
- IMPLICITLY OUT—being open about identity without explicitly naming it, assuming some people know (but not correcting those who think otherwise), not objecting to being seen as gay/lesbian and even implying so through dress, etc., but maintaining a degree of deniability, if needed, by not uttering the words.
- EXPLICITLY OUT—affirming one's gay/lesbian identity, mutually acknowledging one's identity, and wanting to be seen as gay/lesbian.

Adapted from Pat Griffin, "Identity Management Strategies among Lesbian and Gay Educators," *Qualitative Studies in Education* 4, no. 3 (1991): 193.

line. Closeted teachers have usually developed a repertoire of evasions to let students know they will not get an answer. Conversely, teachers could conclude that reprimands and evasions might only exacerbate the situation. Anticipating that the question will keep coming up, at least among the students, he or she could resolve to come out as soon as possible and work the issue out in a relatively controlled environment.

Research by Pat Griffin at the University of Massachusetts has uncovered a continuum (or stage model) of strategies that teachers use to manage their identities at work. They range from being completely closeted to being totally open and affirming. (See box 4.2.)

Like people in other professions, some teachers are more open with certain groups and individuals than with others. But the logic can be convoluted: closeted teachers might avoid coming out to others they suspect of being closeted, because the latter might betray the confidence as a way of disavowing their own sexuality. On the other hand, closeted educators might not disclose to openly gay colleagues who they suspect might betray them or whose company might incriminate them.

Coming out to students is still perceived by most teachers as the last frontier, a leap into a wholly different territory marked by serious taboos. Some of their hesitancy can be ascribed to a menacing political environment. In a 2001 survey by the San Francisco-based Horizons Foundation, only 55 percent of parents would be comfortable having their children taught by openly gay teachers. (In conservative regions comfort is likely even less.) Footage of the Gay, Lesbian,

## BOX 4.3   GAY TEACHER AS BOGEY MAN

Copies of the study, by Colorado psychologist Paul Cameron, were included in the letters that the Christian Coalition mailed recently to every school board chairman, superintendent and legislator in Maine.... "The study demonstrates that homosexual teachers are 8 to 10 times more likely to sexually involve themselves with pupils," [the coalition's executive director] wrote in the letter.... "Knowingly employing homosexual teachers after receipt of this study places you in a precarious legal situation."

Michael Gordon, "Coalition Rips Homosexuals in Letter to School Districts," *Lewiston* [Me.] *Sun-Journal,* April 12, 2000.

and Straight Education Network contingent in a gay rights march was highlighted in the right-wing film, *The Gay Agenda in Public Education,* to incite panic over recruitment and predation. And the Christian Coalition of Maine cited a discredited psychologist's grossly flawed research paper, "Do Homosexual Teachers Pose a Risk to Pupils," in its 2000 campaign against a gay rights bill. (See box 4.3.)

A long history of public anxiety over gay teachers in the United States (see box 4.4.) could give one pause before coming out, even in the enlightened twenty-first century. The Boy Scout bans of 2001 and the homosexual priest panic

## BOX 4.4   GET THE GAY TEACHERS

- A series of political maneuvers were tried in California and Florida, beginning in the 1950s, to deny employment to teachers involved in morals charges, regardless of criminal guilt or innocence.
- There were repeated attempts during Massachusetts legislative debates in the 1980s to exempt teachers and child care workers from gay rights protections.
- The California Briggs Initiative of 1978 called for the dismissal of any school employee who "promoted" homosexuality in a manner that was aimed at, or might come to the attention of, schoolchildren or school employees. It was defeated.
- In 1998, the Oklahoma House of Representatives passed, for the second time since 1985 (when it was ruled unconstitutional), a 1978 law banning homosexuals from working in the public schools.

of 2002 would be easily transferable to the school setting. There is little evidence of active campaigns to seek out discretely closeted teachers; yet there is clear antagonism to open homosexuality—a sort of "don't ask, don't tell" in the schoolhouse. Normalizing of gayness causes alarm, the dread that children will come to believe that there is no inferiority, no disgrace, and no sin in being gay, lesbian, or bisexual.

Yet sometimes teachers are propelled totally out of the closet by a cathartic event, either positive or negative. There are wonderful stories about teachers coming out during antihomophobia workshops and assemblies, inspired by the courage of others or the improving school environment. There are also incidents of teachers being outraged and sorrowful about gay student victimization or suicide or being finally tired of hiding.

Conversely, gay-positive school programs might frighten closeted teachers by bringing unwelcome attention to a subject they have avoided for so long and drive them deeper into hiding. Like some racial minority teachers of an earlier time, they might prefer not to roil the school waters with a civil rights struggle.

Lastly, of course, many teachers come out in teaching a lesson, sometimes on bigotry itself. Such was the case with Rodney Wilson, a St. Louis high school teacher who had kept silent for a long time even in the midst of vile and hostile remarks about gays during student discussions of civil rights. During a 1994 class on the Holocaust, Wilson explained the significance of extermination camp insignia, including the pink triangle worn by homosexual prisoners. He added that had he lived in Europe at that time, he would likely have been victimized as a gay man and then expanded on the history of gay and lesbian oppression.

Most students responded well to his disclosure, but some adults did not. The untenured teacher was eventually sent a letter advising that discussion of "facts and beliefs of a personal nature" was "inappropriate conduct for a teacher." The superintendent warned him not to depart from the prescribed curriculum. Supported by his union, some parents and colleagues, most students, and his principal, he was granted tenure. No parents responded to Wilson's offer to discuss removing their children from his classroom and all students remained.

*Question 3: What are the perils for teachers who don't come out?*

Closeted teachers spend a lot of energy being on guard: keeping track of which identity strategy to use with whom, limiting their confidences, monitoring their language, gestures, and dress, avoiding physical contact, distancing themselves from homosexual students and colleagues, and looking over their shoulders when they are away from work.

Some are driven to perfection as a possible mitigation in the event of discovery. And the sad fact is that, despite their elaborate schemes for deception, many are still unable to protect themselves. Such was the case with a non-tenured

Alabama teacher in 2002. His excellent evaluations, his popularity, and all his ruses could not in the end prevent his being fired on suspicion of being gay. His deliberate accoutrements—female "dates" at school events and a fabricated ex-wife and children—did not work. The poor man couldn't even sue under his own name without jeopardizing his new teaching position in another locality. Although tenure usually means more job security in the event of involuntary disclosure, it seldom removes every fear.

The long-term impact of concealment on closeted teachers' psyches is also problematic. What happens to their self-respect if they are silent while gay and lesbian students and teachers are oppressed? How do they feel, standing on the sidelines of gay resistance and organizing? (Incredibly, some have kept their cover through tacit collusion in the bashing of gay students and the homophobic persecution of colleagues.) The stresses of the teacher closet are known to contribute to drug and alcohol abuse, depression, detachment, and even paranoia.

They should also acknowledge the self-delusion that so often accompanies their evasive dance. While they keep mum, their students are reveling in speculation and grilling other teachers into awkward silences and double-talk.

Los Angeles high school English teacher Martin Bridge, once Teacher of the Month and highly regarded by students and administration, responded to a favorite student's question about whether Bridge was gay with awkward evasion. That implied vulnerability probably explains the torrent of antigay invective he then received from students. Refusing the help of both his principal and the Equal Opportunity Office in a system with sexual orientation protections, he resigned. Later, a faculty training on homophobia occurred and a gay student group was initiated.

Besides the possibility of their individual embarrassment or harm, there is also the likelihood of institutional injury. Sometimes students interpret teachers' attempts to hide in a rather transparent closet as a generational phenomenon— "these old people are just more fearful and conservative." But other explanations are more poisonous: "teachers are ashamed to be gay" or "this school is not as safe for gays as people tell us it is." Closeted teachers should face their role in this damaging fallout.

*Question 4: Short of harassment or job loss, what do teachers fear in coming out?*

Most teachers worry less about vicious harassment or termination than they do about damaged relationships with colleagues and students, especially the latter. Although they depend on cooperation with their peers, most would endure some loss of collegiality more readily than an estrangement from their students. If students lose respect for them, how can glbt teachers be effective in the classroom? (The Martin Bridge tragedy above is an object lesson for that.)

Prospects of recovering peer and student relationships and classroom efficacy can be daunting as well. Might they not be seen as the "homosexual teacher," above all? Will colleagues, students, and parents assume they represent a "special interest" that colors their professional objectivity? Other minority teachers and counselors have aroused such suspicions—and still do in some schools. Only a Pollyanna or a fool would deny the possibility of lastingly crippled relationships as a result of teacher disclosure. Argue as one might that honesty and integrity are at stake, the consequences can still be disastrous. No wonder then that each new occasion of coming out to a classroom can be a worrisome event—sweaty palms and all!

Lost opportunities for career advancement are another real possibility. Yet, discrimination may be hard to prove. Dawn Murray, a biology teacher from Ocean-side, California, had won national honors with a 1995 Princeton fellowship and the title of Outstanding Biology Teacher of the Year. She was out only to a few colleagues, but she still was deprived of a promotion because of "rumors" circulated by security staff and custodians. It was said that she was having sex on the floor with another female teacher, and that she was kissing another employee on school grounds and "fraternizing on campus during school hours" with yet another. Students were hearing about these allegations. Fellow workers penned graffiti and made threats. A janitor was discovered defacing Murray's door.

Murray filed complaints with building administrators showing the rumors to be unfounded. When her harassment and loss of promotion suits were dismissed on technicalities, she bravely stayed on and appealed. Her situation was hellish, and, it must be observed, her mostly closeted stance had made no difference. (See box 4.5.) In 2000 Murray won an appeal to reinstate her case and two years later

## BOX 4.5   SILENCE DIDN'T HELP

"My gay colleagues went further into the closet. I do not have one gay teacher friend now. I'm very hurt over that.... I've stopped all field trips unless there's another adult present. At break, I lock my door, at lunch I lock my door. If a kid wants to talk to me in private, we go to a bench outside under a tree, in full view of everyone. I've talked to kids out there in the pouring rain. When I tutor kids, we do it in the library. I'm just extremely careful.... Whenever my name's in the paper now, it always says 'openly lesbian Dawn Murray.' People look at that and they say, 'She wouldn't have gotten into trouble if she'd kept her mouth shut.' Well, my mouth was shut, and this still happened to me."

Dawn Murray, in Linnea Due, "A Teacher's Odyssey," *San Diego Reader,* May 20, 1999.

her school district agreed to award her $140,000 and to provide annual sensitivity training for employees on sexual orientation discrimination.

There is no law prohibiting glbt teachers from becoming administrators, yet few are out and even fewer come out before they are appointed. The scarcity of openly gay administrators is evidence of a "lavender ceiling" in most systems. Hiring committees and school boards apparently associate administrative credibility and proficiency with heterosexuality or closetedness.

The exceptional glbt administrators who are open appear to be assistant principals and principals, most at the elementary school level. There is no published report of a glbt superintendent, for example, although several are known to exist whose sexuality is undisclosed.

## Question 5: Should parents be notified in advance of a teacher's coming out to students?

Parent notification is a recent tactic aimed at preventing teachers from addressing a broad array of topics to which the conservative Right object. (See chapter 6.) It can muzzle even a brief and general response to a student question about sexuality. On the matter of coming out, there is a flagrant double standard. Few parents construe heterosexual teachers' nonprurient assertions of their straightness as inappropriate. Many answer the perennial student inquiry, "Are you married?" with a casual but specific reference to a spouse or significant other. Some have pictures. Yet when a gay teacher discloses under identical circumstances, he or she can be pilloried for indecency, political activism, or recruitment. For example, a first grade teacher presenting a lesson on biographies at the Burr Elementary School in suburban Newton, Massachusetts, was asked about his family and with whom he lived. He answered that if he had a partner like a husband or wife it would be a man. Asked if he liked being gay, he said that he was proud to be who he was, a good person. The vehemence of some parents' reactions led to press conferences, PTA meetings, and newspaper stories. (See box 4.6.)

Not surprisingly, even parent notification fails to satisfy some critics. Mark French, principal of the Oak View Elementary School in Maple Grove, Minnesota, had been open with his staff. Then, in 2002, he sent a letter to the parents of his seven hundred students prior to his appearance on a national television show about family diversity. He decided to put himself forward to benefit glbt students, staff, and families but wanted to give parents a chance to talk to their children in advance. The response to his letter, which inadvertently had been shared with some students before their parents, was predictably mixed. (See box 4.7.)

Such skirmishes notwithstanding, parent notification requirements seem reasonable compared with giving parents the option of removing their child from a gay teacher's class, a practice that is not rare. The California State Labor Commission ruled in January 2000 that the Hemet School District had discriminated

## BOX 4.6   ALL OVER THE (TOT) LOT

[The] director of a conservative parents' group and the father of a Burr student, [said] "a child's psychology isn't put together for any of this stuff."... "Had the teacher at that point said, 'I'm married and have two kids,' no one would have blinked an eye," [the superintendent] said.... "It's quite clear he handled the situation with sensitivity and discretion," [the mayor] said.... [One parent] sympathized with parents who want to control what their children learn, but, from what they see on television to what they hear on the playground, "there are many things we can't shelter our kids from," she said. "I'm grateful that my child can learn about this in a natural, relaxed manner."

"Gay Teacher's Disclosure Spurs a Debate," *New York Sunday Times*, June 11, 2000.

against a lesbian teacher by allowing parents to transfer their children out of her class because of their religious beliefs. It had ruled similarly when fifteen students were removed from a gay Bakersfield teacher's class. That teacher's employers apologized, yet moved him to a nonteaching position. The Hemet district appealed and a state legislator introduced a bill that would permit such student transfers. The appeal was later denied. In a hopeful sign, California's Hayward Unified School District School Board recently voted unanimously to allow gay school employees to "come out" to students without obtaining parents' permission. Critics were predictably apoplectic.

## BOX 4.7   MAKING THE MOST (BAD AND GOOD) OF IT

"This isn't about homophobia," [one parent] said. "It's about a child's innocence; childhood is supposed to be about fireflies and laughter, and you lose that when you have to deal with something like this." [The president of the PTO], whose son was in the class where the letter was read aloud sees it differently. [She] used the letter to talk about differences and tolerance. She said she role-played some possible scenarios that could occur in school the next day. "I asked my boys, 'Did you like Mr. French yesterday?' " she said. " 'Well, he's the same person today. You shouldn't like him any less.' "

"Gay Principal Notifies Parents of His Sexual Preference," [Statewire] *Minneapolis Star Tribune*, June 6, 2002.

*Question 6: What are the chief rewards of coming out?*

The main benefits of disclosure are integrity, self-respect, and a more honest engagement with students and peers. Young people want their teachers and parents to be truthful about who they are and what they value. Are teachers caring and genuine? Do they know their subjects? Do they really want to find honest answers to the questions we encounter in class and in life? Adult dissembling and hypocrisy foster students' estrangement from teachers and disengagement from studies.

Openly gay teachers are catalysts for school communities to reexamine heterosexist stereotypes. They offer sexual minority youth the chance to observe confident and dignified gay adults in respected positions. Homophobia can sensationalize an open teacher's simplest acts of portraying gay relationships tangibly, but their positive impact on students makes them invaluable. (See box 4.8.)

A teacher's coming out sometimes offers an unexpected gift to straight students, beyond the chance to discard prejudice or learn about gay people. Many find that they can confide in their homosexual teachers as in no others, about their own personal challenges. They divulge their weaknesses, relationship worries, or family secrets. They are moved perhaps by a reciprocity of confidences, but surely also by an expectation of greater understanding and less negative judgment from an adult who has triumphed over misunderstanding and damnation.

---

**BOX 4.8   THE BEST KIND OF LETTER ANY TEACHER COULD GET**

One of my sharpest and most pleasant memories of my years at [the high school] is of you sharing photos of a vacation with Bob. One of the images was of you and Bob holding hands on the beach, and it was from this image that I first understood that there were gay and lesbian people. You taught me so much in school . . . and I have carried and used that knowledge throughout my life, but it is that single lesson that I hold most dear. I am so grateful to you for showing those pictures! I had my first girlfriend within weeks of seeing them, and thus began the long, confusing journey toward discovering my own sexual identity. Your actions went far in ensuring that I was able to make this difficult journey without added burdens. . . . Distorted codes of morality could not stand up against you, my trust in you, and my perception of your goodness and integrity. Thank you for the great, great gift you gave me that day.

Name withheld, unpublished letter to the author, August 12, 1999.

Yet with these rewards, there can also be traps. Gay teachers might assume the impossible burden of infallibility, since the pressures to be the "model minority person" are great. Some are driven to be perfect as a response to homophobia; others don't want to let gay kids down.

Some are induced to take on a disproportionate share of the school change project. It can be flattering to become the resident expert or native informant for the rest of the school on matters of sexual orientation and gratifying to counsel referred students. However, it is also unfair to have to shoulder extra duties and, in the long run, it retards school reform as well. When others become dependent on gay teachers for these services it hinders the faculty development that leads to broad institutional improvement. Schools need to understand that being gay does not render one an expert on antihomophobia campaigns nor a natural leader for them.

*Question 7: Are there any pitfalls in a gay teacher's maintaining an effective professional role with students?*

In addition to the expectations of being a gay expert and role model, openly gay, lesbian, and bisexual teachers are subject to inordinate student curiosity. Students might ask teachers who let their heterosexuality be known whether they are dating someone, are married, or have families. But, when a gay teacher comes out, some students take license to ask about sexual intimacy. Even when it springs from genuine curiosity about unfamiliar eroticism, these questions are inappropriate. The study and discussion of all human sexual practices should not be taboo or even confined to the health class, but they should never be related to the teacher's personal life. All teachers should be prepared to talk with students in a relaxed and informed manner about erotic expression, in general.

Some gay and lesbian teachers want to be out to their students but don't want to risk talking about sexuality, especially when their field appears totally unrelated to the topic. Others are more flexible in departing from their syllabi. Because there are so few opportunities for students to engage with openly gay adults on serious questions about sexual orientation, such "digressions" are perfectly justifiable. When one considers that they could originate in a teacher's coming out in the course of challenging homophobic name-calling between students, such interruptions are mandatory.

Although most teacher coming out stories tend toward positive results, there is always a risk that some students will react negatively to the disclosure. For some, dissonance leads to denial, an insistence that the teacher was joking or testing them. For others, suspicions are confirmed and hostility intensified.

There is no formula to determine the exact response of any student—and there are always surprises. But, there are a number of factors that might logically

## BOX 4.9   RECIPES FOR REACTION

- prior relationship with the teacher (level of mutual respect, affection, and honest exchange)
- student background—ethnic, racial, religious, class, and political
- how and how often issues of difference have been addressed previously
- level of commonality in values
- extent of student leadership in modeling independent expression and tolerance
- teacher's perceived attitude toward his/her sexuality
- teacher's response to negative reactions

predict the outcome. (See box 4.9.) Students' reactions to having a gay teacher are somewhat like reactions to a family member's coming out. Some are confused because they thought they knew someone they really did not. Some are let down. Eventually, a patient, nondefensive teacher and accepting classmates can help restore the relationship.

Like young family members, students may fret over what having a close bond with a gay person says about their own sexualities. Their peers might tease them. Rather than embracing a role model, some who are questioning their own sexual identities may flee or be angry and homophobic. If a student is upset over a loved one's homosexuality, he or she may become hostile toward the teacher as a substitute target.

At the other extreme, some gay students might develop crushes on their gay teachers, idealizing them or mistaking their attention and support for romantic interest.

*Question 8: What can gay teachers do to avoid accusations of seduction?*

Students have always been known to develop crushes on their teachers. They are the natural products of power relationships, role modeling, and the discovery that teachers are flesh and blood after all. Young people can be motivated to superior performance by these attachments. There is danger, however, when the platonic relationship with a beloved mentor is eroticized. Every teacher must take care that the lines are not blurred.

Gay teachers are no more to blame for student infatuation than are their heterosexual peers. Yet, they may find themselves doubly responsible for making sure it does not exceed proper boundaries. The public's facile link between "homosexual"

---

## BOX 4.10   PROTECT THE CHILDREN

"[T]he real risk is that [the gay teacher] may, by presenting himself as a love object to certain [student] members of his own sex at a time when their sex attitudes have not been deeply canalized, develop in them attitudes similar to his own. For nothing seems more certain than that homosexuality is contagious."

Willard Waller, *The Sociology of Teaching* (New York: Russell & Russell, 1961), 147–48. First published in 1932 and twice reissued in the 1960s.

---

and "sex" makes this prudence necessary, as do misconceptions of undue influence and recruitment. (See box 4.10.) Some gay adolescents themselves have been influenced by the dominant culture to see their orientation as highly sexed and adult gay men as predatory. These perceptions could lead students to excess fantasy in the first instance or false accusations of seduction in the second.

Gay teachers must not allow homophobia of either the general or the internalized variety to estrange them from glbt students. They should be careful, not paranoid, about contact and sharing confidences with gay young people.

*Question 9: How much should teachers share with students about their lives as glbt people?*

Gay teachers, like their straight colleagues, have lessons to offer in their personal histories. And a true story—happy, sad, suspenseful, or routinely human—can be instructive. A good story would reflect both the diversity of human experiences and the similarities. But as members of an oppressed minority, a few gay teachers could be tempted to expound on their pain indiscriminately. They may have been ostracized and mistreated as students and professionals and may want to tell all. The approval of straight students might help heal their old adolescent wounds. For these reasons they should conscientiously examine their reasons for coming out and also carefully determine how far to go. (See box 4.11.) Teachers can help students understand and accept differences and fight injustice without focusing too much on themselves. The classroom is not the place for adult therapy.

In counseling glbt students, however, gay teachers should feel freer to detail their struggles for the benefit of those enduring similar difficulties and indignities. GLBT students need to know that obstacles can be overcome and that they can have a generally happy life.

It is also proper for glbt teachers to inform students (as well as parents and other community members) about personal matters that are or will be in the public

## BOX 4.11    TOO MUCH INFORMATION!

[The 6th-grade teacher] told students that she had "gaydar" that enabled her to discern whether individual students are gay or lesbian.... [E]arlier she had told students she had contemplated committing suicide ... including extensive detail about her depression, the specific medications that she had used, the methods for taking her life that she considered and her plans for services following her demise.

Anne Williams, "Parents Get More Details of Teacher Probe," *Eugene* [Ore.] *Register-Guard*, May 23, 2001.

realm—possible dismissal, acts of censorship, harassment, and violence—and to ask, without personal invective or unprofessional attack, for their support.

*Question 10: What kinds of legal protections do glbt teachers actually have?*

As of 2003, only fourteen states, the District of Columbia, and approximately 140 localities provided protections for glbt people against workplace discrimination. And ENDA, the federal Employment Nondiscrimination Act, had not passed. Then-senator John Ashcroft's opposition to ENDA in 1996 was rooted in fears about gay teachers as role models; Senator Orrin Hatch complained that schools would be unable to fire gay teachers who publicly kissed or held hands with their partners.

Because, until their abolition by the Supreme Court in 2003, the sodomy laws of fourteen states still criminalized homosexual sex, teachers convicted of such offenses could lose their credentials with little recourse. Local policy statements, application forms, and teacher contracts may not even reflect existing state protections. Although the National Education Association and the National Federation of Teachers have been outspoken advocates of gay employment rights, some union locals have been less than energetic in supporting glbt members threatened with harassment or job loss. Rather than charging their union with failure to represent them in a hostile environment, some teachers would rather negotiate a quiet departure to seek employment elsewhere.

Without explicit legal protections, judges weigh teachers' rights of free expression and association against the prerogatives of education officials to limit their speech and school activities. Extracurricular speech and advocacy are generally protected, unless they can be proven disruptive to the school. A 1998 federal court order was the first in the nation to require a school system in a state without protections, in this instance Ohio, to rehire a teacher whose contract had not been renewed because he was gay.

*Question 11: How much do legal remedies for discrimination really accomplish?*

Employment and privacy rights are part of the solution, but they do not guarantee changes in homophobic hearts and minds. Therefore, the best-protected gay teacher can still be made to feel isolated, unhappy, and essentially unsafe.

The number of lawmakers and judges who accept the complete equality of gay and straight people is pitifully small and one finds reflections of their heterosexism in their legislative actions and legal opinions. Some of the most progressive senators in the United States voted for the Defense of Marriage Act in 1996. In-school demonstrations of teachers' heterosexual orientation are still normalized, whereas similar homosexual expression can be deemed improperly political or exhibitionistic.

As a rule, civil and employment rights alone do not bring teachers out of the closet. With or without guaranteed protections a good deal of courage is required. And perhaps nothing illustrates this courage better than transgendered educators who are pushing the boundaries of understanding, acceptance, and civil rights despite a relative absence of legal assurances. (See box 4.12.)

*Question 12: Should schools be encouraged to recruit more glbt people into teaching?*

Any school would benefit from having a staff that reflects and celebrates human diversity. Employing identifiable members of marginalized and stigmatized groups is by itself an implicit affirmation. But there is even more to be gained in having them teach about their experiences and those of others like them, encouraging an exchange of ideas and values with colleagues, students, and families, and inviting their critique of the dominant culture.

Recruitment for affirmative action would clearly be a political challenge in many communities. But schools can at least begin by creating an atmosphere in which their current glbt teachers and those with glbt loved ones feel free to speak freely and fully.

## PART 2: FAMILIES

*Question 13: What issues confront glbt families in schools?*

Few schools are meeting the needs of the estimated four to fourteen million children with gay or lesbian parents or caregivers. Many educators harbor incorrect notions about these young people and the homes they come from. Some teachers and counselors assume any problems these students might have can be traced to inherently unhealthy parenting. Most have not given much thought to the

## BOX 4.12   TRANSGENDER AT THE FOREFRONT

1998: Two veteran teachers, one at Lake Forest High School in Illinois and another at Southwest High School in Minneapolis, returned successfully to their workplaces after sex changes.

1999: Male-to-female transsexual teacher Dana Rivers resigned after settling a wrongful termination lawsuit with the Center Unified School Board in Antelope, California, for $150,000. As David Warfield, Rivers was a popular successful teacher, who was also married and a Navy veteran. Rivers had been faulted for discussing her transformation with students. Forty students and two hundred teachers held a rally on her behalf near the school. She also was given back her teaching license and hoped to return to teaching eventually.

2001: A twelve-year veteran, Wilmette, Illinois, middle school principal Donald Reed returns to school in September after gender reassignment surgery as Deanna Reed. Thirty-five parents, concerned about the effects on their pubescent children, organize a petition drive to have her removed. They claim the students are upset about what bathroom she will use and whether they will be punished for laughing or making comments about the principal. Other parents are more open-minded, hoping their children will learn from the experience.

2001: In Northbrook, Illinois, Glenbrook High School science teacher Dayne Travis is about to return to school as Dane Travis, after female-to-male gender reassignment. School officials inform parents in a letter that the matter is personal and will not be discussed with students during classroom activities. After consultation with psychologists and lawyers, they don't expect any disruption to the school.

factors that make school life difficult for these young people and inhospitable to their families.

Educators should learn the truth about glbt parenting and become familiar with the stresses facing glbt families. At the same time, they must implement changes to support these students and make schools more welcoming to their parents.

*Question 14: What prejudices does the public hold about glbt parenting?*

Many people think that children cannot be raised successfully by glbt parents, either singly or in couples. Gay males are presumed to be sex-obsessed pleasure-seekers, rarely monogamous, responsible, or nurturing. The equation of homosexuality and pedophilia renders them a threat to male children. Lesbians are thought to lack the softness for motherhood. The suspected exclusion of men from their lives feeds doubts that they can raise well-adjusted sons, who, it is generally assumed, need proximate male role models.

Moreover, glbt parents are thought by some to be bad models for children of their own gender. At its extreme this idea leads to the conclusion that children raised by glbt caregivers are more likely to become homosexual or gender nonconforming themselves.

*Question 15: What does the research really show about gay parents and their parenting?*

Many studies have examined the mental health of homosexual parents, the quality of their parenting, and their effects on children's psychological health and sexual identity development. They have found no indication that gay parents, despite their stresses, are prone to mental illness. (See box 4.13.) They have also shown

---

### BOX 4.13   GAY PARENTS' MENTAL HEALTH

1. Lesbians have no more mental health problems than heterosexual women do; some are more self-confident and independent, and enjoy support from alternative family constellations.
2. Single lesbian mothers share concerns similar to single heterosexual mothers relative to providing for their children.
3. Divorced lesbian mothers have added worries about disclosure of their identities and its ramifications regarding custody and family relations.
4. Lesbian mothers with female partners have stresses about earnings, since female couples, particularly in the working class, earn less than heterosexual ones.
5. Gay parents are more likely than straight ones to try to be supermoms and superdads.
6. Lesbian families in which one woman or both are stepparents to their divorced partners' children may face a more difficult adjustment than similar families with heterosexual remarried parents, because of secrecy, legal status, and stigmatization.
7. Noncustodial divorced gay fathers are subject to grief over losing quality contact with their children and stress over the integration of their parental self-concept/role and their often newly forming gay identity.
8. Gay fathers who are open with their children about their homosexuality appear to have better relationships with them than closeted fathers.

## BOX 4.14   GAYS AND LESBIANS AS PARENTS

1. Lesbians do not value their motherhood any less than heterosexual women do nor do they perform differently in child rearing and problem solving.
2. Lesbians and gay men are not less effective parents than heterosexuals are.
3. Gay parents are far less likely to use physical punishment as opposed to reason and conversation to modify children's behavior than straight parents are.
4. Gay fathers are more likely to play an active role in parenting than straight ones and are less likely to be constrained by gender roles in parenting.
5. The nonbiological parent is likely to bond closely with the child and assume increasing responsibility for rearing after the child's infancy, although biological mothers are more likely to be childcare-givers, and nonbiological mothers are more often in paid employment.
6. The nonbiological lesbian parent is usually more involved in child rearing than fathers in heterosexual couples.
7. Lesbian mothers are as likely as, or more likely than, single or divorced heterosexual mothers to ensure children's contact with adult men, including their fathers.
8. Lesbians and gay men are not likely to molest their own children or anyone else's. (Heterosexual men have been found to be most involved in such abuse.)
9. The only evidence of parental dysfunction appears in cases of opposite-gender couples where the homosexual parent is closeted to the child and in cases of closeted gay fathers, even those living apart from their families.

that lesbians and gay men make good parents. (See box 4.14.) They conclude that children of gay parents are no less well adjusted than are their peers from heterosexual households. (See box 4.15.) To no one's surprise among gay families, in 2002 the American Academy of Pediatrics, after reviewing two decades of research, concluded that children of gay or lesbian parents are as likely to be as socially and psychologically well adjusted as the children of heterosexual parents.

Questions and suspicions about the influence of gay parents on the sexualities of their offspring, however, continue to vex both researchers and the public. The issue garnered considerable attention after the publication of a paper by two University of Southern California sociologists, Timothy Biblarz and Judith Stacey, in

## BOX 4.15  HOW ARE THE KIDS DOING?

1. Differences in mental and emotional health have not been observed between children of lesbians and those of heterosexual mothers. Marital discord and divorce are greater predictors than parental homosexuality of children's psychological problems.
2. If there is any discomfort with a parent's sexual orientation, it comes when the child's situation is disclosed to others.
3. Cognitive functioning and behavioral adjustment of the 3-to-10-year-old children of lesbian couples are comparable to those of heterosexuals' children.
4. Self-esteem of daughters whose lesbian mothers live with their partners may be higher than that of daughters whose mothers live singly.
5. Children are better-adjusted and lesbian mothers happier when child-rearing responsibilities are more evenly divided.
6. Absence of a father has no correlation with sex-role behavior in homosexual or heterosexual families.
7. Children with homosexual parents are aware of societal disapproval and are often compelled to secrecy. However, children of lesbians are no more likely to lack self-esteem or feel less social acceptability than their peers are.
8. Some parents and teachers see children of lesbian couples as more affectionate, responsive, and protective of younger children than are heterosexual couples' children, who appear more domineering and negativistic.

2001. In their review of previous research (mostly on children of lesbians), they found that, although adolescents raised by gay parents were as emotionally healthy and academically successful as their peers were, they exhibited some differences with regard to gender role and sexuality. First, they were somewhat more likely to depart from traditional gender roles in both recreational, dress, and occupational choices and in personal behavior. Teenage boys with same-gender parents were more sexually restrained, for example, and teenage girls from gay households were more likely to be sexually adventurous. Both appeared to be more open to same-sex relationships than the children of heterosexual couples.

The conclusion to be drawn from this review is that because they are raised to accept differences in sexual and gender expression, children in gay households are less inhibited about exploring their own sexual and gender ranges and more inclined to challenge traditional sexual and gender norms. The American Academy of Pediatrics report took the Biblarz and Stacey paper into consideration but still found no basis on which to assume a parent's homosexual orientation would "increase the likelihood of or lead to a similar orientation in his or her child."

Despite this finding, might we not expect that a child with a homosexual capacity raised by openly gay parents would be more likely to accept his or her orientation than a similar child brought up by rigidly homophobic parents? And if there are indeed genetic components to sexual orientation, then would there not be a greater chance of a lesbian mom and a gay sperm donor having a homosexual child?

We should rely on scientific research for the answers to these questions, of course. But that must not prevent us from asking why gay parents' influence on their children's sexualities should really matter. Why should we fear the sexual orientation effects of gay parents more than we do the orientation effects of straight ones? The underlying assumption is that children need to be protected from becoming gay. Thus, both the hostility of some heterosexual people and the defensiveness of some gays are driven by heterosexism. What if more young people did turn out gay? Why would that be an undesirable outcome for the children, their families, or the community? Those who respond that gay kids have such a tough row to hoe might just as well argue that other oppressed people ought not bring children into a hostile world.

## Question 16: What stresses do glbt families face?

Many of their concerns are caused by the legal system. Although many states have recognized the rights of gay parents, a number still regards them with suspicion if not hostility. Only Florida specifically prohibits all gay adoptions, but twenty-nine states will not allow both partners in a same-sex couple to be a child's legal guardians.

Custody and visitation decisions are among the most painful obstacles they face. Courts have denied custody to both divorced and never-married gay people; they have set unreasonable conditions for awarding custody or visitation rights; and they have taken children from a gay parent and placed them with a questionably fit parent, foster parent, or relative. (See box 4.16.) The 2003 Supreme Court sodomy decision should nullify one historic argument for denying gay parents' rights, that is, that they are criminals by virtue of their sexual expression.

Children in glbt families may also have stresses that lead to home and school problems. Those with divorced or divorcing parents experience some of the same pain that any other child would have under those circumstances. When the cause of the breakup is a closeted parent's homosexuality or gender identity, however the child might be especially puzzled about the changes at home. If a parent comes out in the process of divorce, the child might react negatively as well as worry about public exposure and peer rejection.

Younger children and late adolescents seem to adjust more easily than early or mid-adolescents. Very young children would naturally be less dismayed by something that is beyond their interest and comprehension. Older children with

## BOX 4.16   LOSE SOME

A Bonneville County magistrate says a gay father has a choice: stop living with his partner or lose visitation rights with his children.

"Judge Gives Gay Dad Ultimatum," *Idaho Statesman*, July 11, 2002.

The [Alabama Supreme] Court last week awarded custody of three Alabama teens to their father rather than their lesbian mother.... Chief Justice Moore wrote, "common law designates homosexuality as an inherent evil, and if a person openly engages in such a practice, that fact alone would render him or her an unfit parent."

"NGLTF CONDEMNS REMARKS BY ALABAMA CHIEF JUSTICE," *National Gay and Lesbian Task Force* [press release], February 19, 2002.

Shelley M. Zachritz is the primary caregiver for five children who live with her and her partner.... She also participated in the birth or adoption of each child. But two courts have ruled she's not a "parent."

Kimball Perry, "Court: Same-Sex Partner Not Legal Parent," *Cincinnati Post*, February 23, 2001.

established identities would be less likely to doubt their own sexualities as a result or fret that someone else might. Early and mid-adolescents, on the other hand, might be less sure of themselves. In fact, young people seem to have a harder time when the glbt parent is of their own gender. When mothers are lesbian, more daughters than sons are worried about becoming homosexual; when fathers are gay, the opposite is true. Gender may also play a role in children's acting out. Some girls compete for attention with their mothers' partners. Some boys become angry and belligerent with their peers.

Children's worries about peer reactions are legitimate. They may encounter teasing and harassment, even physical assault. Their friends may turn from them, on their own or because their parents have forbidden further contact. (See box 4.17.) Many adolescent children with glbt parents employ protective strategies against peer hostility, such as limiting others' contact with their parents, controlling parental behavior, and hiding sexuality and gender evidence at home.

Clearly children manage the stigma of a parent's homosexuality or gender nonconformity in a way that mirrors the manner in which glbt people themselves manage it as they come out. (See chapters 2 and 3.) It has also been found that the

## BOX 4.17    FAMILY VALUES?

[H]aving two moms isn't easy. When you're from south Texas, he says, being different in any way is like wearing a "Kick Me" sign on your back.... [H]e's fought twice over his moms. Lost a friend. Switched churches. Had crude sex toys thrown on his porch. He knows he should stand up for his moms more. When his girlfriend's dad made her break up with him, he knows he should have said to her dad, who always liked him before: "What's the problem? Why do you have to be that stupid? I'm not gay and your daughter's not dating my mother. All the stuff I know I learned from two gay parents. I'm who I am because I was raised by gay parents." But he never said these things. He knows he should have, but he didn't.

Reilly Capps, "Family Week Gives P-Town New Slant on the 'Gay Lifestyle,'" *Boston Globe*, August 15, 2002.

happier the parent is with his or her own homosexuality, the better equipped the child is to handle the hostility of others. If parents are closeted and seem ashamed, it is harder for their children to develop a positive attitude and resilience.

Children are also compelled to deal with a parent's homosexuality and gender expression in a cultural context, often determined by race, ethnicity, religion, class, geography, and so on. They can be torn between community condemnation and their love for and loyalty to their parent. They may become conflicted, frustrated, and angry, if shame keeps them silent in the face of homophobia. Their anger can even be directed at their parent for being glbt—the perceived cause of their problems.

If geography or culture isolates these children from others who have glbt parents, their adjustment may be retarded. Those from communities in which glbt families are open and affirmed have an easier time.

Finally, some children must grieve over the loss of the parent they thought they knew, before they can fully accept the person that parent has become. The pattern is so like parents' mourning when a child comes out. (See chapter 3.) Ultimately the child may come to appreciate the gift that having a glbt parent bestows. (See box 4.18.)

*Question 17: What can schools do to help glbt parents and their children?*

School officials can safely assume that children from glbt families, as well as glbt students and staff, are present in their school community. As always, educators must interrupt homophobic teasing and harassment. Moreover, glbt people and families must be acknowledged and celebrated in school activities and curricula.

## BOX 4.18   GRIEVING AND GIFTS

The first crack in my purposely-indifferent teen exterior came when I saw my father fully dressed as a woman.... My God, I thought, she is really doing this.... I wonder now if my family could have used a mourning period.... But instead, we believed our own rhetoric—that he was the same, only different, and that our family was still intact and loving, only divorced and a little confused. We did not acknowledge that the change my father was making was more than cosmetic, and that even if it was ultimately for the better, it still entailed profound loss.... But now her struggle is ours together, and in the pact we have made, I found a father I never had.

Noelle Howey, "Studying Womanhood," *Ms. Magazine*, October 1999.

Such steps improve the school environment for all students. They should also promote better relations between straight young people and their glbt family members and friends, not to mention between glbt youth and their loved ones. When glbt youth and families can be out and comfortable, not only they, but also those with whom they have been open, are relieved of the psychic burden of concealment and monitoring and the resentments they both engender.

While the long-term projects of developing and implementing inclusive counseling and curricula proceed, schools should make themselves more welcoming with easier, more immediate steps. (See box 4.19.)

Parents' homosexual orientation and gender identity are not always related to the difficulties that their children might have in school, even when these students are conflicted over these issues. Nor is their own sexuality or gender necessarily on glbt parents' minds when they engage with schools. Indeed, many gay parents say that parenthood feels more central to their self-concept than being gay does. Neither possibility, however, relieves the school from its obligation to reach out to glbt families and to provide support for them when needed. (See appendix D.)

Schools should also be prepared to refer families with glbt parents or children to outside help, when it is requested. Some community-based social service providers can assist with such matters as gay men raising daughters, lesbians parenting sons, foster parenting of gay/lesbian youth, and gay/lesbian big brothers/sisters or other mentoring programs.

The respect and inclusion afforded to all nontraditional families demonstrates a school's commitment to diversity and to the proposition that such differences should not be disadvantages. GLBT parent visibility and support also enhance the hopes of glbt students who may want to be parents themselves one day.

(For further reading, see appendix R.)

## BOX 4.19   A TO-DO LIST FOR SCHOOLS

1. Drop the assumption that all parents are heterosexual.
   - School forms, intake interviews, and questionnaires should be modified so as to use inclusive terms.
   - School personnel who call or write to parents need to be sensitized.
   - PTAs should explicitly welcome glbt parents.
2. Encourage parents and children to be open with faculty and administration. It may be advisable to designate a school liaison (perhaps a glbt) with whom parents can make a comfortable first contact.
3. Be clear about who will or should be informed about glbt parents (e.g., student teachers) and who is responsible for transmitting the information (principal, teachers, or the parents themselves).
4. Understand that some glbt parents and their children may not want to disclose to students or to adults other than the child's teachers and administrators.
5. Be prepared to deflect questions on behalf of those children and help them deal with their impact.
6. Encourage and train teachers to break the silence discreetly with parents who have not disclosed.
7. Be prepared to respond sensitively when children reveal more than their parents wish them to.
8. Use the relationship names that children use for their glbt parents (e.g., mommy and mama, Leo and dad).
9. Use acceptable terms in addressing both coparents directly (e.g., "your daughter").
10. Recognize that a coparent may want as much as a biological one does to be involved in the child's life.
11. Be prepared for reactions of educators, parents, and community people who disapprove of glbt parenting.
12. Be aware that homosexual parents and families from conservative subcultural and religious traditions may have needs and coping behaviors different from the majority.
13. Be sensitive to the possible unease of closeted gay and lesbian teachers who have children of openly glbt parents in their classes. Parents may feel awkward disclosing to and/or dealing with these teachers too.

# 5

# Effective School Reforms

*Question 1: What should be the goals of school reform regarding gay and lesbian issues?*

Considering the levels of glbt student harassment, their invisibility in the school culture, and their curricular omission, the initial objectives should be tolerance, support, and inclusion. Sexual minorities are part of the school community and their concerns matter, yet 53 percent of high school seniors in a 2001 Zogby poll reported that gay issues were never discussed in any of their classes.

Schools should adopt and enforce antiharassment policies, provide support services for glbt youth and families, and integrate gay-related topics into appropriate subject areas of the curriculum. But schools should also combat homophobia to enhance the intellectual, ethical, and psychosexual development of heterosexual students. A majority of educators think gay-positive education is only about glbt student safety and self-esteem. They don't see the connections between homophobia, hypermasculinity, school violence, and dating violence—or between sissy phobia and boys' aversion to academic success. (See chapter 7.)

Finally, educators should understand that homophobia is embedded in heterosexist oppression, which the school and community have a responsibility to eliminate, along with other oppressions based on gender, race, class, religious belief or nonbelief, and physical ability. This goal demands a level of self-examination, political analysis, and commitment that is rare among individuals and rarer yet at the institutional level. As instruments of social conservation, schools are not expected to foster such an understanding or embrace such a mission. (See question 16.) Still, we hope that they will try, despite the discouragement and risks they encounter along the way.

*Question 2: What is the strategy for achieving these reforms?*

Waiting for progressive political leadership on controversial issues can be frustrating. Besides, top-down mandates, if they do come, can evoke local resistance. A two-track approach is best: persuading school boards and other legislative bodies to change policy, and a simultaneous collaborative effort among like-minded faculty, administrators, and community supporters at the school level to move forward on their own.

A critical mass of teacher, student, and parent support for antihomophobia education can pull policy makers along. And, credit for each advance can be shared among all partners in the process. The campaign for each facet of reform—whether for antiharassment policies, student support services, or curricular inclusion—must target individual attitudes, institutional policies and practices, and community norms.

*Question 3: How can we change individuals' attitudes toward gay issues in schools?*

Homophobia is not just about feelings and discomforts that require soothing or psychoanalysis. Most homophobes are not victims of irrational hatred. Deeply held beliefs about the world and legitimate concerns about the familiar social order usually influence their attitudes and behavior toward gay people. They need to be convinced that homosexuality is compatible with their moral system or that their values should change to be fair to gay people. They have to rethink what homosexuality is and what would happen if gay people were afforded the same rights and respect as anyone else. Because there *would be* social consequences—good ones, we believe—and it is either shortsighted or disingenuous for educational reformers to pretend otherwise.

A propagandistic approach that employs only positive images of gays and lesbians to sell people on homosexuality is likely to fall short. Granted, there is nothing intrinsically wrong with classroom posters of famous gay and lesbian heroes, especially when they depict the racial and gender diversity within gay communities. Yet, ultimately, tolerance should not depend on exaggerating gay virtue or airbrushing homosexual nonconformity. Gay people (and other minorities) should not have to seem like everyone else or behave better than everyone else to be less threatening or deserving of rights.

Some antiprejudice educators put their faith in the idea that contact leads people to conclude that "the other" is really more like "us" than we thought. But sometimes coming together fails to uncover the commonalties between groups and just sharpens the differences. At this time in human history homosexuality is an indicator of significant "otherness." Schools need to talk plainly about sexuality differences and how important they are to us individually and to our society. Of course gay people bleed when they are pricked, but like Shylock in a Christian culture, they conduct one aspect of their lives so unconventionally they are not easily accepted. Homosexuality would be unremarkable only in a nonpatriarchal, sex-affirming environment. Those conditions are hard to find.

That is not to say that lessons about homosexuality should begin with the aspects of gay life that are most alien to heterosexual people and, therefore, the most difficult to relate to. We must think about meeting people where they are and bringing them along. Our educational practice must have an underlying developmental strategy.

*Question 4: Are there any educational theories that can inform these strategies for individual persuasion?*

Because antihomophobia education seeks to expand an individual's moral judgment to include respect for gay people, the work of some developmental and feminist psychologists is useful. The most valuable research and theory explain how to nurture the cognitive evolution that leads students to a more humane ethical system and how to support students as their values are challenged and shaken.

U.S. and Australian research indicates that *fag* and its British equivalent *poofter* are the most frequent and feared elementary school insults. But, elementary school kids do not knowingly shout *faggot* to defend the adult system of heterosexual superiority. They are sometimes parroting adult put-downs to appear grown-up and earn adult approval and they are using an insult that is clearly effective among their peers, even if none of the children knows exactly what it means. Later, their homophobia grows more complex and their investment in it deepens, both personally—as sexually maturing adolescents—and socially—as new players in a heterosexist culture.

Sensitivity training and values clarification are a good beginning, but the best tolerance education goes beyond promoting sensitivity and good feelings to fostering genuine understanding, empathy, and long-term cooperation. If teachers want to have a lasting impact on students' notions of difference and on their behavior toward minorities, they must pay attention to bigotry as a manifestation of moral development. That requires understanding how people move from a self-centered to a more highly evolved moral system, that is, from punishment-avoidance and reciprocity, through conventionality, and finally, to principled thinking.

*Question 5: Does this moral development approach minimize the importance of students' feelings?*

It does make a priority of changing people's ideas, but it does not ignore their feelings. When students begin to see that their old principles can't satisfactorily resolve a moral question, they experience both intellectual dissonance and psychological unease. They search for a better moral perspective that will satisfy both mind and heart.

Moreover, the relationship of moral judgment to moral action often hinges on affective factors. Once they figure out what's right, their ego must be strong enough to support their acting on their highest principles. People in transition need to hear convincing moral arguments, but they also need reassurance that they are valued and loved.

The topic of homosexuality can throw even the best and brightest heterosexuals off balance because sexuality goes to their emotional core. Patience and kindness are better tactics than confrontation in easing their initial discomfort. (See box 5.1.) We want students to internalize new nonheterosexist values, not feel forced into "correctness" that might be abandoned when politically fashionable thinking changes.

*Question 6: Doesn't having contact with gay people also have a positive impact?*

The right kind of contact can help change people's attitudes. Those who say they know someone gay generally report fewer negative feelings about homosexuals.

## BOX 5.1   DEGREES OF COMFORT AND DISSONANCE

Polls indicate that many Americans are more comfortable being fair to gay people than they are with homosexuality itself.

*Source: Public Agenda,* www.publicagenda.org (February 2002).

While 62 percent [of high school seniors] said they would be comfortable in a class taught by a gay man, only 43 percent were comfortable with the idea of a gay, same-sex, lab partner. Thirty-eight percent were OK with a gay teammate who used the same locker room. Only 31.5 percent said they would be comfortable at a party with both gay and straight couples.

Christopher Michaud, "U.S. Students Hold Mostly Pro-Gay Views—Survey," *Reuters,* August 27, 2001.

I am not saying that one must support homosexuality....But the hate towards diversity needs to stop. We all need to take time to learn about things we do not know. If it's not for you then it's not for you. But either way, it's not wrong...it's human.

Heather Brown (student), "Letter to the Editor: A Plea for Tolerance," *San Luis Obispo Tribune,* April 1, 2002.

That is why many gay leaders promote coming out as a strategy for greater acceptance (e.g., National Coming Out Day). However, key to the effectiveness of coming out is the relationship between the discloser and the audience. Coming out to admirers, friends, and loved ones, who are already predisposed to accept the glbt person, is likely to have a more productive result than coming out to strangers. Yet, the "exceptional case" rationale for continuing bigotry is also common, "Oh, she's an okay lesbian, because she's not like the rest of *them*." (See box 5.2.)

As part of a prejudice-reduction program, contact must be carefully planned and executed. Just mixing people together and hoping for the best is naïve. Physical integration is a first step and can even change behavior in the short term. But if we want students to enter the world beyond the classroom with a commitment to human equality and justice that extends to strangers, even those who make them uncomfortable, we have to change fundamental attitudes about "the other."

There must be joint endeavor and opportunities for meaningful exchange so that deeper relationships can build familiarity and trust. Then, to get at the roots of bigotry, differences must be aired and misunderstandings thrashed out in an environment that encourages the expression of the most humane moral arguments.

*Question 7: Is it really advisable for schools to promote contact with gays?*

In general, the school should facilitate equal status contacts between different groups and set expectations for their success and continuance. Of course, there is a history of resistance to "forced" racial integration, especially from those who fear losing their own status, opportunities, or values. One could, therefore, predict resistance to contact with gays and lesbians from those who benefit from

---

### BOX 5.2   TOLERANCE NOT TRANSFERABLE

"[T]here is a certain student who, when around my best friend seems tolerant and OK with [my friend's homosexuality], but when he is around me, it is totally opposite and he is insensitive when choosing certain words to call me. A lot of people want to change, they want to be accepting, but it is hard to shake stereotypes that have surrounded them for their whole lives."

Gay sophomore, in Cam-Tu Dang, "Out in the Open," *Las Vegas Review-Journal*, December 9, 2001.

heterosexual privileges and patriarchal values, not to mention those who fear sexual molestation and other horrors.

Gays and lesbians do not have to be imported into most schools; they are already there. It is their coming out or the mention of their anonymous presence that provokes reaction and creates an opportunity for dialogue. Clearly, it is never easy, especially for young people in a homophobic school, to urge tolerance of homosexuality. Even adults can be intimidated by the prospect of having to oppose prevailing values and possibly having their own sexuality questioned.

When it is possible, having glbt students speak is of paramount value. With good preparation, they can usually be effective reform agents. Moreover, the school performs a tangible restitution by giving them an opportunity to heal the wounds of concealment and self-censorship. Having a genuine public voice, perhaps for the first time, gives them more power and dignity than other advocates can confer on their behalf.

*Question 8: How does a school create a respectful and productive dialogue about homosexuality?*

Antiprejudice interventions work best in schools that promote justice, caring, and a sense of community. The school's decision making should be democratic, involving faculty and students in significant issues like rule making and discipline. Moreover, the science and humanities curricula should feature engaging ethical issues that foster group discussion. Large bureaucratic schools should be broken down into smaller learning communities to permit group bonding and honest dialogue. Where such "small schools" are not feasible, the classroom has to suffice.

Students at every level of ethical understanding must be called upon to care for and be fair to each other. These exhortations have the greatest impact when they come from peers, but teachers should underscore the ethos too. Then, to coax the community of caring to extend to sexual minorities, the sentiment must be expressed that gays and lesbians in our town and in our school should feel as comfortable as any other member of our community feels. The number of gays and lesbians in the population is irrelevant, since the rights and respect due to a minority group is not proportionate to their numbers.

Especially for young people, concrete examples are more persuasive than abstractions. The more a gay individual is perceived as "one of our own," the more effective the "be nice" argument is. Openly gay, lesbian, and bisexual students and their families have good leverage, as do gay, lesbian, and bisexual teachers and staff. Popular and respected student leaders who come out can influence attitudes and behavior. Male athletes are often in a unique position to challenge common gay stereotypes. (See box 5.3.) If no current students can be open, recent graduates might also be credible.

## BOX 5.3  THE SPECIAL POWER OF THE GAY ATHLETE

"I am Dan Bozzuto. I am just another student here at Cheshire High School, just another student who happens to be gay." The oxygen was suddenly sucked out of the gym. . . . He was the junior class president. . . . [T]his three-sport captain. . . is a born leader. . . . During two assemblies in which Bozzuto addressed more than 1,000 students, his speech was greeted by thunderous ovations. . . . "A few students have come up to me and thanked me for what I did," he said. "They said they have family members who were gay, and they did not know how to deal with them. And some have said they now have the strength to deal with this themselves."

Joe Palladino, "Personal Torment Set Aside," *Waterbury* [Conn.] *Republican-American*, June 11, 2002.

Our high school athletic department sponsored an evening meeting for everyone on school teams . . . plus their parents . . . to discuss the problem of homophobic language and attitudes in sports. More than 500 people attended. Among the speakers were a varsity football captain from another school who is gay and the mother of a boy who committed suicide after being hazed and harassed. This educational event did a lot to challenge stereotypes about homosexuality and make antigay remarks and behavior a lot more unacceptable.

Alexandra Early [9th grader in Arlington, Mass.], "Gay-Straight Club That Breeds . . . Success," *Los Angeles Times*, March 26, 2000.

Gay youth testimony is very effective not only among their classmates but also with adults who know them. For example, a Natrona County, Wyoming, gay student's letter to the Casper *Star Tribune* in 2003 elicited support for the student, classroom discussions, and a commitment from his school to lessening harassment. When they cannot speak up personally or in writing, youth from other schools or film segments can be substituted. High school students have spoken powerfully to their former middle school teachers, for instance. Most teachers and administrators want to do the right thing for young people. It is not easy for them to hear that current or former students were in pain and that they failed them. Perhaps they were oblivious to having sexual minority youth in the school or avoided acknowledging their needs because they did not know how to meet them or dreaded parent reaction. Most want to make amends by improving the school and being more aware in the future.

**BOX 5.4  TURNING POINT FOR AN ELOQUENT ALLY**

When students make any type of homophobic remarks, my usual response is to squelch the issue by explaining that such comments "aren't
allowed".... This time, I realized, my continuing silence on the issue was
unacceptable.... "The names on the board are people I know and love. They
are friends of mine, and they are gay. The stars are for ones who have AIDS
or who have already died. One of them is my brother. One star is next
to a person who cut my hair for eight years.... [L]ast summer someone
who did not like gay people killed him.... He was one of the nicest, most
gentle people you could ever know.... I can promise you that someone in
this class may be gay or have a gay relative or a gay friend. If you say that
homosexuals should be excluded from society, or call someone a 'fag,' you
will hurt someone. You will hurt me."

Jamie Rhein, "The Names on the Board," *Teaching Tolerance Magazine* 13
(1998).

Heterosexual teachers or students can say that they feel bad when people make
homophobic remarks, because someone they respect and love is gay. It may not be
as dramatic as having gay students and teachers testify to their own victimization,
but it shows that homophobia can also hurt straight people and it sets an example
for being an ally. (See box 5.4.) At this level of appeal the moral principle is that
students be nice—that they respect the feelings of others in the group. When
heterosexual community members testify that they don't have gay relatives or
friends but still think gays deserve respect, they model that one doesn't need to
have a personal stake in the matter to speak up for glbt people. This higher stage
plea to extend an ethic of fairness beyond one's "near and dear" probably appeals
to fewer adolescents yet still must be made.

When we invite glbt people to testify to the injuries they have suffered because
of homophobia, our purpose is to evoke empathy for our equals, not sympathy
for misfits who shouldn't be blamed for their affliction. We want heterosexual
students to consider how they would feel as objects of bigotry and to take responsibility for their hurtful words and deeds. Condescension further wounds glbt
youth's self-esteem and might even erode their safety.

The truest indicator of a school's acceptance of diversity is how it regards gender
nonconformity. For any environment to be judged safe for sexual minorities, it
must welcome a range of gender identity and expression. When sissies, butch girls,
transgender, and transsexual youth are understood and respected in the school
community, the environment is healthy for all. (See box 5.5.)

## BOX 5.5  RESPONSES: GOOD AND PRACTICAL

Keala Chow was born a boy, but on Sunday walked with the girls during the [high school] graduation, covering up a "very seductive" dress with a graduation gown.... "It really wasn't a hard decision," [the principal] said. "We do respect the individual, and of course she wanted to graduate as a young lady...."

Treena Shapiro, "McKinley Lets Male-Born Student Graduate in Dress," *Honolulu Star-Bulletin*, June 8, 2002.

He is a well-liked and attractive 13-year-old.... He is also a regular at the school's weekly gay, lesbian, bisexual and transgender student group, although none of his friends know that.... He likes girls. He has a girlfriend.... [T]he support-group members presume... that he is probably secretly gay or bisexual or maybe just confused.... He isn't gay. He isn't confused. He isn't even a boy. For the last four years, M., who was born a girl, has secretly lived as a boy.... [A teacher who knows] created a safety plan for M.... [H]e consulted with the principal, a counselor, a nurse and a representative from the school district... then hand-selected M.'s other teachers, choosing those he thought would be sensitive to M.'s situation.

Benoit Denizet-Lewis, "About a Boy Who Isn't," *New York Times Magazine*, May 26, 2002.

*Question 9: What is the role of teachers and other adults in the community-building dialogue?*

For adolescents, peers are pivotal. They are best positioned to influence other students' opinions. Still, only a few students are willing to speak up against homophobia and they *do* need adult support. A 2002 National Mental Health Association survey found that, although nearly 80 percent of teens witness antigay bullying in schools, only 5 percent say they defend the targets of such attacks. Adults should, however, try to limit their role to restating students' positions and reminding them that caring and fairness are central.

Generally, students are inclined to make the "kindness to people we know" argument. Those who can present a higher, more abstract plea for minority rights should be encouraged to speak up. If adults are the only ones who can articulate a broader perspective they should avoid preaching too far ahead of the group. At the same time, students who are grasping for a higher principle need to hear it presented by someone.

If parents of homosexual youth are available to speak, faculty and students can be moved by their stories of the love that prevented or healed their estrangement from their children.

Openly gay and lesbian faculty are important members of the school community as well and deserve respect and honor. They are in a unique position to influence student opinion, but their participation in student debate should still be restrained. As gay adults with power over students, they should avoid any perception of intimidation or stifling honest expression. (See chapter 4.)

*Question 10: Why shouldn't school authorities just "lay down the law" about homophobia?*

It is tempting to reach for the zero tolerance strategy manual to stop homophobic behavior. Clear rules and penalties devised and imposed by adults may indeed work in curtailing harassment in supervised areas of the school. But they have limited impact on student reasoning. Those who act fairly only because they fear being caught and punished can't be trusted to be fair when they are out of the authorities' sight. (See box 5.6.)

## BOX 5.6   PUNISHMENT NO SOLUTION

Each week, Tom Sutter carefully records... his encounters with intolerance.... "While I was walking down to the music room I heard the word fag three times.... People called me 'gay guy' in the hallway.... Today in the hallway some kid elbowed me. In the drama class, this one kid... tried to put his hand on my legs."... Recently, Sutter found threatening notes by his locker.... [School] officials have tried to deal with Sutter's complaints, detaining and suspending a few students. Officials called some students' parents into the school. Teachers attended an awareness session on harassment and gays. A hall monitor often meets Sutter at his locker and follows him to class to try to catch the students who assault him. But Sutter still complains of students hitting him and sexually harassing him when officials aren't looking. He wore headphones one week trying to block out the name-calling.

Mei-Ling Hopgood, "Teens Work for Tolerance," *Detroit Free Press*, May 2, 2000.

Too many students view school disciplinary codes as arbitrary means of adult control. If we want them to internalize more humane values, they should be involved in setting *and enforcing* the highest standards they can arrive at as a community of students and adults together. Effective antiharassment rules depend on a range of moral arguments, from punishment and revenge-avoidance to group kindness norms to real empathy and respect for human rights. It is never enough to say to a school-aged child, "you should be punished for breaking a rule," without elaborating the rule's rationale at the next ethical level he or she can begin to comprehend.

This endeavor is not the most convenient quick fix for homophobic harassment. It is nearly always messy and time-consuming. It entails disagreement, of course, yet with good refereeing by teachers and tolerant peers against threatening speech and hostile behavior the best can be evoked. Older students should be trained to moderate debate, serving as role models for younger students and using language they both understand. Gay-straight high school alliance members, where there are such groups, might be best prepared for that role.

The stresses and divisions of the democratic process can be soothed by other community-building activities that help students get to know and trust one another. Group music, art, writing, video, and theater projects, outdoor adventures, field trips, and shared meals are just a few of the other modalities for cultivating friendship and understanding.

*Question 11: Isn't the chief aim of these school reforms to protect the safety of gay, lesbian, bisexual, and transgender students?*

School safety is crucial, of course, but that minimum standard is not the only goal of antihomophobia education. After all, schools are expected to protect all students from harassment and violence. If physical safety were the sole object, strict rules and harsh penalties might be enough to achieve it in all policed settings.

Some might see safety—an assurance of being left alone—as a society's greatest benefit to the individual. But few would argue that tolerance is as significant a social blessing as understanding and empathy. And the safety that comes from those sources is far more dependable than the security that depends on fear. Despite the political qualms some advocates have in saying so, our stated goal should be to persuade students that homosexuality is as natural and good as any other sexual orientation for the individual, for the school, and for society. We want to elicit the same level of acceptance and affirmation of sexuality differences as we do for diversity in gender, race, ethnicity, and faith.

Even liberals have a hard time owning up to these objectives when homosexuality is on the table. (See box 5.7.)

## BOX 5.7   RESPECT WITHOUT ACCEPTANCE?

[A Dubuque Community School] Board member ... said the district is stating zero tolerance for [antigay] harassment ... not advocating a lifestyle. "We're not telling you whether it's right or wrong, ... it's about the level of expectations or respect in our learning environments."

Diane Heldt, "Sexual Orientation Added to Policy," *Dubuque Telegraph-Herald*, February 13, 2001.

Ron Peiffer, [of the] Maryland State Department of Education, said the amendment would protect homosexuals from discrimination, not require that sexual orientation awareness be included in multicultural curriculum. "This does not have anything to do with curriculum," Peiffer said.

Tara Reilly, "County Schools Would Observe Gay Anti-Discrimination Rules," *Hagerstown* [Md.] *Herald-Mail*, July 12, 2001.

"We're not trying to change anybody's beliefs. We're just looking to make people safe."

Dade County PTA president Karin Brown, in Analisa Nazareno, "Gay Rights Advocate Loses Fight," *Miami Herald*, December 19, 2000.

*Question 12: How should the school respond to parents and staff who object to these goals?*

They should have the same opportunities for discussion and debate as students do. Opponents, too, might argue on behalf of student safety, claiming that homosexuality is a physically and morally "dangerous lifestyle" from which gay students themselves should be protected. And, if they concede that some adolescents are irredeemably gay, they still want schools to warn other students away from the evils those victims represent, as if a homosexual potential in all youth must be expunged. They seem to fear that children could become gay as a consequence of being persuaded not to harass gays. The logical progression they want to interrupt is that if gay is good enough to respect, it might be respectable enough to *be*. In many communities, homosexuals seem to be the single minority group public officials, parents, and teachers can defame freely.

Students want to know what grown-ups think about these issues, but teachers especially have to hold back from expressing antigay opinions that could acrimoniously divide the school or lead glbt students to believe they would not be treated fairly in a classroom. (See box 5.8.)

## BOX 5.8   INTENDED EFFECT?

Six high school teachers have accused the Portland School District of promoting homosexuality with a list of reading material for students and teachers aimed at better understanding gays and lesbians.... The group of teachers asked that the school purchase 10 copies of the book "Homosexuality and the Politics of Truth" [which purports] that gays and lesbians ... can change.... Dajah Kilgore, 16, a Cleveland junior, became visibly upset as she read the [teachers'] memo.... Dajah, who said she is openly lesbian, said gay and lesbian students no longer would feel comfortable in the teachers' classes.

"Six Teachers Claim Portland Schools Promote Homosexuality," *Associated Press*, November 19, 1999.

When a teacher's or a parent's personal or religious views about homosexuality conflict with the school's values of acceptance, they must at least be circumspect when students are present. In the public schools, religious conviction can be expressed but must ultimately surrender to secular values. When challenged by the ACLU in 2003, officials in Jacksonville, Arkansas, had to concede that it was wrong to force a fourteen-year-old junior high school student to read passages against homosexuality from a bible because he told a peer that he was gay. Egalitarianism and secular humanism are not relativistic, as some detractors claim. They set a clear and appropriate standard for schools that welcome diversity. Educators simply cannot defy their school's promotion of that diversity. (See box 5.9.)

## BOX 5.9   THE LIMITS OF TEACHER EXPRESSION

Los Angeles schoolteacher Robert Downs ... posted pictures of a traditional family, texts of a federal law against same-sex marriage and a Supreme Court ruling against sodomy—and, eventually, a biblical passage calling homosexuality "detestable." The principal ordered him to stop.... Downs can express his views "[anywhere else] but not on bulletin boards that are overseen by school officials and are the official voice of the school," the [9th U.S. Circuit Court of Appeals ruled]. A school district ... "may decide not only to talk about gay and lesbian awareness and tolerance in general, but also to advocate such tolerance if it so desires, and restrict the contrary speech of one of its representatives," said [the judge]...."

Bob Egelko, "Gay Rights Opponent Loses Case in Federal Appeals Court," *New York Times Syndicate*, September 8, 2000.

To allow otherwise would invite animosities and balkanization among faculty and students.

Teachers, parents, administrators, school boards, and other adults must try to negotiate a common stance on antihomophobia education. Civic responsibility and good will should propel them toward a consensus that values all students and families equally. To plan the promotion of that same consensus among students, schools can devise staff development workshops and other teacher trainings. (See box 5.10.)

*Question 13: Shouldn't schools be concerned about the well-being of sexual minority students during these debates?*

Of course they should. Anyone can feel battered in the arena of free expression, but stigmatized minorities are more vulnerable because they enter the public discourse at a disadvantage. Even gay adults can find debates about their rights hard to endure, so we can't expect glbt adolescents to take homophobic arguments for hypothetical abstractions. They could also interpret the public restraint of their teachers as a lack of support. (Schools should also be aware of Internet bullying, which has raised anonymous homophobic graffiti to a new level of potency.)

When teachers and counselors know who the gay students and those from gay families are, they should reassure them privately and help them work through their injuries. A gay–straight alliance (gsa) is also a good venue for both adult and peer support.

### BOX 5.10   WORKSHOP AND TRAINING BASICS

- Express the general objectives of understanding, safety, equity, and action.
- Provide clear goals for the session(s).
- Invite introductions that express personal motivation for coming and what the participant hopes to get from session(s).
- Acknowledge the goodwill and prior experience of participants.
- Encourage genuine expression of both thoughts and feelings.
- Assure confidentiality.
- Provide information (e.g., identity development and counseling concerns of sexual minority youth, needs of gay families, curriculum inclusion, stopping harassment, etc.).
- Facilitate questions and discussion.
- Provide an evaluation tool that includes both responses to the session as well as intended actions by the participant to improve the school.

Teachers should convey to all students that the school cares for them whatever the community debate might be. Bigoted students need to hear that they are personally valued, even if the school does not accept their views.

*Question 14: Aren't rules against student hate speech justified?*

Because all students require a safe environment in which to learn, schools must have rules against outright verbal and physical harassment directed at individuals or groups (e.g., sexual orientation, race, religion, disability, body shape). Spurred by researcher-activists like Ian Rivers in England, recent international antibullying campaigns are a promising indicator. (See box 5.11.) Education Week's Quality Counts 2003 report found that thirty-three states require or recommend antibullying programs. But speech codes are no answer to competing values and no cure for prejudice. When administrators try to protect gay students with broad prohibitions against hate speech, they may end up stifling the very debate that schools need to progress as well as violating the law. (See box 5.12.) The trick is to assure sexual minority students' well-being, while at the same time providing all students a forum for their ideas—but not for personal insults or threats.

Teachers and counselors need to set an example as respectful listeners. They should also try to mend the rifts and soothe the hurts that inevitably occur. Every school has a credo of equality and respect, sometimes emblazoned over its entryway and always printed in its rulebooks and manuals. The reformers' advantage lies in calling the community to live up to its own standard.

Recent successful suits against speech and harassment codes in Pennsylvania and elsewhere were brought by people who believe that homosexuality is a sin and who think they have a duty to share their beliefs. Their rights were correctly upheld and such speech will continue. Consequently, as most glbt young people and those from gay families do not easily distinguish between "homosexuality is evil" and "you or your family are evil," it is essential that they have affirmative counseling and that the school have a curriculum that honors the gay experience.

## BOX 5.12   STRUGGLING WITH SPEECH

"[T]he free speech clause protects a wide variety of speech that listeners may consider deeply offensive, including statements that impugn another's race or national origin or that denigrate religious beliefs. . . . When laws against harassment attempt to regulate oral or written expression on such topics, however detestable the views expressed may be, we cannot turn a blind eye to the First Amendment implications."

From the majority opinion of 3rd U.S. Circuit Court of Appeals, in Robyn E. Blumner, "Free Speech Intimidated by Harassment Charges," *St. Petersburg* [Fla.] *Times*, February 25, 2001.

A high school violated a student's constitutional rights last year when the principal ordered him not to wear a sweat shirt with the words "Straight Pride" on it, a judge ruled.

"School Dress Code Ruled Illegal," *Associated Press*, January 16, 2002.

[Tom Martin of GLSEN Modesto] worries that the [antigay school newspaper editorial] could inflame other students to take action against gay teens. He said schools need to ask "at what point does that opinion hurt other people?"

Molly Dugan, "Student Editorial Causes a Ruckus," *Sacramento Bee*, February 5, 2002.

(See chapter 7.) They also need openly glbt educators teaching with dignity and demanding safety and respect in the school and in the community.

*Question 15: Should sexual minority youth ever be transferred from less accepting to safer schools?*

Try as we might to make all schools safer, some students may require it. Those who choose to be open or whose appearance or demeanor makes it difficult to hide could be in real danger at some schools. If they are victimized, school authorities may agree with them and their parents that a transfer is warranted. Some systems have established alternative public schools like the Harvey Milk School in New York City specifically for sexual minority students.[1] Los Angeles provides teachers for its OASIS program (Out Adolescents Staying in School), which consists of four schools housed in churches and other facilities. Dallas has an unaccredited private alternative, the Walt Whitman Community School, which enrolls seven to twenty-six students a year and meets four days a week. And the Toronto, Canada, district school board funds the Triangle Program, a "one-room schoolhouse" for students ages fourteen to twenty-five.

It is unfair to send students away who would prefer to remain in their own schools if they could be made more hospitable. Sexual minority youth are not the problem, but rather the homophobia that drives them out. Transferring them does nothing to make the school safer for the "invisible" or quieter gay students who remain behind. (See box 5.13.) Alternative placements should serve, therefore, as a last resort and should be seen at best as a temporary solution until reform takes hold.

*Question 16: Is it reasonable to have to wait for such reforms when anything less is an injustice?*

Liberalism has often disappointed gays and lesbians with its gradual imperfect advances. Advocates of a more insistent radical reform, sometimes called social reconstructionist schooling, are critical of human relations approaches to diversity education. They are right to find fault with assimilationist pleas for tolerance that fail to challenge conventional values. They are also right to call for coalition building among marginalized groups and a critical examination of shared oppressions.

Social reconstructionists, like C. E. Sleeter and Colleen Capper, are skeptical of a democratic model that depends on a learning community, persuasion, and moral development. They want to offer students explicit lessons in social transformation and empower them with direct social action skills, while linking homophobia to larger issues of power and privilege.

---

**BOX 5.13   DERELICTION OF DUTY**

"We haven't been particularly successful at sending students back to mainstream schools," says [the Institute's Carl] Strange. "For this to happen, a certain level of community transformation has to take place. And so far, it hasn't." ... Educators at Harvey Milk and Walt Whitman point out that the principal intent of their institutions is to provide essential and immediate services for young people who can't afford to sit by and expose themselves to harm while waiting for change—change that may come too late.

Tim Walker, "School's Out," *Teaching Tolerance Magazine* 21 (2002).

Their aims are unassailable, but their language is not likely to be understood by students. Moreover, this approach would appeal to few but the most progressive teachers, administrators, and communities. It is therefore more advisable to employ the school's own professed ideals and vocabulary as a means of achieving genuine school democracy and a community of caring. These can lead to both individual and group growth—and to wider social change. This strategy for social transformation is admittedly less direct and more gradual, but a developmental approach should embrace both rationality and a caring democratic practice as valid and necessary means and ends of education.

*Question 17: Is comparing homophobia to other kinds of bigotry a good idea?*

Heterosexism depends on sexism and has some features in common with racism and religious intolerance, but they are not all the same. Nor are all of these oppressions experienced in the same way. In fact, individuals within the same stigmatized group can have quite different experiences with bigotry.

Because racism is a familiar concept and is widely condemned, white teachers might be tempted to compare homophobia to racism. For example, they might say to a student who is calling someone a fag, "You would never call a person the 'N-word,' would you?" Such a stance invites not only the "being black isn't a choice" response; it also risks provoking resentment on the part of students of color who could reasonably question the right of a person with white privilege to make such a comparison. Teachers of color are more credible in drawing parallels between racism and homophobia, particularly when they are gay themselves and can speak to the weight of both oppressions, even if different, in their own lives.

Another analogy might be made to religious intolerance, such as anti-Semitism. Since freedom of religious affiliation and practice are generally honored, one could make a case that, even if there is some degree of choice in sexuality, it too should be respected.

Finding commonality with others is one aim of moral education, but teachers should be careful when comparing one people's suffering with another. Some victims think their pain is worse than anybody else's and cling to a "hierarchy of oppression." Teachers have to be both knowledgeable and tactful in helping students understand what they have in common and how their differences are not to be feared. Comparing and contrasting is intellectually valuable and should not devolve into a competition.

*Question 18: How important are school administrators in the reform process?*

They have an important role to play in setting the school tone, rallying the faculty, and reassuring parents and the rest of the community. Their primary message should be that antihomophobia education is both ethically imperative and in the best interests of all students.

Administrators must convey to the school community that everyone, including cafeteria personnel and bus monitors, is responsible for making the school safe and affirming. The best school leaders are proactive and positive. They don't depend on a crisis to justify reform and they know progress is not achieved by fiat.

Unfortunately, the topic of sexuality is personally discomforting to some administrators. Many also fear public opposition to discussing gay issues in schools, so they avoid the subject and block others who would raise it. Even worse, some male administrators display a pattern of disrespect toward women and gays and condone or ignore sexism and homophobia in others.

Administrators often find it easier to believe there are no gay students or families in their schools than to face the likelihood that they are hiding because the school is dangerous. Year after year student surveys testify to a cacophony of homophobic invective to which adults in schools are somehow deaf.

## Question 19: How can administrators be enlisted in this reform?

They can be influenced by higher level administrators, school boards and other governmental authorities, parents, faculty, students, and their professional peers. But, they must be persuaded by convincing arguments to lead on a potentially controversial issue. If they do not believe in the merits of the enterprise, pressure alone usually elicits a tepid response, just enough to fulfill the letter of the mandate. They merely cross their fingers and hope to get through some token gesture without incident.

The most powerful proactive arguments come from students, but the most reassuring ones are made by fellow administrators from schools that have already had positive experiences with antihomophobia programs. They need to hear from someone who walks in their shoes, "I was apprehensive like you, but we did the right thing and our school is better for it."

School personnel are often galvanized by educator-led trainings, featuring the testimony of students, parents, and experts on glbt youth—and *rarely* attended by administrators. Because they are often preoccupied with crisis management and burdened with other meetings, one can understand why they might ask a gsa advisor, health teacher, school nurse, or a counselor to go in their stead. Too often administrators feel that delegating a "gay meetings" person relieves them of further responsibility to the issues.

If superintendents, curriculum directors, and principals are to be enlisted as leaders in this effort, they must themselves attend student, parent, expert, and peer presentations. (See box 5.14.) Rather than waiting for them to show up at workshops, reformers must find a way to reach administrators where they already gather, at meetings of professional associations or at districtwide administrative sessions, for example.

## BOX 5.14   CONVERSION

"Because the previously existing nondiscrimination policy did not explicitly state that LGBT students should be protected, schools just did not enforce it. Hearing the heartfelt stories of the isolation experienced by current and former gay students truly changed the way in which I viewed this issue. Every child deserves a safe school environment in which to learn."

Anchorage Alaska School Superintendent Carol Comeau, in Courtney Snowden, "They've Got the Power," *Respect* [GLSEN National Magazine] 9 (2002).

The organizers of such events must be convinced beforehand to feature antihomophobia speakers during plenary sessions. A few optional presentations on gay issues among hundreds of other offerings will reach a mere handful. The need for school change is too urgent for that haphazard approach.

*Question 20: Aren't administrators more likely to respond to legal pressures than humanitarian arguments?*

The prospect of having to pay a harassed student money damages could certainly influence school authorities to pay more attention to the safety of sexual minority youth.

Only a few states (California, Connecticut, Massachusetts, Vermont, Wisconsin, Minnesota, and New Jersey) and local school systems have explicit legal protections for gay students that they could be forced by courts to uphold. Such was indirectly the case when Jamie Nabozny sued his former school district and officials in Ashland, Wisconsin, for failing to protect him from harassment and violence that began in middle school and eventually forced him to leave high school.

Nabozny's middle school principal told him he brought harassment (i.e., being kicked unconscious, mock raped, and urinated upon) on himself by being openly gay. Later he was offered a private bathroom and separate seat on the school bus. None of his attackers was ever punished, but eventually the school system tried to avoid responsibility by blaming their parents for raising brutes. A lower court ruled that the school system had not supported or totally overlooked the harassment and that they could not be required to protect Nabozny from such violence. But a 1996 federal jury found three administrators guilty of violating Nabozny's rights to equal protection regardless of gender. In finding that the school system had not enforced its antiharassment policies equally for boys and girls, the decision skirted the issue of sexual orientation protections per se. Nabozny was awarded $900,000 in an out-of-court settlement.

Over the next six years, the Nabozny case was followed by many other discrimination and harassment lawsuits. Maine's attorney general brought a civil rights action on behalf of a fifteen-year-old who was attacked and harassed for months, despite police intervention. A former high school student in Kent, Washington, was awarded $40,000 after an uninterrupted gang assault near the school security office and another beating, witnessed by teachers, one of whom remarked, "I already have twenty girls in my class. I don't need another." A harassed twelve-year-old in Pacifica, California, was given $125,000 in an out-of-court settlement. In 1998 a rural Kentucky girl, tormented for four years with no response from school officials, was awarded $220,000. And in 2003, a federal district court upheld the right of six former Morgan Hill, California, students to sue the school district for not protecting them from antigay bullying and violence. The first in the nation ruling stipulated that the United States Constitution's Equal Protection Clause had been violated because the schools had taken "minimal action" to enforce its antiharassment policies.

In 1998 the federal Office for Civil Rights (OCR) had found the Fayetteville, Arkansas, public schools in violation of Title IX sex discrimination regulations for overlooking antigay harassment. Fayetteville agreed to prohibit, monitor, and punish homophobic behavior and to train teachers. But for Title IX to be used in instances of homophobia, there must be a "sexual" component to the harassment. (See box 5.15.) Therefore, the success of a suit is best assured when state or local policies explicitly cover offenses based on actual or perceived sexual orientation.

---

### BOX 5.15  TITLE IX CLARIFICATION

[I]f a male student or a group of male students target a gay student for physical sexual advances, serious enough to deny or limit the victim's ability to participate in or benefit from the school's program, the school would need to respond promptly and effectively.... On the other hand, if students heckle another student with comments based on the student's sexual orientation (e.g., "gay students are not welcome at this table in the cafeteria"), but their actions do not involve conduct of a sexual nature, their actions would not be sexual harassment covered by Title IX.*

U.S. Department of Education: Office of Civil Rights (OCR), "Revised Sexual Harassment Guidance: Harassment of Students by School Employees, Other Students, or Third Parties," *The Federal Register*, January 19, 2001.

---

*However, sufficiently serious sexual harassment is covered by Title IX even if the hostile environment also includes taunts based on sexual orientation.

As a cascade of lawsuits and settlements continues to make headlines, from Titusville, Pennsylvania, to Kansas City, Missouri, to Visalia, California, we should not conclude that legal threats are the best means of enlisting administrators in antihomophobia reforms. Just as punishment avoidance is a low-level motivator for moral behavior among students, so is fear a crude instrument among adults. Do we want school boards hiring lawyers to get them off the hook? Wouldn't we rather have administrators supporting school change because they recognize the injustices of homophobic discrimination and the suffering of sexual minority youth?

Admittedly, legal action can be effective when school leaders refuse to discuss these issues or are unresponsive to moral arguments. Such was the case in progressive Cambridge, Massachusetts, in the mid-1980s. After the administration denied gay teachers' requests for educator training and gay youth supports, a harassment complaint by a gay teacher against a colleague produced a formal agreement requiring a mandatory antihomophobia faculty workshop. That single event led to the formation of the first public high school glbt student support group in the East.

Almost twenty years later, action on behalf of Nevada high school student Derek Henkle yielded similar results after a protracted legal struggle. Henkle's suit, including Title IX claims, brought in 2000 and joined by the ACLU, alleged that Washoe County school officials had failed to protect him from harassment at three different schools. At the first students had thrown a lasso around his neck and threatened to drag him from a pickup truck. At the second, the principal had warned him against "acting like a fag." When he was repeatedly punched in the face at the third, school police officers had done nothing. In 2002, county school trustees finally approved a settlement of $451,000, granted the right to disclose and discuss sexual orientation in schools, and agreed to require regular staff training and student education on harassment, sexual harassment, and intimidation.

Regrettably, lawsuits are sometimes the only practical means of rescuing students or faculty from dire situations. (See appendix E.)

*Question 21: How can we change community attitudes toward gay issues in schools?*

On a subject as incendiary as gay issues in schools, reasonable community dialogue can be difficult. Few average citizens are prepared to participate in town square debate in the first place. Only a handful of schools and colleges instill a commitment to democracy or teach the skills of democratic practice by involving students in important decision making. Four to eight years of individualism, authoritarianism, and paternalism do not encourage young people to take responsibility for the welfare of the community. In our communities the field is too often ceded to extremists and demagogues, and political opportunism replaces genuine concern for child welfare.

If progressive arguments are to prevail, antihomophobia proponents must base their case on civic principles to which even their opponents claim allegiance. When religious values are invoked (as they invariably are in the imperfect church-state separation in the United States), let school reformers, including clergy, cite the most humane tenets of the major religions. People of the cloth have significant power to correct the impression that all churches oppose glbt affirmation in school policies and curricula.

By all means, however, avoid the trap of scriptural debate. Arguments about what God thinks about homosexuals are irresolvable and have no place in civic life. If we choose to be governed by our core values of liberty, equality, and tolerance, we will have enough work guaranteeing each without violating any.

Heterosexual allies are as important in the community as in the school. Even social conservatives find it hard to ignore straight parents of gay children who can speak about their own path to acceptance. The essence of their message is, "We know how you feel, because we have felt the same way. We did not accept homosexuality right away just because our children are gay. We had to work at it. We had to rethink all we have been told." Straight allies without gay loved ones are also assets because they cannot be accused of rationalizing due to a special interest.

## Question 22: How do we respond to "family values" arguments?

Homosexuality and family are not mutually exclusive concepts. Gays and lesbians are just as likely to support their families of origin as any other members are. Sometimes they are expected to bear a greater burden of family care than straight relatives are because the significance of their gay relationships is ignored or minimized. Many glbt people create intentional families of their own, bringing family values to friendship, domestic partnership, and child rearing, despite social stigma, legal impediments, and the lack of those affirming social customs that bolster heterosexual relationships.

Moreover, the conservative "family values" extolled by the Right are not always good for families or communities. There is no love or nurturance in a family's rejection of its gay members. And when excessive family cohesion fosters insularity and prejudice, schools may be called upon to mitigate tribal values with democratic ones. Conflict between home values and school values may be politically difficult, but it is not unhealthy for democracy. Educators should be confident that the more just perspective will prevail in the end.

To build a base of support and to minimize public posturing and acrimony, PTAs and parent councils should organize small group discussions with clear goals, personal stories, factual information, and invocations of the democratic values of the community. For example, the first of its kind Gay Lesbian PTSA of Greater Puget Sound, chartered by the Washington State PTA in 1999 with the blessing of the national PTA, borrowed the activist segments of the PFLAG agenda. Like a special interest caucus, it was founded to advocate for the welfare of gay and lesbian parents, students, and teachers in schools and also within the larger PTA organization.

## Question 23: What specific school policies should be enacted?

The school must have explicit policies protecting students who are, or who are perceived to be, glbt from discrimination, harassment, and violence. Most schools already have harassment policies to which sexual orientation and gender expression protections may be added. They should be clearly stated in school board regulations, faculty and student handbooks, and the like. (See box 5.16.) Sometimes teachers and counselors are legally required to report alleged abuses to superiors but not necessarily to intervene directly. Administrators, on the other hand, may be obligated to take remedial action.

Whoever is responsible for reporting procedures and enforcement should exercise the same sensitivity that is called for in cases of alleged rape or other sexual abuse. Victims might anticipate an unsympathetic response from school authorities. They might fear increased harassment, the usual result of snitching, but more virulent because of the perceived weakness of the gay target. Closeted, uncertain, or heterosexual youth might dread scrutiny of their sexuality and

---

### BOX 5.16   GOOD POLICY COMPONENTS

Regulations should:

- include in their preamble a school ethic of caring and respect for diversity;
- employ the language of municipal and state laws, where they exist regarding protections for sexual minorities;
- include procedures for bringing a complaint, for adjudication, and for appeal;
- encourage documentation by students and parents (see next item) of incidents of abuse and the responses of school personnel;
- assure confidentiality and discretion in parental reporting (when legally permitted);
- assure protection from and penalties for retribution;
- provide for peer mediation where appropriate;
- delineate a specific appeal process to school board, state administrative authorities, and the courts;
- allow for appeal of the decision, the penalty, or the pace of the process;
- guarantee swift and decisive response to incidents of physical violence.

the equation of their complaint with coming out. Where parent notification is mandatory, young people could well conclude that calling their family's attention to their sexuality would be worse than risking further peer harassment by not reporting at all.

Students, parents, or schools who want to pursue sexual orientation harassment charges should know what must be proven to get a conviction and what questions are likely to be asked by the judging authority. (See box 5.17.)

Some states and localities have established gay-inclusive hate crimes prevention and reporting projects in which schools are encouraged to participate. They may offer school presentations, website and toll-free phone access, posters, and literature.

*Question 24: How can a gay–straight alliance (gsa) be an effective part of school reform?*

Biology teacher Virginia Uribe founded Project 10, the first public school gay support group, at Los Angeles' Fairfax High School in 1984. Gay–straight alliances

### BOX 5.17  HARASSMENT: TYPICAL CONDITIONS AND QUESTIONS

The behavior has to:

1. be unwelcome;
2. pervade the educational environment;
3. focus on sexual orientation;
4. affect the student's ability to learn.

Questions:

1. Does the school have a published policy and procedure?
2. Has the behavior been documented and reported to the administration?
3. Has the administration investigated as confidentially as possible?
4. Has the administration taken prompt remedial action, including various levels of discipline, on a case by case basis?

Mary Bonauto, civil rights project director, Gay and Lesbian Advocates and Defenders, Boston, Mass. (www.glad.org).

> **BOX 5.18   WHAT THE GSA MEANS TO ME**
>
> - A place for me to take a breath from the rest of the school, from the name-calling in the classrooms and the halls. A place where I know there will be someone to talk with about a problem or concern I am having. Here I am Julie, rather than a label or assumption.
> - Safety, creativity, individuality, and respect. A place to be together with friends, intellectuals, actors, writers, creators. Freedom, advice, camaraderie, etc.
> - A place where I can feel comfortable and be myself. Participate in some form of social action.
> - A place to come and be safe, hang out, eat lunch, have deep conversations, meet people, do socially good stuff.
>
> Student survey, Project 10 CRLS (Cambridge Rindge and Latin GSA), September 2001.

were begun in Massachusetts in 1989 and there are now over sixteen hundred high school gsas in forty-eight states (there are none in Mississippi and North Dakota). That rapid growth is a historic accomplishment, but there are still some twenty-five thousand high schools in the United States without gsas.

In its many guises (e.g., Pride Alliance, Safe Haven, Spectrum) the gsa is a crucial standard of the antihomophobia school reform movement. A school may institute antiharassment policies and conduct teacher trainings, but it has not really begun to meet the needs of its gay, lesbian, bisexual, and questioning students until it has created an environment where a gsa can flourish. (See box 5.18.)

If they don't already have a gsa at their school, workshop participants almost always leave antihomophobia presentations resolving to start one. They take their proposal to an often overly cautious and sometimes obstructionist bureaucracy. In 2001, for example, administrators in Indiana tried to dilute or kill a proposed high school gsa. First, they insisted it be a Diversity Club, covering everything including obesity; then they said it would provoke homophobia; and finally they claimed the faculty sponsor had not completely filled out the application. After a year long struggle, a court gave the gsa a green light, but the superintendent vowed an appeal. In late 2002, after a long haul, students at Kalaheo High School in Kailua were the first in Hawaii to win approval of a group with *gay* in its name. On the advice of the state attorney general, the principal yielded, but not before requiring a change in the gsa's charter to eliminate "advocacy of a lifestyle." Also in 2002, under the eye of the ACLU, the Neenah, Wisconsin, School Board overruled the superintendent's and high school principal's refusal to allow a gsa. Such resistance is not unusual. (See box 5.19.) And besides administrative barriers, gsas also face

## BOX 5.19  ADMINISTRATIVE HURDLES

"Sex isn't an appropriate topic for schools. So the appropriate place for these conversations is with their parents.... Besides, we wouldn't allow a heterosexual club, so why have one for gays?"

Administrator Sid Bailey, in Mel Meléndez, "Gays Being Heard," *The Arizona Republic*, February 6, 2002.

Even though school officials finally acquiesced to [student Jesse Brown's requests for a gsa],... [they] told him not to talk...to the media until after school closed for the year.... Brown said one former school official in 2001 told him that the group would be formed over the official's "dead body."

David Webb, "Formation of Gay-Straight Alliance Caps 18-Month Effort," *Dallas Voice*, June 7, 2002.

"We have to be discreet," says [Maria] Slagle of their own [suburban Washington, D.C.] GSA. "We can only put up very small posters, and we can't say the word 'gay' anywhere on them. All we can write is 'GSA' and then a time and place to meet."... [Lisa Saesee adds,] "We can't even say 'Come to our group' or 'Please join us' because it's considered recruiting."

Will Doig, "Sunny Day: Out in the Park with Youth Pride," *Metro Weekly*, April 17, 2003.

outright hostility. Posters are routinely torn down or defaced and student organizers are sometimes harassed or physically attacked. Although a few gsas meet off campus to protect student safety and confidentiality, most choose to meet at school both for convenience and as a public gesture for tolerance.

GSAs may also encounter challenges getting started and maintaining momentum. Some are common to many youth organizations and others are particular to gsas. (See box 5.20.)

*Question 25: Which of these challenges is most difficult?*

The answer may depend on the school. Location and political demographics often determine community resistance, for example. A gsa in a remote conservative town may find it hard to meet at all. For many gsas, however, the most important challenges are leadership, diversity, goal setting, and isolation.

## BOX 5.20  GSA CHALLENGES

- balancing student privacy with the need for visibility vis à vis other school clubs
- developing student leadership
- depending on overcommitted students
- getting new members
- reflecting the diversity of the school
- mitigating cliques within the group
- making the group comfortable for new, perhaps intimidated, students and still exciting the veterans
- dealing with different levels of openness—those who come out to the advisor and some peers, but not to the group, or come out in the group but not more widely in the school
- maintaining trust and confidentiality
- keeping the group focused
- harmonizing educational, activist, counseling, and social agendas
- motivating student follow-through on projects
- combating isolation by communicating with other gsas
- working out relationships with community-based youth and adult groups
- dealing with community resistance and hostility

GSAs' enrollment often fluctuates alarmingly from year to year. The changes might merely reflect social justice issues going in and out of style—"this year, gay rights, next year, the environment." But the problem could relate more to leadership than to trendiness. GSA advisors frequently look back on the golden years before great leaders graduated and worry whether they and the students can make the group vibrant again, a concern shared by advisors to other school clubs too.

Clearly, underclass students have to be prepared in advance for leadership roles. Key components of such training are power sharing, group decision making, creative thinking, delegation of tasks, and leadership by inspiration and example. Such leadership development goals are rarely achieved in adult organizations, let alone undertaken at all in secondary schools.

Over the long term, numbers are less important than group cohesion and effectiveness. An energetic few students with a dedicated advisor can create a distinguished record. (See box 5.21.)

*Question 26: How is diversity in the gsa a challenge?*

The question of who chooses to participate is vexing. The gsa may be a haven for alienated misfits ("freaks") or a bohemian countercultural enclave (like the

## BOX 5.21   SIZE ISN'T EVERYTHING

When the Alliance was first formed, a large number of gay and straight students attended the meetings to show support for the beleaguered group, numbering as high as 50 for a while. Once established, however, the size of the group diminished to about 15 students, a number that has stayed constant for the past seven years.... I'm not saying there is no homophobia ... or that we've solved all our problems, but we're at least heading in that direction. This support group's existence is a statement of tolerance in itself, and that commitment is not lost on our students.

Christine Baron [high school English teacher], "What Adults Can Learn," *Los Angeles Times*, March 1, 2000.

prototypical drama club) or both. Moreover, its composition tends to perpetuate itself as like attracts like and other kinds of students are put off by its image in the school.

As a purported safe space for sexual minority youth, it is no wonder that other nonconformists seek it out. A youth group who won't hassle its members about homosexuality is likely to be nonjudgmental about other characteristics like weight, drug use, music and clothing preferences, and intellectual interests that evoke ridicule and worse among more conventional adolescents. Regardless of their sexuality or gender identity, teens who deviate from traditional gender role and presentation can find respite in a gsa.

Sexual minority youth who cannot pass for straight or who choose not to are most likely to need a gsa as a support against victimization. They are already at disproportionate risk for depression, suicide, substance abuse, and so on. (See chapter 3.) Other gay youth who can stay closeted or are better supported outside school and therefore less needy might not associate with the gsa, if it meant "outing" themselves or being seen in "bad company."

Many gsas are composed mostly of straight, bisexual, and nonlabeled girls. They apparently suffer fewer negative consequences in the larger school because of their gsa membership than boys do. That result is consistent with girls having greater latitude in gender expression generally and with sexual minority females being less threatening to straight people.

Racial and ethnic diversity is also a clear challenge. Students of color may not feel welcome in a group that does not reflect or offer evidence of understanding their cultural identity and experience. No matter how sincere their outreach, a gsa that looks like a bunch of white hippies or goths could have little success recruiting racial and ethnic minorities. Moreover, the heteronormative pressure within their cultural peer group prevents many minority youth from entering a gay setting, especially in the school where detection is likely. Community-based gay youth support groups outside their own neighborhoods could offer them a safe alternative to the gsa but do not always provide one. (See box 5.22.)

The gsa should still do everything it can to appeal to a variety of students. It could recruit adults of color as advisors, elect students of color to leadership positions, sponsor joint activities with other more diverse school groups, and bring in speakers and films to initiate discussion about nonwhite, non-European gays and lesbians. It is also imperative that majority-white gsas develop and act on an antiracist agenda and cooperate with other school organizations in social justice projects. Tokenism, often detected and always off-putting, must be avoided.

There is evidence that students of color whose ethnicity is shared by the majority in a school often find it harder to join a gsa because of racial group pressure. Even other glbt youth of color in a school may resent one of their own joining the gsa. Urban schools with higher numbers of students of color may therefore need extra resources. For example, when it became apparent in 2000 that the Boston public schools lagged behind the suburbs in gsa formation, they were given

## BOX 5.22   GSAS AND COMMUNITY GROUPS: SOMETIMES A TOUGH SELL

"There's a whole separate gay culture for black kids," says [19-year-old Jaison] Gardner. "If you were to take kids from SMYAL and put them together with a group of white kids . . . , they would still have trouble interacting." . . . [O]nly five D.C. schools have functioning [gsas]; four of them are private schools. . . . Most of the efforts have lacked faculty or community support and—especially—student initiative. . . . The lone public school [gsa] is . . . in the wealthiest part of town.

Laura Lang, "Below the Gaydar," *Washington* [D.C.] *City Paper*, May 19, 2000.

Celeste Morgan, SMYAL's health programs manager, said one of the greatest challenges has been getting gay Latino youths to take advantage of the support group and other initiatives created specifically for them. . . . "I don't know if it's a matter of getting [Latino youths] to SMYAL or making them feel comfortable here." . . . "Being a youth, living with your mom and dad . . . I just think it's incredibly difficult to come out to yourself or to your family," [Lena Hernandez, an SMYAL assistant] said. "There's this huge feeling that if you tell your parents you're gay, you will be an outcast."

Rhonda Smith, "Study to Examine Unique Challenges of Coming Out as a Teen," *Washington* [D.C.] *Blade*, August 14, 2002.

a $40,000 state grant for a citywide gsa coordinator of color and for technical assistance.

The diversity problem illustrates why school support for sexual minority youth should not be limited to a gsa. The only way to extend support to all glbt students is through culturally sensitive counseling and an inclusive curriculum that represents the diversity of the gay experience.

Finally, a disproportionate gsa membership of alienated, troubled, gay and straight young people inhibits the formation of a healthy youth culture. The counseling needs of individual students can overwhelm the advisor and detract from the group's necessary focus on group needs and objectives. This observation is not meant to blame students for their problems, only to underline how hard it is to focus any group on communitarian ends when a critical mass of members are emotionally disabled. The tensions between individual counseling and community building can be exhausting, especially for advisors who are not trained mental health service providers and substance abuse counselors.

As much as compassionate adults might wish to defer to a counseling model, they should not abandon the democratic peer community as a means of advancing the group's collective goals. Responsibility to the group as well as the self can also be therapeutic for the individual.

## Question 27: How is goal setting a challenge for the gsa?

Quite simply, different students want different things from their gsa. Some join to learn about gay and lesbian issues. Some want to change the school and the community through political activism. Some want support and counseling for coming out. Some want to hang out, socialize, and do things that are fun.

The trick is to meet as many expectations as possible without spreading the group (or its advisors) too thin. Subcommittees are an attractive approach to multiple objectives, but follow-through is also an issue for often overcommitted students. Better to have fewer projects at hand and more hands available. It is also a great idea to organize some events with gsas from neighboring communities.

## Question 28: What are the National Day of Silence and National Coming Out Day?

National Day of Silence is a springtime event coordinated by GLSEN (Gay Lesbian and Straight Education Network) during which students (and some staff) elect not to speak for a day to represent those who are silenced by homophobia. They may wear a ribbon or some other signifier and carry a handout explaining their action as support for those who cannot be open about themselves or their loved ones. Some students may choose to speak on that day but still wear a signifier

## BOX 5.23   DAY OF SILENCE

"[I]f we fear what people might do to us then nothing will ever change," said [Spencer] Davis, 17, who came out earlier this year through a column he wrote for the school's newspaper. . . . Davis was one of the students at the high school who chose to spend the day without talking to dramatize what it feels like to be unable to speak one's heart. . . . [A freshman] whose face was marked with a red circle with a slash over her mouth, said in a typed statement that many of her classmates taunted and teased her for her silence, causing her, as a heterosexual, to experience homosexual discrimination first hand.

Danielle Samaniego, "Silence Lends Voice to Rights," *Los Angeles Times*, April 11, 2002.

[The principal] said he would send teachers a list of students observing the day of silence, with instructions to accommodate the protest by working around those students at class time. . . . "This, in itself, is a learning experience," he said. "It's a trade-off. It's one educational experience for another for one day."

Scott Williams, "Students Hope Their Silence Will Make a Statement for Gay Rights," *Milwaukee Journal-Sentinel*, March 29, 2002.

in solidarity. Organizers should plan the day in cooperation with their teachers and administrators as much as possible, publicize it, and invite everyone to participate. (See box 5.23.)

National Coming Out Day is an October event coordinated by the HRC (Human Rights Campaign) that encourages glbt people to come out in their workplaces, families, schools, and places of worship. Some schools hold assemblies to mark the occasion. Individual students or gsas can have a "coming out" impact through school and community publications as well. (See box 5.24.)

*Question 29: How is isolation a challenge for the gsa?*

It takes courage to join a gsa. Whether it meets openly in the school or more privately elsewhere, membership is hard to keep confidential. Gay students and allies alike find their sexuality under scrutiny. (See box 5.25.) Both are subject to teasing and harassment. Whether the gsa consists of a few brave souls in a rural

## BOX 5.24   THE POWER OF THE SCHOOL PRESS

This is one of the hardest things I have ever had to write, but it is necessary to write it. You may be asking, where is this going? Well, I'm going to tell you; keep reading. I have been the topic of some conversation in recent years. The question is always, "Is he or isn't he?" In this editorial I am answering that question. Yes, I am gay.

Josh Hoffer, "Columnist Spills Guts...KEEP READING," [commentary], *BROBOCA* (Monthly newspaper of Brookings High School, Brookings, S.D.), November 22, 2000.

community or a larger group in a big city, its members can feel besieged, alone, and dispirited.

GSAs can combat this isolation by reaching out to other gsas in their area and by communicating with even more such groups around their state and across the country through gsa networks. (See appendix F.) There is utter exhilaration in actually being together in regional and national gsa confabs, sponsored by state education departments or independent agencies like True Colors (Conn.), SMYAL (D.C.), Safe Schools Washington, and GLSEN. Among the topics for discussion

## BOX 5.25   CRIPPLING SUSPICION

Only months after Safe Haven started meeting at the Wales school to help promote tolerance about sexual orientation, its members decided to disband it two weeks ago, said [its teacher sponsor]. "It got dubbed 'the gay group.' We were stereotyped right away, and kids who are tolerant were afraid to be part of it."

Amy Hetzner, "Students' Gay Tolerance Group Ends," *Milwaukee Journal Sentinel*, December 18, 2000.

Most of the students in the [gsa] club identify themselves as heterosexual, and most of the gay students at Skyline [High School] aren't in the club, because they would rather not be pegged as gay, students say.

Alex Katz, "Response Is Mixed to Gay School Clubs," *Alameda Times-Star*, November 17, 2002.

and strategizing, networking events should include gsa successes and obstacles in achieving membership, diversity, and activity goals.

GSA advisors sometimes feel even more alone than students do. They should have a sustained block of time at such conferences for mutual adult support.

*Question 30: Is a gsa more advisable than a school support group for gay youth?*

A gsa often brings straight allies to the mission of making schools safe for all. It also encourages students who are fearful of coming out or uncertain of their sexual orientation to participate, usually without assumptions or pressure to identify. GLBT students are free to come out at their own pace or not at all.

A gsa appears to be a more moderate step than a gay support group. Cautious administrators who want to deflect the focus from sexuality and would prefer a "diversity club" for all minorities might agree to settle for a gsa.

A gsa is more likely to be an advocacy group for gay rights, school safety, and inclusion than to be a direct service provider to sexual minority youth. Students who need support with coming out, dealing with family, and other personal sexuality issues may need more than a gsa can offer. They often require complete confidentiality and glbt peer advisors. Some students organize a gsa spinoff for sexual minority youth only or locate a community-based program for counseling, identity solidification, and socialization.

Outside support groups are often freer to discuss sex-related issues and are usually more relaxed about sexually expressive behavior than schools are. Being comfortable in their sexualities is key to glbt students' safety and health. But of course, in or out of school, sexual minority youth have more on their minds than sex. (See box 5.26.)

---

### BOX 5.26   IT'S NOT ALWAYS ABOUT SEX

The kids at District 202 [glbt teen center] chat about homework, school papers and teachers. They talk about their plans for the night and what tomorrow night's drag show will be like. They talk about celebrities, their new music videos—who's hot and who's not. They discuss the latest fashions out in the stores, but there's very little talk about things directly related to homosexuality—only that there should be more places like this. Jacob, 15, explains. "I get harassed a lot at school. It hurts."

Ben Fornell, "Minnesota Youth News: Gay Teens Aren't So Different from Their Straight Peers," *Minneapolis Star Tribune*, May 14, 2001.

## BOX 5.27  RECRUITMENT?

[The past president of the American Academy of Child and Adolescent Psychiatrists] wonders whether [gsas] might lead some . . . to identify themselves as gay, lesbian, or bisexual when they haven't yet sorted out their sexuality. " . . . [A]dolescents . . . tend to feel alienated, they tend to feel isolated," he said. "As a result, they're very prone to pick up whatever is being espoused by a group, and I think we have to be aware of that." [Another] psychiatrist who works with teens [observes], "All kids explore and experiment sexually as part of their normal development . . . " he said. "The experimentation in itself doesn't determine someone's sexual orientation."

Scott S. Greenberger, "Gay Alliance Taking Hold in Schools," *Boston Globe*, April 15, 2001.

*Question 31: Do gsas influence some students to become gay?*

Opponents of gay positive programs and curricula in the schools regularly make that charge, but there is no evidence to support it. Students who become less fearful of or hateful toward homosexuality may have fewer inhibitions in exploring the full range of their sexual interests. Some find confirmation of their gay or bisexual desires, others do not, and some become less invested in sexuality labels overall. Adult observers, however, are quite divided. (See box 5.27.)

*Question 32: What does it take to be a gsa advisor?*

It is discouraging that students often have trouble finding faculty advisors for their gsa. (See box 5.28.) It can be a difficult role. Besides encountering political opposition, advisors may have their sexuality questioned and actions monitored. One Tennessee gsa advisor was accused by a colleague of "running a sex club for fags" and another in California received 2,000 hate e-mails from one address. Other stresses arise from the gsa itself. They may find glbt youth risk behaviors worrisome. Some become targets for students' displaced anger with the system or their families. Helping gay youth balance coming out fears or enthusiasms with schoolwork and other responsibilities requires special skill. Advisors who themselves are gay, lesbian, or bisexual face additional challenges as role models and advocates. (See chapter 4.)

Because there is little available training for the job in most localities, too many take the assignment out of compassion, having only goodwill to sustain them. They should read as much as they can about glbt youth, talk to other advisors,

## BOX 5.28   MENTOR SEARCH

One teacher who agreed to be the [gsa's] sponsor this year backed out, concerned about how her involvement would affect her professionally, [a student] said. He later found a couple of married teachers willing to take the project on.

David Webb, "Formation of Gay-Straight Alliance Caps 18-Month Effort," *Dallas Voice*, June 7, 2002.

[A senior] wants to start a gsa, but he can't find a sponsor.... Teachers thought they would be labeled gay, [a veteran teacher] said.... [I]n other cities...teachers' cars were vandalized or they lost their jobs when they supported gay students.

Alliniece T. Andino, "Gay Students Say Schools Should Help Fight Prejudice," *Florida Times-Union*, January 11, 2001.

and reach out to school and community-based counselors and social workers for advice and intervention when needed.

*Question 33: Are faculty trainings and gsas good indicators of school progress?*

They are positive signs. Research indicates that students in schools with clear antiharassment policies, faculty antihomophobia workshops, and gsas *feel* safer and more comfortable than do students in schools without those variables. Schools that care enough to take such steps might have felt (and *have been*) safer than other schools to begin with. "Before and after" studies have yet to be done. Nevertheless, in Massachusetts, with its history of teacher workshops and numerous gsas, the proportion of gay-identified youth who report being threatened or injured with a weapon at school has declined steadily from 33 percent (1995) to 18 percent (2001). No decline is registered among self-identified heterosexual youth. Still, complete safety is elusive: even an established gsa is no cure-all. (See box 5.29.)

Reform is a long-term, all-school proposition. Sending a few earnest faculty members to a conference is a beginning gesture. Asking them to help devise a subsequent training for the whole faculty and inviting outside experts to participate is even more promising. Sole responsibility for reform should not fall to the gsa and its advisors. Devising a schoolwide action plan and ongoing assessment strategy is best. (See box 5.30.)

## BOX 5.29   REAL WORLD INTRUSIONS

"It's one thing to have a group, in the abstract, that meets," said ... a Chapel Hill High senior and four-year member of the Gay-Straight Alliance. "But it's different to actually be an out bisexual person at high school. Classmates are always throwing around homophobic phrases and offensive insults. That's the kind of thing I experience on a daily basis."

Sumathi Reddy, "Gay-Straight Alliances Persevere," *Raleigh News & Observer*, April 5, 2001.

Finally, no school system can be serious about reform unless it provides appropriate funding for its implementation. On this measure, even the most progressive might fall short.

*Question 34: What should be the goals of school reform on gay and lesbian issues?*

First, schools must recognize that these issues are important. Sexual minorities are a part of their schools and their concerns matter. Moreover, homophobia is related to the school problems of heterosexual youth as well. Second, schools

## BOX 5.30   SOME CRITERIA FOR THE LONG TERM

- Are policy changes actively enforced and what impact has that had on student behavior and attitudes?
- What are the effects of teacher trainings? Have faculty altered their perceptions of student and family diversity? Are they more aware of harassment, more inclined to intervene, and more effective in doing so? Have they changed their curricula? Have they read more about homosexuality or enrolled in graduate courses on gay topics? Have they asked school trainers for more workshops or technical assistance?
- Has the gsa been well advised? Has it received material and community support? Have other faculty besides the gsa advisor helped it thrive? Have students in need of services been appropriately referred?
- Has the school formed an ongoing task force of faculty, administrators, counselors, parents, and other community members to help plan, support, and evaluate ongoing goals and activities?

must adopt and enforce antiharassment policies and support services for glbt youth and families. Lastly, the school must understand that homophobia is embedded in a heterosexist system of oppression that the school and community have a responsibility to eliminate along with other oppressions based on gender, race, class, ability, and the like.

This ultimate goal demands a level of self-examination, political analysis, and commitment that is rare among individuals and rarer yet at the institutional level. As instruments of social conservation, schools are not expected to foster such a critique or embrace such a mission. (See question 16.) Still, we hope that they will try, despite the discouragement and dangers they will invariably encounter on the way.

*Question 35: Can the certification process be improved as a part of these reforms?*

Prospective teachers, administrators, and counselors (and those seeking recertification) can be required to show some knowledge of gay issues in education. (See box 5.31.) In 1994, for example, the Massachusetts State Board of Education added "sexual orientation" to the equity competencies of their teacher and administrator certification standards, demanding mastery of "effective strategies within the classroom and other school settings to address discrimination based on each student's race, sex, religion, socioeconomic class, or disability." After this modest change, reformers quickly related sexual orientation to other parts of the equity

---

**BOX 5.31   CERTIFICATION COMPETENCIES**

Competent educators should be able to:

- understand the significance of glbt issues in education;
- teach more comprehensively about the human experience through the integration of glbt subject matter into the core of learning in their disciplines;
- promote the psychological and physical health and intellectual development of all students;
- reduce bigotry, self-hatred, and violence by increasing tolerance for sexuality differences;
- aid communication between glbt youth and their families and schools;
- facilitate the integration of glbt families into the school community;
- nurture the well-being of faculty, staff, and administrators of all sexual orientations;
- collaborate with the greater community in achieving these ends.

standard, namely: regard for freedom of expression, nurturing of self-esteem, attention to unique developmental and cultural needs, and awareness of diverse family backgrounds.

The Governor's Commission on Gay and Lesbian Youth persuaded the Department of Education to begin the Project for the Integration of Gay & Lesbian Youth Issues in School Personnel Certification Programs. Faculty from about half of the state's nearly seventy college and graduate education departments attended a three-hour training to introduce them to sexual minority youth and family concerns and to help them alter their teacher education syllabi.

*Question 36: Is there anything that teachers can do in a school that will not undertake any gay-related reforms?*

Teachers in conservative districts shouldn't feel helpless. (See appendix G.) Even where progress must be sub rosa and slow, the key catalysts for change are still information and allies.

Reformers should learn as much as they can about glbt young people in general and in their communities. They should read from the growing literature on the development and school experiences of sexual minority youth. Where possible, they should have conversations with local glbt students and their families in venues where they feel comfortable. Published accounts and organizations like GLSEN can help them learn from the triumphs and failures of reformers in communities like their own.

They must reach out to others to join in this research and discussion. Even a few colleagues, families, youth, and community supporters will reduce the isolation. Further outreach from the core group should eventually be possible. Some members may prefer a private one-on-one approach. Others might be willing to have a dialogue with administrators, teachers, PTAs and parent councils, and church and civic groups. Planners should include clear goals, personal stories, facts, and invitations to reform couched in the highest values of the community itself.

Such a meeting may not yield immediate strategies for school change, yet it will have succeeded if invited participants begin to understand that school silence about glbt issues is not neutrality—it is harm by omission.

(For further reading, see appendix R.)

## NOTE

1. In July 2003 it was announced that the Harvey Milk School would be a "full-fledged" public school, featuring a $3.2 million renovation and an enrollment of one hundred glbt students. Since 1984 the Hetrick-Martin Institute had operated and co-funded it as a two-room alternative program with as long as a three-year waiting list.

# 6

# Progress and Resistance

*Question 1: What are the political issues in educational reform regarding sexual orientation?*

Students' political values are contested daily both in and out of school by means of unprecedented channels of communication. Finding common civic values and learning to live by them in peaceful communities is a challenge that students must begin to undertake in school.

Most school curricula, even the "pure" sciences, have political dimensions or ramifications. Moreover, deciding what will be studied and how it will be presented nearly always involves political considerations. National and community politics impact policy and funding. The decisions of local school boards, even nonelected ones, are clearly politicized. Politics influences professional decision making in schools all the time and can determine whether a particular school reform succeeds or fails.

Because both sex education and gay positive programs raise the intensity of educational politics, any meaningful progress in this arena demands effective advocacy and lobbying by a range of constituencies—parents, students, teachers, and so on. When reforms are approved, moreover, the politics do not evaporate. The concerns of each group must be continuously addressed and balanced against the greater goal of making schools safe and affirming. Consulting with other constituencies, educators should be allowed the time and resources to develop and implement programs using their best professional skills and judgment. They are accountable to elected officials and the community but should not be micromanaged by them.

A cautionary example is evident in Massachusetts. For over a decade the volunteer Governor's Commission on Gay and Lesbian Youth has instigated unparalleled advancements for gay and lesbian youth in schools and communities.

Yet they have sometimes favored ephemeral public relations events over more substantive programming geared toward lasting change. The commissioners know that good headlines help oil the legislative machinery, so they are right to cultivate splashy conferences and rallies. But they have also sometimes been deaf to experienced gay and lesbian youth workers and have pressured state agencies to ignore their own contractors' recommendations for improved youth services and ongoing training/technical support for providers. Some of this imbalance has been redressed under new commissioners, but the tension between political expediency and professional priorities will likely persist. It may be feasible only to acknowledge these often-competing aims and to insure respectful communication between their proponents.

*Question 2: What is the federal government doing to aid school reform?*

Until the late 1990s references to homosexual youth by federal departments were almost nonexistent, even in studies of high-risk youth and suicide. Former Secretary of Health and Human Services Louis Sullivan would not publicize or comment substantively on a 1986 paper that was part of his own department's study—Paul Gibson's famous, if somewhat limited, "Gay and Lesbian Youth Suicide." The HHS secretary merely stated that the paper's views "undermine the institution of the family."

The limited applicability of Title IX is frustrating. (See chapter 5, box 5.15.) Still, a number of federal departments have offered general resources that are useful, provided they are taken off the shelf and taken seriously by local school officials. A 1994 *Guide to Enhancing the Cultural Competence of Runaway and Homeless Youth Programs* from HHS was a first exception to gay omission, followed by 1997's "Healing the Hate," a middle school bias crime prevention curriculum, funded by the Justice Department. Then in January 1999 the U.S. Department of Education Office for Civil Rights (OCR) and the National Association of Attorneys General Bias Crime Task Force Education Subcommittee issued "Protecting Students from Harassment and Hate Crimes, A Guide for Schools." These guidelines identify sexual orientation–related offenses in elementary and secondary schools and recommend sample policies for prevention and enforcement. (See box 6.1.) Some conservatives strongly oppose these documents.

Surgeon General David Satcher's 2001 report on sex education, "The Call to Action to Promote Sexual Health and Responsible Sexual Behavior," dealt with what he himself called "the most controversial and sensitive" issue he faced in office. This glbt-inclusive document calls for "equity of access to information for promoting sexual health" and notes that "anti-homosexual attitudes are associated with psychological distress for homosexual persons and may have a negative impact on mental health, including a greater incidence of depression and suicide, lower self-acceptance and a greater likelihood of hiding sexual orientation." At

**BOX 6.1   PURPOSES OF PROTECTING STUDENTS FROM HARASSMENT AND HATE CRIMES, A GUIDE FOR SCHOOLS**

- Offer strategies for long-term solutions to the problem.
- Increase awareness of the need for organizing school-parent-community partnerships to respond to the problem.
- Offer information that will help schools to write, revise, and enforce written antiharassment policies that cover all kinds of unlawful discrimination.
- Assist school personnel to recognize harassment when it occurs and respond effectively to stop the harassment and deter recurrence or escalation.
- Review support strategies for victims.
- Provide advice to schools on ways to establish formal reporting and complaint procedures.
- Provide information to schools regarding when and how to refer incidents to law enforcement authorities for investigation or prosecution.
- Make schools aware of the advantages of accurate incident reporting.
- Identify the components of crisis intervention plans that will help to avoid disruption of the educational process, should incidents occur.

From "Protecting Students from Harassment and Hate Crimes," available at www.ed.gov/offices, through ED Pubs, or at 800-USA LEARN.

the end of 2001 the Centers for Disease Control (CDC) published "School Health Guidelines to Prevent Unintentional Injuries and Violence." It makes several important references to sexual orientation and gay and lesbian students and to their "right to safety." (See box 6.2.)

Focusing on safety, risk, and prevention, the OCR and CDC reports and recommendations highlight pathology rather than resilience. It is not surprising that the federal voice on sexual minority youth would be more protective than affirmative. Despite that drawback, they can lend muscle to local efforts.

*Question 3: What kinds of action have state and municipal governments taken?*

Eight states (California, Connecticut, Massachusetts, Minnesota, New Jersey, Vermont, Washington, and Wisconsin) and the District of Columbia have added "sexual orientation" to their antiharassment regulations. Many local school boards in those states and others have done the same (including Decatur, Georgia, and Lawrence, Kansas!).

## BOX 6.2   SCHOOL HEALTH GUIDELINES TO PREVENT UNINTENTIONAL INJURIES AND VIOLENCE: HIGHLIGHTS

- Regardless of a child's ethnic, socioeconomic, religious, sexual orientation, or physical status, all children have a right to safety. When victimization through bullying, verbal abuse, and physical violence is prevalent in a school, the entire school community experiences the consequences. (p. 18)
- Students who are different from the majority of their classmates because of their race, ethnicity, sexual orientation, religion, or other personal characteristics are at increased risk for being bullied. Gay, lesbian, or bisexual students, and students perceived to be gay by their peers are often victims of repeated verbal abuse and physical assault. (p. 18)
- Support nonviolence and protect students, staff members, and faculty from harassment, violence, or discrimination based on personal characteristics (e.g., race, sex, sexual orientation, religion, physical or mental ability, and appearance). (p. 19)
- Rather than using curricula focused directly on suicide prevention, schools might target risk and protective factors (e.g., alcohol use, bullying, and school connectedness), educate students regarding the consequences of suicidal behavior, and focus on specific subpopulations that might be at higher risk (e.g., gay and lesbian students). (p. 25)
- Issues of social class, race, ethnicity, language, sexual orientation, and physical ability might be considered when choosing and implementing prevention strategies.... Activities that promote tolerance and respect for differences are critical. (p. 26)
- Gay, lesbian, and bisexual students are at increased risk for attempting suicide. (p. 33)

CDC, "School Health Guidelines to Prevent Unintentional Injuries and Violence," www.cdc.gov/mmwr/preview/mmwrhtml/rr5022a1.htm (December 7, 2001).

But even that small step has provoked intense debate across the country. (See box 6.3.) Opponents regularly claim that all students are protected by general antiharassment language and that there is no need to single out gays and lesbians. It appears they have never objected to the inclusion of religion, race, and gender in the law and only find their voice when the addition of sexual orientation is proposed. From Omaha to Honolulu, some officials would rather abandon all specific categories than permit that "divisive" addition.

## BOX 6.3   POLICY PROBLEMS

The state school board backed away yesterday—for at least the third time in as many years—from explicitly protecting gay and lesbian students from harassment in Maryland's public schools ... as a response to legislative—and community—fears that the policy's new wording would require the teaching of homosexuality in classrooms. ...

Stephanie Desmon, "School Board Defers Vote on Policy to Protect Gay Students," *Baltimore Sun*, June 27, 2002. (A Maryland regulation inclusive of sexual orientation was finally passed in June 2003.)

Despite recommendations for policy changes by the Iowa Department of Education ..., relatively few school districts in Iowa have added sexual orientation to the list of protected classes under their harassment policies.

Ben Godar, "Gilbert Case Has Impact on Other Districts," *Ames* [Iowa] *Tribune*, April 13, 2002.

Virginia's Fairfax district's antiharassment policy was not amended in 2002 to prohibit antigay harassment, even though the student handbook had been so changed in 2001. After prolonged and, according to the chairman, unprecedented dissension among the school board, Virginia's attorney general ruled that Fairfax officials could not amend the policy without a change in state law.

Explicit glbt references in official policy are important because they improve the chances of successful lawsuits on behalf of sexual minority youth. Additionally, gay and lesbian student protections have been used to justify government expenditures for teacher training, gsas, student support services, and the like. The $800,000 Massachusetts' Safe Schools Program for Gay and Lesbian Students has sponsored up to eleven regional conferences annually for gsas and their advisors. It has also awarded school grants of up to $3,000 for gsa support, $5,000 for "Mentor GSAs" to assist other gsas, and a number of $5,000 "Middle School Climate Improvement Grants," to challenge *all* categories of discrimination. (In 2002, broad budget cuts eliminated the Safe Schools program at the Department of Education. $700,000 for community-based glbt youth programs at the Department of Public Health was left intact. In 2003 that amount was halved.)

In September 1999, the California Assembly approved by just one vote bill AB 537, banning discrimination against gays and lesbians in public schools and universities. Its comprehensive recommendations can serve as a model for other states. (See appendix H.) Because AB 537's provisions are as yet voluntary and unfunded, the GSA Network has developed "Make It Real," a strategic manual for maximizing the local impact of the law (www.gsanetwork.org/ab537). Activist vigilance in "making it real" is no small matter. Too often, in California and elsewhere, laws are passed to mollify minority constituencies and there's the end of it. (See box 6.4.)

New York's Dignity for All Students Act passed the state assembly in April 2002 by a 144-2 margin and moved on to the senate, where it remained dormant through June 2003. If it is enacted, the state will finally have gained official momentum for reform. Later that year the state board of education agreed to add a sexual orientation variable to its Youth Risk Behavior Survey (YRBS) to determine the bases on which students are bullied. However, their YRBS does not investigate any other glbt-related risk. New York City's Board of Education includes "sexual preference" in its antidiscrimination policies yet provides little leadership or support beyond what it gives to alternative programs like Harvey Milk School.

With St. Paul schools' Out for Equity and Minneapolis's Out4Good, the Twin Cities are in the vanguard. Out4Good has confidential support groups for glbt

## BOX 6.4  AFTER THE LAW, THEN WHAT?

Since a state law took effect last year prohibiting harassment against gays in the schools, few districts in California have taken major steps to implement [it]. . . . [S]tudents away from urban centers . . . still don't realize . . . that they can file grievances with their school administrator.

Christopher Heredia, "Gay Students Demand Schools Recognize Law," *San Francisco Chronicle*, June 3, 2001.

The Chicago Public Schools passed a non-discrimination policy in 1997 that extended protection to students and employees based on sexual orientation. But GLSEN officials said the district has never really implemented those protections or trained its staff to deal with these issues.

Tracy Dell'Angela, "Bullying Said to Be Worse for Gay Teens," *Chicago Tribune*, May 31, 2001.

The Governor's Commission for Gay and Lesbian Youth yesterday sent a letter to the Board of Education asking the state to more stridently enforce the Gay and Lesbian Student Rights Law enacted in 1994. . . . About 30 percent of the schools in the state still have not added the law to their policies or spelled it out in their student handbooks, [the commission chair] said.

Doreen Iudica Vigue, "Safety of Gays in School Is Urged," *Boston Globe*, September 3, 1999.

teens run by social workers or guidance counselors in all seven Minneapolis high schools and some alternative schools. Out for Equity has two gsas. Both districts also have Safe Staffs—educators or other adult volunteers available to students dealing with their own or their families' sexual identity issues.

Other school districts with full-time counselor/advocates for sexual minority students and/or families include: Madison and Milwaukee, Wis.; San Francisco and Los Angeles, Calif.; Seattle, Wash.; and Cambridge, Mass. In 2001, the Milwaukee School Board mandated its counselor "to improve the academic achievement, emotional security, and personal acceptance" of glbt students and staff, and to be "a source of support and information to all students."

*Question 4: What are national professional organizations doing to aid school reform on glbt issues?*

Over the last twenty years, and particularly the last decade, many professional organizations that deal with health, education, and welfare have passed resolutions to support gay and lesbian youth. These mainstream groups, including the American Psychological Association, the National Association of Social Workers, and the National School Boards Association, have proven to be significant allies because they are perceived as having a less partisan agenda than gay organizations. Significantly, many of these groups have gay and lesbian caucuses that have initiated their progress.

A 1999 National Association of School Psychologists' position statement recognizes the increased risk sexual minority students face and supports their equal access to education and mental health services as well as targeted HIV prevention. The NASP supports school and community advocacy on behalf of gay youth and calls for research on programs that serve them. In its 1999 Position Statement on Gay, Lesbian, and Bisexual Youth, this organization goes beyond victimology in recognizing that "a successful program to address these issues educates both those who discriminate and those who are discriminated against because of sexual orientation."

The American Psychological Association's Healthy Lesbian, Gay and Bisexual Students Project (www.apa.org/ed/hlgb.html) is designed to help school counselors, nurses, psychologists, and social workers prevent health risks and promote healthy outcomes for sexual minority youth. In collaboration with six major school counseling, health, and mental health associations, HLGBSP has begun training events at professional conferences.

*Question 5: How has the PTA been involved?*

The National Parent Teacher Association has taken some bold steps. It includes sexual orientation in its antidiscrimination statement, which applies to both children and families. National PTA has commended the Washington State PTA for creating specialty groups focusing on those, including homosexual people, who may feel disenfranchised by traditional PTAs. Of the PTA's hundreds of resolutions and suggestions promoting respect for human differences, the gay-related ones have been the most controversial.

*Question 6: What other organizations have weighed in on behalf of sexual minority youth in schools?*

Organizations promoting civil rights and liberties have made significant contributions to the campaign. The ACLU Lesbian and Gay Rights Project (www.aclu.org/issues/gay/safe_schools.htm) offers to help communities make their schools safe for all students, preferably without litigation.

Human Rights Watch's (www.hrw.org) 2001 report, "Hatred in the Hallways: Violence and Discrimination Against Lesbian, Gay, Bisexual and Transgender Students in U.S. Schools," the product of a two-year study, had an immediate public impact. A subsequent survey by the National Mental Health Association in 2002 found that nearly eight in ten teens observe antigay teasing and bullying in their schools. These studies are being used effectively to counter denial of this ubiquitous problem.

Likewise, People for the American Way (www.pfaw.org) has regularly produced two substantive national reports. "Hostile Climate" documents antigay incidents among other hate crimes and "Attacks on the Freedom to Learn" includes glbt-related cases in reports on school censorship.

Gay and lesbian issues are also being increasingly featured in the work of organizations that promote antibias curricula. (See appendix I.)

*Question 7: How has the National Education Association contributed?*

The NEA, a historically progressive union, has made significant strides, despite a few slipups. A resolution passed at its 1990 representative assembly demanded equal opportunity for all, "regardless of sexual orientation," professional counseling for "students who are struggling with their sexual/gender orientation," and "staff development" efforts to reduce homophobia and discrimination. The NEA urged school systems to consider positive role models in person and in the curriculum for gay students.

These actions were groundbreaking. Their only shortcoming was that their focus on victimized and needy gay students seemed to ignore peer homophobia, teacher indifference, and the need for education *about* sexual minorities. The 1994 NEA Representative Assembly began to address the last point in a comprehensive Resolution B-9 on Sexual Orientation Education, which called for "effective ongoing training programs for education employees for the purpose of identifying and eliminating sexual orientation stereotyping in the educational setting." (See box 6.5.) Because B-9 linked the protection of gay youth with the

> ## BOX 6.5   FROM NEA 1994 RESOLUTION B-9
>
> Such programs should attend to but not be limited to:
>
> - Accurate portrayal of the roles and contributions of gay, lesbian, and bisexual people throughout history, with acknowledgment of their sexual orientation.
> - The acceptance of diverse sexual orientation and the awareness of sexual stereotyping whenever sexuality and/or tolerance of diversity are taught.
> - Elimination of sexual orientation name-calling and jokes in the classroom.

need to educate both staff and students about homosexual people, it represented a significant move forward.

Just a year later, however, the passage of a previously defeated Gay History Month Resolution led to a setback. This simple amendment to B-9 called for "the celebration of a Lesbian and Gay History Month as a means of acknowledging the contributions of lesbians, gays, and bisexuals throughout history." Inspired by a GLSEN (Gay, Lesbian, and Straight Education Network) History Month project, it was modeled on existing NEA history month observances for African Americans and women.

The right-wing reaction, led by the Concerned Women for America (CWA), was immense. In large newspaper ads CWA characterized the history month resolution as a "threat to morality and decency"—another move by the nefarious NEA and the homosexuals, 49 percent of whom, they claimed "admitted to having sex with a minor." Despite official support for Gay History Month from governors (Connecticut, Massachusetts, and Oregon) and mayors (St. Louis, Boston, and Santa Fe), protests broke out all over the country.

Conservative state and local school boards disavowed the history month project and condemned any gay positive education. One NEA state official defensively claimed the resolution was nonbinding and not about curriculum but about helping students struggling with their sexuality. Others pointed to an emotional and divided convention that produced an impotent unfunded resolution. Utah's 110 delegates boasted that none of them had supported it. Union leaders in Oklahoma, Louisiana, and Nebraska joined the chorus.

Regrettably, national NEA folded. A spokesperson announced that the history month resolution dealt only with gay and lesbian teens and vowed that NEA was not preparing any curriculum on the topic. Another claimed the language was directed only at teachers, adding nonsensically, "The resolution deals principally with tolerance and has nothing to do with anything going on in the classrooms or hallways." The NEA president issued a semi-disclaimer. Neither African American nor Women's History months had ever evoked such a weak defense. (To be fair, even the National Gay and Lesbian Task Force was unprepared in that environment to embrace the broad educational purpose of Gay History Month, stating it was intended for isolated homosexual youth.)

On the rebound, the NEA consulted with its various minority caucuses to refashion its resolutions. By a wide margin the 1996 representative assembly eliminated previous sections on racism, sexism, and sexual orientation education as well as History Month recommendations for all six minority cultures previously listed. A new B-6 on Diversity called for tolerance and celebration of specifically named minority statuses, including sexual orientation, and stressed the importance of "programs and observances which accurately portray and recognize the roles, contributions, cultures, and history of these diverse groups and individuals."

A new "B-7: Racism, Sexism, and Sexual Orientation Discrimination" sought the elimination of discrimination and stereotyping on the basis of various characteristics, including sexual orientation. (See box 6.6.) Further, the NEA encouraged its affiliates to develop and implement trainings on these matters.

*Question 8: Did these revisions signal progress or retreat?*

These steps were taken in reaction to right-wing attacks. The majority of the NEA Gay and Lesbian Caucus voted against the changes. Still, it would be progress

---

### BOX 6.6   THE NEW B-7

[The NEA supports] plans, activities, and programs for staff, students, parents, and the community [to]:

- increase tolerance and sensitivity;
- eliminate discrimination and stereotyping in the curriculum, textbooks [et al.];
- foster the use of nondiscriminatory, nonsexist, and nonstereotypical language, resources, practices, and activities;
- eliminate institutional discrimination;
- integrate an accurate portrayal of the roles and contributions of all groups throughout history and across the curriculum;
- identify how prejudice, stereotyping, and discrimination have limited the roles and contributions of individuals and groups;
- eliminate subtle practices that favor the education of one student on the basis of race, ethnicity, gender, and sexual orientation over another.

if all multicultural constituencies would work together regardless of school demographics to advance the common goals of these resolutions. It would also be progress if the NEA committed resources to the related education and training of its members.

There have been clearly positive developments since 1996. The NEA's president in 1998, Bob Chase, spoke forcefully to his board on the need both to protect gay students from harassment and to "teach tolerance." In 1999, along with nine other professional organizations, including the American Federation of Teachers (AFT), the NEA helped GLSEN prepare and distribute "Just the Facts about Sexual Orientation and Youth: A Primer for Principals, Educators, and School Personnel." Written in support of sexual minority students and sent to over 15,000 school district superintendents, this pamphlet warned educators against "remedies" for homosexuality. "Just the Facts" was a decisive challenge to reparative therapy proponents and provoked their boilerplate responses. In the end, only one of the pamphlet's sponsoring groups, the American Association of School Administrators, backpedaled, noting the booklet would likely be used "based on community values." On October 7, 2000, Bob Chase became the first NEA president to address a GLSEN annual conference. Citing vicious attacks on his participation, he eloquently defended NEA's efforts on behalf of gay and lesbian students. He declared, "This is not a matter of promoting a quote 'unsafe and abhorrent lifestyle,' as one of our members put it, but a matter of protecting one of the most vulnerable populations from unsafe and abhorrent behavior." In that spirit, after the release of the 2001 Human Rights Watch study of antigay harassment, the NEA and AFT joined GLSEN in a letter to U.S. Secretary of Education Rod Paige, urging his department to take an active role in protecting sexual minority students.

Notwithstanding Bob Chase's courage, NEA's internal struggle has not abated. In 2001, resolutions were proposed on Diversity, on Racism, Sexism, and Sexual Orientation Discrimination, on Multicultural Education, and on Student Sexual Orientation. They addressed the needs of glbt students and called for lessons for all students on the contributions, heritage, culture, and history of glbt people. They also proposed to eliminate stereotyping in instructional materials and to teach how prejudice hurts individuals, groups, and society.

These proposals reignited the opposition and became a national story on the eve of the July representative assembly. The groups Focus on the Family and the Traditional Values Coalition organized six hundred "Christian activist" protesters outside the Los Angeles Convention Center. President Chase characterized the picketers' actions as "demagoguery." Nevertheless, the furor, including some rebellion in the ranks, resulted in the withdrawal of the resolutions and the formation of an NEA task force to recommend ways to make schools safer for glbt students. The NEA Gay and Lesbian Caucus backed the move in hopes that the task force report would increase support for the scuttled resolutions.

The ensuing well-documented 2002 report featured recommendations against employment discrimination, for the formation of a standing advisory committee on sexual orientation/gender identification, and for the appointment of an official observer to the NEA board and executive committee. They were approved by the NEA board of directors and submitted to the executive committee. Rather than propose new glbt resolutions to the 2002 Representative Assembly or resubmit those withdrawn the year before, the board agreed to refer to the executive committee a set of recommendations to "help foster an environment of respect and safety" in the schools. Again there was emphasis on the "needs and problems" of sexual minority youth, but this time the NEA president characterized discussion of those topics as a key to understanding and respect—and just a starting point for all NEA members.

## Question 9: What can school reformers learn from the NEA experience?

Several important points are clear in the NEA's encounters over gay issues. First, the struggle within the NEA, which represents 2.6 million school workers, will likely go on for some time, with continuing steps forward and some hedging and outright contravention by conservative locals.

Second, policy resolutions from above can be most effective when they are unequivocal and accompanied by implementation assistance, both strategic and material. Even symbolic resolutions, however, can serve as inspiration to reform at the local level.

Finally, proposing to support gay youth as victims of harassment, violence, and self-destructive behaviors is less controversial than proposing to teach all students to understand and accept homosexuality. *Curriculum* is always a scary word to those who think it means increasing the chances that students will *become* homosexual. This motive for anti-NEA stridency is notable among those who fear the effects of normalization on impressionable young boys.

Substantive reform demands leaders who take a stand, shun divisiveness, and embrace each opportunity for principled action and moral suasion. Bob Chase made an impressive attempt to do so and is a model for his successors and for district leaders nationwide.

## Question 10: Are professional educational research and training organizations doing their part?

The largest and most prominent group of education professors and researchers, the American Educational Research Association (AERA), has an active Gay and Lesbian Special Interest Group (SIG), founded in 1987. AERA annual conferences feature a significant number of research panels and less formal "poster sessions" on sexual minority issues. AERA's several journals have also been inclusive. Gay educational issues are also represented at the Association for Supervision and Curriculum Development's (ASCD) Gay and Lesbian Network.

Still, multiculturalism and diversity are often construed narrowly in professional training and publications. After more than a decade of gay activism in education, erasure of sexual minority youth concerns is too common, even in articles and forums (e.g., on risk and resilience, victimization, suicide, or dropouts), where one would most expect to find them.

## Question 11: What are gay organizations doing?

For years, although youth often served important roles in them, national and state gay and lesbian organizations shied away from school issues. They had other priorities—from hate crimes to civil rights to AIDS. But they also seemed to reflect institutionally the disinclination of gay and lesbian adults to be associated with youth. Already under attack for the work they were doing, they had no appetite for further slander, so they did not push the "youth button." The only group that could safely advocate for glbt youth were their families, yet even PFLAG's Respect All Youth Campaign did not include the schools. Perhaps school bureaucracies were too intimidating for PFLAG at first.

With the possible exception of legal organizations like Lambda Legal Defense and Education Fund (www.lambdalegal.org), National Center for Lesbian Rights (www.nclrights.org), and Gay and Lesbian Advocates and Defenders (www.glad.org), gay teachers and students had the major responsibility for school activism, a challenge they bravely undertook.

In recent years, youth needs and youth leadership are priorities of the National Gay and Lesbian Task Force, among other national and international gay rights groups. School-related work is also more broadly shared, thanks to the persistent example and repeated pleas of teachers and students. PFLAG, for instance, now makes schools a major focus. Its 2001 "From Our House to the School House: A Recipe for Safe Schools" is a multiyear, nationwide initiative. It provides tools to assist activists in starting or expanding their safe schools efforts in coalition with similarly dedicated groups. PFLAG's chapters in over 440 communities can employ the cogent personal appeals and political leverage of families in reaching school authorities, even in some of the nation's smallest schools.

The Safe Schools Coalition in Washington state is one of the most productive change agents in the United States (www.SafeSchoolsCoalition.org and www.SafeSchoolZine.org). In addition to its yearly harassment and violence reports, it has issued the third edition of its *Resource Guide* and a new *Safe School eZine* with resources specifically for youth.

Without question, GLSEN (www.glsen.org) has been a primary catalyst for over a decade, enlisting other gay organizations in the cause and making the nation itself aware that schools have not been safe for glbt youth.

*Question 12: What is GLSEN doing now?*

With its National Headquarters and Northeast Regional Field Office in New York, and other offices in Atlanta, Chicago, San Francisco, and Washington, D.C., GLSEN (Gay, Lesbian, and Straight Education Network) has been involved in many aspects of safe schools work: advocacy, training, curriculum, and collaboration. Its contributions to school reform have included: national school harassment surveys, the Day of Silence campaign, the GLSEN Lunchbox teacher training materials, the *GLSEN Workbook* for school improvement, the membership magazine *Respect*, the *GLSEN Yearbook* by and for student leaders, its media relations, and its national conferences. GLSEN proved its tactical acumen by commissioning the first national poll of parents of school-aged children regarding attitudes toward glbt school matters. The results were both encouraging and politically useful. (See box 6.7.)

GLSEN collaborations like "Just the Facts" (see question 8) and "Stop the Hate" (public service announcements with MTV) prove that it brings important allies on board. Likewise, the 2002 publication with Lambda Legal Defense and Education Fund of *A Guide to Effective Statewide Laws/Policies: Preventing Discrimination against GLBT Students in K-12 Schools*. The collaborative spirit is reflected in GLSEN's chapters as well. For example, GLSEN Fort Lauderdale produced a twenty-minute training video with PFLAG and the Broward County Schools' Office of Diversity and Cultural Outreach.

---

**BOX 6.7    A STELLAR POLL FROM GLSEN**

Of parents polled:

- 86% favor policies to protect GLBT students from harassment and discrimination;
- 80% favor sensitivity training for teachers to help them deal with anti-gay harassment;
- 82% are bothered by gay kids being "abused" at schools;
- 79% are bothered by gay kids being "isolated" by other students;
- 51% want "positive information" about gay people included in middle and high school English and social studies classes.

*Source*: Nationwide telephone survey conducted by Lake Snell Perry & Associates, July 31–August 7, 2001. 1,000 parents of students ages 5–18. Poll included over-samples of African American and Hispanic parents. Margin of error: +/− 3.1 percent.

In 2002, GLSEN announced a new focus on providing direct support at the grassroots. A reassuring sign of organizational priorities, this new tack seems modeled on the emphasis of the NGLTF to think creatively and even globally about policy and best practices but act locally in enabling implementation.

### Question 13: What is the international situation?

The European Union funds the GLEE project (http://glee.oulu.fi) for teacher training, curriculum development, and research initiatives to combat homophobia in schools throughout Europe. Coordinated by the Department of Educational Sciences and Teacher Education at Finland's Oulu University, GLEE has partner institutions in universities in Italy and Portugal, as well as with the Terrence Higgins Trust, the United Kingdom's leading HIV/AIDS charity. GLEE also consults with GLSEN in the United States. GLEE conducts a summer Leadership Training Course and maintains an interactive network (GLEENET).

In the United Kingdom, School's Out! National (www.schools-out.org.uk) provides a support network for glbt educators. It also advocates research and curriculum development and campaigns on glbt issues.

Section 28, banning "the promotion of homosexuality in schools," was a long-term obstacle in England. The 1988 law, championed by Margaret Thatcher's Conservative Party and church figures, including the Archbishop of Canterbury, was not repealed until July 2003, despite opposition from 2000 by Prime Minister Blair and a majority of the House of Commons. As among some conservatives in the United States, supporters of the law seemed more disturbed about the effects of a gay-positive curriculum on straight students than about protecting sexual minority youth from harassment. The chilling effects of Section 28 (e.g., the virtual absence of school-based gay–straight alliances) were demonstrated by a 2000 study in which 80 percent of teachers were unclear about what was permitted and over half believed the law made it difficult to meet the needs of glbt pupils. When it appeared that its prohibitions might be repealed, Blair's education minister tried to placate the Right by insisting that he still wanted teachers to "emphasise the importance of marriage." Gay rights organizations like Schools Out and Stonewall continued to push for abolition, aided by European Union antidiscrimination requirements.

Although government ministers in Scotland pledged to highlight marriage in legally required sex education curricula, the Scottish Parliament repealed Section 28 in June 2000, after seeing the issue dominate its deliberations for a year. Scotland's largest teachers union followed with a commitment to an antihomophobia campaign that includes wide distribution of materials for enhanced health education and social development programs. That does not mean, of course, that debate over the subject has ended. In 2002, for example, conservatives attacked the performance of an antibullying play in Edinburgh schools as "homosexual propaganda." In 2003, moreover, teachers still awaited promised guidelines and materials for dealing with homophobia.

A new code announced in 2003 will allow Irish students legal recourse for harassment and discrimination based on sexual orientation, race, and so forth.

In Canada, where about fifty gsas had been formed by 2001, mainly in the provinces of British Columbia, Manitoba, Ontario, and Nova Scotia, a number of organizations are active. GALE-BC (www.galebc.org), a GLSEN analogue, sent its 250-page book, *Challenging Homophobia in Schools*, to every public school in British Columbia. The B.C. Teachers Federation and twenty-seven affiliates shared the cost. Seventy-five percent of the federation's delegates also backed a resolution calling for gsas in middle and high schools. In 2003, two GALE-BC members took a case to the provincial Human Rights Tribunal asking for gay-affirmative curriculum in every classroom.

In Ontario, the Rainbow Classroom Network (www.dezines.com/rainbow) serves a similar function to that of GALE-BC. The Alberta Teachers' Association's Diversity, Equity and Human Rights GLBT website (www.teachers.ab.ca/diversity/Sexual_Orientation/Index.htm), and the Gay, Lesbian, Bisexual, Two-Spirited Youth Outreach Project (www.glbtalberta.com), sponsored by PFLAG and Planned Parenthood, provide many resources in Alberta. And in Ottawa the Rainbow Youth Coalition has supported formation of glbt high school youth groups.

Despite raucous protests from some Muslims, the Toronto District School Board passed significant recommendations to complement its inclusive equity policy. (See box 6.8.) The Toronto Coalition for Lesbian, Gay and Bisexual Youth (www.tcglbty.com) works to create both school and community services for glbt youth.

### BOX 6.8   TORONTO'S POLICY (EXCERPTS)

- Determining whether bias against gays, women, the disabled or the poor are present in learning materials;
- Providing money for workshops to train staff to become "agents of change" by challenging homophobia or stereotypes against gender, people with disabilities or a particular socioeconomic class;
- Ensuring the classrooms and school libraries accurately reflect the range of Canada's lesbian and gay communities, disabled and socioeconomic classes;
- Supporting student leadership programs in antihomophobia education;
- Developing academic supports for underachieving lesbian and gay students.

Louise Brown, "School Board Talks Gay Rights," *Toronto Star*, December 8, 1999.

A few years ago homophobia in Australian schools was described as "endemic, extensive and savage." PFLAG, university researchers, gay activists, and teachers have had the most success changing that dire situation in Tasmania and Queensland. The former is the only state where antihomophobia education is mandatory. A law barring school promotion or encouragement of homosexuality inhibits Western Australian teachers even from interrupting name-calling. Officials in New South Wales, where only antiracism lessons are required, employ the familiar dodge that they oppose all forms of school violence. Consequently, Outlink (http://outlink.trump.net.au/) has been devised to support isolated rural sexual minority youth and provide an antihomophobia kit for teachers.

In New Zealand, research on anti-glbt violence and harassment by New Zealand's academic institutions like the Otago University's Children's Issues Center has been invaluable in supporting the need for glbt youth programs. One of these, Rainbow Youth Inc. (PO Box 5426, Wellesly St., Auckland), presents school workshops for teachers, counselors, and health professionals.

The new international *Journal of Gay & Lesbian Issues in Education* (www.jtsears.com/jglie.htm) publishes research studies, scholarly essays, and practitioner articles on educational policy, professional practice, curriculum development, and pedagogy. It presents scholarly investigation and portraiture from every continent in accessible language.

*Question 14: What are the major categories of resistance to school reforms?*

Opposition predictably targets the "promotion of homosexuality" and its signposts: antiharassment policies, gsas, faculty trainings, and student activities/support. Oregon, Vermont, California, and Virginia have experienced attempts to adopt "nonpromotion" laws like Britain's Section 28 and worse. (South Carolina statutorily prohibits mention of homosexuality outside the context of AIDS.)

Conservative religious and political organizations have taken aim at the panoply of antihomophobia initiatives. (See box 6.9.) Concerned Women for America, Focus on the Family, The Family Research Council, and others weigh in on every gay-related school issue, excoriating GLSEN and other activists at every opportunity. As part of its "know the enemy" tactic the Family Research Council published "Top 10 Strategies Used by Homosexual Activists in Schools" (FRC Insight paper by Peter LaBarbera, 11/23/99, IS99F4HS).

In some localities, sexual minority youth in schools have been purposely cut off from any positive information, even lists of community resources. School administrators in Iowa went so far as to delay the Creston High School Band's May 2002 trip to Orlando Disney World to prevent any student's even catching sight of homosexuals during the theme park's annual "Gay Days." One glbt support group, Time Out Youth in Charlotte, North Carolina, leased five public billboards in 2001 to break through the wall of school censorship.

## BOX 6.9  RIGHT-WING BLUNDERBUSS

[Focus on the Family] publishes a how-to book telling members how to get their message out.... The book supplies outraged form letters as well as practical advice on tracking down offensive material in textbooks, AIDS and sex education curriculums, and school libraries. (The group also wisely counsels parents against quoting scripture or using clichés like "God created Adam and Eve, not Adam and Steve" in school board meetings.)

Sharon Lerner, "Christian Conservatives Take Their Antigay Campaign to the Schools," *Village Voice*, May 2, 2001.

Preventative Actions and Novel Strategies

1. FIND OUT ABOUT FACULTY TRAINING.
   ...(Use the terms gay-oriented or sexual orientation-related, since the educators may deny that such programs promote or affirm homosexuality.)...Has the school ever worked with [GLSEN or PFLAG] or sent teachers to their seminars?
2. OPT OUT.
   ...ask that your child be "opted out" of [pro-homosexuality lessons]....
3. PROTEST PREEMPTIVELY....
4. DEMAND FAIRNESS.
   ...demand that both sides of the homosexuality issue be presented....
5. TEACH STUDENTS HOW TO RESPOND TO IN-SCHOOL "GAY" ACTIVISM.
   ...work with and educate a group of student-leaders who can correctly apply Christian principles on this issue. They may be far more effective than you in reaching their peers with the truth about homosexuality, and at the very least, they can demand that school administrators not subject students to just one side of this controversial issue.

From Peter LaBarbera, "How to Protect Your Children from Pro-Homosexuality Propaganda in Schools," *Family Research Council Web* (www.frc.org/get/if99j1.cfm) (June 2002).

Resistance to school reforms occurs in a broad spectrum of schools. It would be wrong to assume, for example, that highly educated, wealthy, or even liberal parents and administrators are immune to homophobia. Genteel people are usually just more covert in expressing their bigotry—but not always. For example, in 2002, a Tennessee woman removed her daughter from Oldfields, an elite private school for girls in Maryland, and sued, claiming that the school "has a permissive homosexual agenda, which is encouraged by a number of the faculty members." Her allegations included hand-holding and sexual activity between female students, as well as health class instruction on lesbian safe sex. The school's feeble defense—that sexual orientation is a "private matter"—emanated perhaps from the common aversion of single-sex institutions to developing a gay reputation.

## Question 15: What kinds of opposition have antiharassment policies faced?

Resistance to harassment policies comes from politicians and parents, churches, conservative organizations, and sometimes from students in the classroom. (See box 6.10.) Having a lesbian sister did not stop Speaker of the House Newt Gingrich from denouncing gay and lesbian curricula as "clearly propaganda and clearly recruitment" in 1995. When the Winston-Salem, North Carolina, Board of Education reaffirmed its decision not to extend its antidiscrimination policy to cover gay students, accolades came from adults and students alike. One might have thought that the end of the world had been averted. (See box 6.11.)

Parents may oppose antiharassment policies and lessons as a violation of their parental rights. They do not want their children exposed to explicit tolerance for glbt people. Some teachers also want an exemption. To have to acknowledge the mere presence of sexual minorities in the school community and the world can be taken as an affront to their moral and religious sensibilities, if not their persons. (See box 6.12; see also question 22.) Assuming the role of offended citizens resisting a sinister "gay agenda" is a clever and often politically effective ploy.

It is also cunning to rue the passing of the good old schooldays when race and sexuality were not mentioned and "everybody got along." But this regret is only another version of blaming the victim—"It's only since you minorities began calling attention to your differences, that we've had such controversy." Their amnesiac argument begs the question, "On whose pain was that alleged prior harmony built?"

## Question 16: What kinds of opposition have gsas faced?

In addition to administrative obstacles and school hostility (see chapter 5), gsas have been targeted since they began to multiply in the mid-1990s. An infamous battle occurred in Salt Lake City, where the courts ruled that, pursuant to the

## BOX 6.10  DON'T GIVE THEM AN INCH

[E]xisting policy already makes any kind of assault or threats of violence against any student a punishable offense. Who the student is makes no difference. . . . At the core, this is an issue of promotion of a lifestyle, not protection.

Gary Cass and Priscilla Schreiber (members of the Grossmont Union High School District Board of Trustees), "Commentary: District Will Not Be Hijacked by Homosexual Activists," *San Diego Union-Tribune*, March 28, 2002.

Gay students lobbying for discrimination protection in Florida schools got a jolting civics lesson Monday from a lawmaker who welcomed them into his office only to declare: "God . . . is going to destroy you. . . . You are going to cause the downfall of this country that was built on Christian principles."

Ann-Marie Manchise, "Senator's Antigay Lecture Shocks Students," *Tampa Tribune*, April 10, 2001.

For years, Keith Uselton has been harassed almost daily at school for being gay, he said. A recent confrontation seemed sadly familiar—until a teacher stepped in. "The teacher told the guy, 'If you don't stop, I'm going to write you up,'" said Uselton. . . . "It was amazing. . . . But then there was another guy in the back of class who said, 'Why are you writing him up? Why not write the [gay slur] up?'"

Paula Caballero, "Struggling in School," *Fort Worth Star-Telegram*, March 24, 2002.

1984 federal Equal Access Act, schools could not discriminate among noncurricular clubs. Then, rather than allow the gsa to meet, the school board abolished all noncurricular clubs, including racial awareness clubs, pep clubs, Young Republicans and Democrats, and Students Against Drunk Driving. Trying to finish off the gsas, Utah then banned student clubs that "promote bigotry, encourage criminal behavior or involve human sexuality."

The Utah Board of Education allowed gsas so long as they were student-directed and supervised or monitored by a school employee and did not advocate sexual activity outside of marriage or engage in mental health counseling. It also permitted local boards to change "disruptive" group names and to forbid both advocacy of illegal sexual activities and presentations that violate sex education and privacy laws. These actions led to a confusing discriminatory hodgepodge. Some

## BOX 6.11    PILING ON

[A] member of Berean Baptist, told board members that if they changed the policy they could be following in the footsteps of such places as San Francisco that are "being overtaken by homosexuals." . . . [A] senior at West Forsyth, said that any harassment of homosexual students at school has "been blown out of proportion." [Another senior] said that many students get teased. "If you're part of a minority, you're going to get picked on," he said. "That's just the way it is."

Dawn Ziegenbalg, "Christian Group Says Gay Policy Unneeded," *Winston-Salem Journal*, March 13, 2002.

gsas were banned outright. Five, forbidden to put up posters and barred from the yearbook, met as a private organization in rented high school space. And some other noncurricular clubs went on meeting as before.

Salt Lake students attempted to form a curricular club, PRISM (People Respecting Important Social Movements) to discuss gay perspectives on sociology, U.S. history, government, and politics. After an assistant superintendent ruled

## BOX 6.12    WHO'S THE VICTIM?

Four Tennyson High teachers want to be excused from a gay sensitivity training session, saying they object to it for religious reasons. . . . According to a statement . . . the teachers should not attend the . . . training because of a federal law protecting religious employees.

Elizabeth Schainbaum, "Some Say 'No' to Gay Sensitivity Class," *Hayward Daily Review*, March 30, 2002.

Paul Scott's complaint, filed last month, alleges discrimination and intolerance of him and his daughter by "not addressing a very clear right of privacy violation that requires my child to share restrooms, dressing rooms and showering facilities with those who by their own, and societies [sic] definition, are attracted to the same gender. . . ."

Jill Spielvogel, "District Denies Discrimination Complaint by Student's Dad," *San Diego Union-Tribune*, March 28, 2002.

PRISM would not be academic because it would be "viewpoint exclusive," the students sued, claiming violation of free speech. In 2000, a U.S. District Court judge issued a temporary injunction against the district. She observed there was no rule that curricular clubs address every viewpoint and, if there was an implicit one, it was not being applied equitably since, for example, the Polynesian Club was not banned because it focused only on Polynesian culture. (One had to wish her ruling had authority in the case of a Niskayuna, New York, school board member who refused to authorize a gsa because she saw its antidiscrimination mission as "inherently political.") The court's last word on the matter was that during the alleged all-club ban, the Salt Lake City school district had denied the gsa equal access to school facilities, while permitting other noncurricular clubs to meet.

In the late summer of 2000, the Salt Lake School Board overturned the 1996 ban. Noncurricular clubs, including the gsa and PRISM Club, were designated as "student clubs." They would have school meeting space during noninstructional time and be student-initiated but not school-sponsored. They would be monitored by a nonparticipant and membership would require parental permission. On the other hand, curriculum-related "school clubs" would be directed by a teacher and would receive school financial support and priority in booking facilities. They could not advocate any political, theological, ideological, or partisan view on curriculum subjects. No club could defy state regulations (i.e., advocate sex outside marriage) and all club names would be subject to administrative approval.

GSAs in California's Orange Unified School District were faced with both outright bans, distinctions between official clubs and "equal-access groups," and, as in the Saddleback Valley Unified School District, vague definitions of *curricular* and *noncurricular*. Only court action in 2000 forced a lifting of the ban on the El Modena High School gsa. Despite the judge's finding that gsas "involve the protection of life itself," new rules were adopted blocking club discussion of sexual activity and allowing parents to keep their child out of any school group.

Utah and Orange Unified are indicative of many schools' method of dealing with gsas through begrudging compliance with the Equal Access Law of 1984, ironically proposed to allow school Bible clubs to meet. Administrators in numbers of schools agree to gsa formation; then they hobble them by such means as requiring after-hours meetings and restricting and monitoring their activities and speech.

Many school officials feel the additional need to distance themselves from the gsa. On the pretext of safety, some advise against gsa formation or warn them to stay underground. It's no wonder that gsa members feel as if the schools are ashamed of them. But, more likely, administrators are just trying to protect *themselves* from rampant hostility. (See box 6.13.) Faced with an American Civil Liberties Union suit, Texas's Klein Independent School District officials

**BOX 6.13   A COLD, LONG DISTANCE FROM
THE GSA MENACE**

The [GSA] will not be sponsored by the school.... "We are not providing them any services," said [the principal]. "All they will get is space after school." Unlike most other clubs ...the GSA's meetings will not be
announced over the school intercom and the group's meetings cannot
take place during school hours. The chapter will not have a faculty adviser.... [The superintendent said,] "We're not really fired up in support of
gays and lesbians. We're not trying to endorse this group or oppose them.
We are following the law."

Michael Biesecker, "Taking a Stand," *Winston-Salem Journal*, August 25, 2000.

"Our children's future is in jeopardy if you allow gay clubs in schools," said
[a] parent.... "We cannot allow this evil to triumph." Some parents, who
believe values should be taught at home, said approving the club would
create a "mass exodus" of students from Clovis High.

Jennifer Fitzenberger, "Clovis Unified Board OKs Students' Gay-Straight Club,"
*Fresno Bee*, February 14, 2002.

made clear they would allow a gsa to form in 2003 as "a matter of law," despite their own objections and the opinion of the community. And when a
U.S. district court judge ruled in 2003 that a Boyd County, Kentucky, noncurricular gsa club could not be banned on the grounds of "school disruption," he
wryly noted that the group's opponents were solely responsible for the turmoil.
In 2003, public campaigns against gsas were waged in such locales as University City, Missouri, Christiansburg, Virginia, and both Gull Lake and Rockford,
Michigan.

*Question 17: What kinds of opposition have faculty trainings faced?*

Overt attacks on pre-service and in-service teacher education are less common
than those directed against student education and glbt student support, but they
do occur. Parents in Anoka, Minnesota, tried to scuttle a faculty training in 2002,
warning that teachers would be persuaded to "push" healthy students struggling
with sexuality into a "gay lifestyle." Teachers themselves have raised similar objections. (See box 6.14.)

## BOX 6.14   DERAILING THE TRAININGS

Four high school teachers are renewing charges that Portland schools promote homosexuality through library books and teacher workshops, and
vow to support a ballot measure to stop it. The ... teachers say the district
has failed to respond to complaints they raised last year that the district's
Committee on Sexual Diversity promotes homosexuality.

Bill Graves, "Teachers Renew Objection to Sexual Diversity Committee," *The
Oregonian*, September 8, 2000.

Massachusetts' progressive preservice requirements (see chapter 5, question 35)
were dealt a severe blow in 2000. A conservative majority on the state board of education weakened the hitherto gay-inclusive teacher certification standards under
the direction of a new deputy commissioner, the author of a book called *Losing Our
Language: How Multicultural Classroom Instruction Is Undermining Our Children's
Ability to Read, Write, and Reason*. The revised equity provisions eliminated all
multiculturally specific criteria, substituting language that stresses academic rigor
and collective citizenship. Under the new requirements, the certifiable teacher
merely "encourages all students to believe that effort is a key to high achievement and works to promote high achievement in all students ... [and] helps all
students to understand American civic culture, its underlying ideals, founding political principles and political institutions and to see themselves as members of a
local, state, and national civic community."

Despite such high-profile reversals, negativity in the teacher-training arena is
chiefly hidden, localized, and even personal. In an era of high stakes standardized
testing in "the basics," homophobia and glbt student needs are at best a low staff
development priority. In the rare event that gay-related workshops are approved
and funded, few systemic incentives encourage participation in them. They are
almost never mandatory. Teachers who seek out information may be compelled to
attend workshops after hours, off site, and at their own expense. Moreover, some
who organize and attend them become objects of subtle teasing or ugly suspicion
and derision.

Even when opponents fail to prevent teacher trainings, they don't necessarily abandon the field. The American Family Association's video, *Suffer the Children: Answering the Homosexual Agenda in Public Schools*, for instance, takes aim at
the video, *It's Elementary*, which has had remarkable success convincing educators to teach young students why antigay name-calling and stereotyping are hurtful and wrong. *Suffer the Children* protests that films like *It's Elementary* are part
of a campaign to trick students, through spin and mind control, into accepting

family-wrecking homosexuality. It warns teachers that the self-destructive behavior of glbt youth is the result of their unnatural pernicious lifestyle—not prejudice and harassment.

### Question 18: What is the opposition to gay-related activities for all students?

These activities are at the core of the charge that schools are "promoting" homosexuality. Student activities lie within the curriculum domain. Although some critics say they would support putting homosexuality in school lessons alongside drug addiction, alcoholism, and other pathologies, they condemn any affirmative curriculum as proselytizing. Positive portrayals of glbt life are the censors' red flag because they threaten the sociosexual order from which conservatives benefit and which they are loath to see examined critically in schools.

Since in-depth classroom instruction on homosexuality is not yet common, opponents more often draw battle lines around preserving emblematic cultural expressions like proms, from which openly glbt couples are routinely (and illegally) excluded, and yearbooks. (See box 6.15.) They also target consciousness-raising activities like the Day of Silence. A high school teacher in Collier County, Florida, actually ordered a girl to remove her rainbow-colored shoelaces—an allegedly too flagrant symbol of gay pride—in 2001. (The sophomore responded by organizing the county's first gsa, approved grudgingly the next year by administrators on advice of counsel.) In 2002, the Rich Township, Illinois, superintendent had "safety-zone" rainbow triangles removed from classrooms after some parents complained the schools were "promoting one side against the other."

Critics also object to modest curricular content in displays (see box 6.16) and one-time informational events like Diversity Days. For example, after a high school Day of Dialogue in 2000, parents in Santa Rosa, California, demanded that the school board prohibit schools from addressing homosexuality. Despite the fact that the event offered forty optional discussions on topics that ranged from being gay to understanding a Christian worldview, the opponents rallied against the schools' "legitimizing the homosexual lifestyle." The school board president sought a legal opinion about whether the state parent notification law had been followed and whether there had been a "balance of viewpoints expressed by the speakers." Would opponents have been satisfied to hear that the Taliban had participated in both the homosexuality and the Christian worldview sessions?

At about the same time, in Naperville, Illinois, two high school gsa members were featured speakers at three 25-minute freshmen "Respect" assemblies. Their opinions on the "benefits" of being gay—clearly a response to negative characterizations—were construed as raw recruitment by some furious students and parents. Apparently seeing no justification for their advocacy, the principal sent an apology to all parents.

## BOX 6.15   NO POSING, KISSING, OR LOVING

[W]hen it came time to sit for her ... senior yearbook photos at Bryn-Alan Studios, Nikki and her mother decided the best attire for her would be a black suit jacket, white dress shirt and tie. But her wardrobe choice didn't jive with the school. They were told only male students could wear shirts and ties. ... [Her lawyer wrote,] "The shirt and tie ... is the attire that is consistent with Nikki's gender identity and expression."

Melanie Ave, "No Drape, No Photo, Leaves Teen Wondering," *St. Petersburg* [Fla.] *Times*, January 25, 2002.

[The protest was] organized as a reaction against keeping a photo showing two bisexual girls kissing out of the yearbook. ... The yearbook adviser ... said she wouldn't run the photo unless the staff of the yearbook got permission from the parents of the two girls. ... [P]hotos of male-female kisses were allowed to run without parental approval.

Monte Whaley, "Protesters Lock Lips at Kiss-In," *Denver Post*, May 24, 2001.

Two girls will be listed as "class sweethearts" in their high school year-book after a dispute over whether same-sex couples were eligible for the honor. [They] overwhelmingly led other couples when the yearbook staff conducted its annual "senior superlatives" survey. ... [The principal had] declared the vote invalid because the ballot asked students to choose one male and one female.

J. M. Hirsch, "Dover Lesbian Couple Allowed to Remain as 'Class Sweet-hearts,'" *Associated Press*, December 4, 2001.

This principal's retreat is not uncommon. In 2001, a discussion of homosex-uality, one of a series of teacher-led, twenty-minute, tolerance conversations in the wake of September 11, created a stir at a Connecticut high school. Some par-ents demanded the administrator be censured. Like-minded parents in Oregon were outraged that gay speakers had taken part in a 2002 high school diversity week. The principals at both schools groveled in apologetic equivocation. (See box 6.17.) They set the standard for a Santa Barbara junior high principal's 2002 letter, regretting not informing parents that a lesbian would be included in her school's Diversity Day, along with a Holocaust survivor, disabled man, and so on.

In California in 1998, Karl Debro, an eighteen-year veteran teacher who cofounded the San Leandro High School GSA, was reprimanded for making

## BOX 6.16   INFORMATION VERSUS TEACHING?

The . . . school district has been ordered to apologize to two gay teachers who were forced to tear down gay history month displays at West Middle School and Salem High School. . . . [The arbitrator ruled that the teachers] "were not teaching anything by putting up the displays; they were merely presenting information which they hoped would improve the climate of the school by enhancing understanding and acceptance of gays and lesbians . . . their purpose . . . was to help create a safe, accepting, affirming learning environment for all students. . . ."

Tony Bruscato, "Ruling Favors Gay Display," *Plymouth Observer*, December 7, 2001.

pro-gay remarks in his classroom. The heterosexual African American said he was responding to student concerns about antigay initiatives in the community and rampant racism and homophobia in the school. Administrators held that their "Controversial Issues Policy" required Debro get the principal's permission before addressing such matters. A parent suit that Debro was indoctrinating their son in

## BOX 6.17   TEPID SUPPORT

[The principal] said the discussion was about tolerance, not gay pride. Discussions did not dissect what constitutes a lesbian or gay person, nor whether or not they should be proud, he said. One of the primary goals was to talk about hurtful phrases like "soccer fairy" and "faggot" that students sometimes use.

Brynn Mandel, "Gay Tolerance Discussions at School Supported, Criticized," *Waterbury* [Conn.] *Republican-American*, October 26, 2001.

"We didn't set an appropriate staging for this issue to be addressed in a right way," [the principal] said. . . . "I'm not saying this shouldn't be covered, but it does not represent our curriculum. This is kind of new stuff that public schools shouldn't jump to. The issue is so political and reaches into the religious value systems of so many families."

Tracy Jan, "Centennial Apologizes for Allowing Gay Speakers," *The Oregonian*, February 18, 2002.

his "gay agenda" was thrown out of court, but the ramifications of the teacher's prior punishment had already taken hold and lasted for years. Debro had filed a civil rights suit on his own behalf and was awarded $500,000 in 2002. Proof of the district's malice meant that its insurance policy did not apply. The possibility of the superintendent's personal liability could serve as a warning to other censorious administrators.

The Harborfields School District in New York cancelled an entire three-day antibias program for fifth-graders in 2002, after members of a local Baptist church disrupted a PTA meeting to protest one planned segment on bullying of gay students. The state attorney general's antibullying program, attacked as pro-gay and anti-Christian, was nixed in 2002 by the West Virginia Board of Education. And a 2002 showing of the Anti-Defamation League's film, *Teen Files: The Truth about Hate*, to the students at Granite Hills High School in California was permitted only after its segment on antigay discrimination had been edited out.

In 2001, in Torrance, California, where the health curriculum includes no gay content, but where teachers are trained to answer questions about homosexuality, PUSHES (Parents United to Stop Homosexual Education in Our Schools) ran a full-page newspaper ad attacking "pro-homosexual activists and propaganda on our school campuses." The cause of their concern: PFLAG speakers on an optional panel among a dozen seminars at a high school Human Relations Convention—a one-day, voluntary, nonschoolday event requiring parental permission to attend. A year later, the Torrance school board banned a convention presentation by GLIDE (Gays and Lesbians Initiating Dialogue for Equality), a respected nonprofit that makes hundreds of school, government, and church presentations a year.

An undercover right-wing operative secretly recorded an HIV prevention session at GLSEN Boston's Teach Out 2000 conference. The voluntary workshop was one of a handful specifically directed to teenagers at the weekend event. Two acclaimed youth educators from the Department of Education's HIV/AIDS Program responded explicitly to anonymous written questions from students. These DOE employees led the workshop on their own time and did not represent the department. Although the conference program book included greetings from the commissioner of education, the state had not sponsored the conference.

After edited copies of the workshop tape were disseminated, every right-wing figure in the country excoriated GLSEN and Massachusetts. Demagogic presidential candidate Alan Keyes, imported to a state house rally for abolition of the Safe Schools program, warned the crowd about homosexuals' spreading a "plague" to their children. Speakers demanded that the governor disband his Commission on Gay and Lesbian Youth and fire the education commissioner.

Safe Schools supporters rallied. A state senator came out as a lesbian in a Boston *Globe* op-ed piece. Although neither the legislature, nor the governor, nor the commissioner abandoned Safe Schools, the protests did make them all flinch. The two HIV educators were forced from their jobs, on the grounds that their presentation was "prurient." Despite years of successful partnership, the state DOE did not renew its contract with GLSEN Boston for school workshops and trainings. Henceforth, only DOE employees would conduct them and then under new restrictions: they were to "confine their work to train and educate adults" and the Safe Schools Program would limit its concerns to safety and suicide, not sexuality.

As the GLSEN fallout spread, Outright Vermont lost its $12,000 state DOE contract for antiharassment workshops, despite assurances that it had never brought safe sex education materials from its HIV prevention work into a single school. In October 2001, amid death threats and bomb searches, the Broward County, Florida, school board refused to renew a partnership with GLSEN-Miami for teacher, counselor, and student trainings. The opponents feared students would be exposed to sexual language, but they did not change their position even after student involvement was dropped from the proposal. They were wary of GLSEN, they said, especially after a local talk show host showed them GLSEN Connecticut student materials with explicit sexual language. Eventually, a split board approved the teacher-only agreement, with the exception that gay and lesbian students might make presentations to adults. Seven months later no trainings were planned.

A dismaying consequence of the GLSEN Boston controversy was GLSEN national's declaration that its mission was safety, not sex education, and GLSEN Boston's decision to exclude sexual content from future conferences. This policy barred HIV/AIDS presentations by organizations, many with government funding, whose prevention and treatment work is specifically targeted to youth. It also prevented Planned Parenthood from distributing sex education materials at its usual information table, effectively weakening its participation.

*Question 19: What's wrong with state and school officials requiring employees and contractors who conduct school workshops to avoid sex education?*

It may make political sense to some, since few legislators publicly support funding of explicit sex education for anyone. Few politicians placed themselves between the presidential firing squad and Surgeon General Jocelyn Elders when she suggested that students be taught about masturbation as a healthy form of sexual expression.

However, to answer the accusation that glbt school reform is only about sex, we do not have to retreat from the conviction that part of our mission must be sex education. Safety, suicide prevention, and risk reduction cannot be severed from issues of sexual identity, self-esteem, promiscuity, and safe sex. To pretend otherwise is to concede the high ground to the hysterical right.

It is morally indefensible to purge gsas, health classes, and glbt youth conferences of lifesaving sexual explicitness because of puritan opposition. At the very least, school-based advocates should challenge medical and public health professionals, the masters of "best practices" in health, to take responsibility for the sex education component of our work. When GLSEN Boston was under attack, even the Department of Public Health was silent. In the shadow of growing sexual transmission of HIV among young people, retreat is unconscionable.

A 2002 Lambda Legal toolkit—"Tell Me the (Whole) Truth: School Supplies to Get Real Sex Education"—offers strategies to counter the effects of "abstinence-only" programs on glbt youth. Such resources should be welcome.

## Question 20: What kinds of opposition has an inclusive academic curriculum faced?

Antipathy toward curriculum is ubiquitous. In 1999, Georgia legislators only narrowly defeated a mandate that "cultural diversity" in the statewide school character curriculum "shall mean ethnic and regional differences but shall not include sexual orientation." Also in the south, the Memphis office of Facing History and Ourselves has faced resistance to the gay content in its materials. In order to pass a state gay rights law in 2000, Maine lawmakers had to stipulate that schools do not have to include homosexuality in their curricula. Iowa's governor ordered his department of education to drop a proposed 2001 requirement that schools provide diverse programming and an inclusive environment because it mentioned information about "alternative lifestyles."

After the passage of Assembly Bill 537 the San Ramon Valley, California, school board was compelled to state repeatedly that the district has no plans to incorporate homosexuality into its curriculum. In conservative Novato, school board member Bill King, defending the use of the gay-inclusive video, That's a Family, was similarly adamant that he was not advocating teaching "about homosexuality." In overstatement or naïveté, he added that Novato schools are not supported in teaching about heterosexuality either.

Changes in Massachusetts' curricular policy are a clear setback, yet another reminder that progress, even in liberal states, must be carefully guarded. In 1993, the State Board of Education amended its equal-educational-opportunity provisions to include sexual orientation, but it took until 2000 for the board to revise the regulations that are part of the law's implementation phase. Before the addition of sexual orientation, the regulations had mandated that school curricula reflect the diversity of the student body and that, in the aggregate, new books and materials should depict minorities and women "in a broad variety of positive roles." Progressive activists hoped the state would maintain the same curricular standards in 2000.

Instead, the board replaced them with the requirement that curricula should "encourage respect for the human and civil rights of all individuals regardless of race, color, sex, religion, national origin or sexual orientation." Such regulations could be satisfied with the adoption of a generic "respect everyone" curriculum, lacking any reference to specific minority experiences.

In an even more egregious change, the board called on teachers to "review all instructional and educational materials for simplistic and demeaning generalizations, lacking intellectual merit, on the basis of race, color, sex, religion, national origin or sexual orientation." What simplistic and demeaning generalizations have intellectual merit? Furthermore, in the event that such stereotypes are found in classroom materials, the regulations specify that "appropriate activities, discussions and/or supplementary materials shall be used to provide balance and context for any such stereotypes." Why would the remedy be found in context and balance rather than in reasoned refutation? (The board had rejected a prior draft, mandating curricula to "counteract ... demeaning generalizations.") As for curricula that avoid stereotypes by omitting stigmatized minority groups entirely, the new regulations say nothing. Indeed they implicitly encourage erasure by not requiring inclusion as the old ones had done.

The board's leaders did not conceal their motive for hobbling the curriculum requirements, namely in obeisance to cultural conservatives. (See box 6.18.) For nearly thirty years, while the regulations applied to race, gender, religion, and national origin, *but not to sexual orientation*, the board made no concessions toward validating home-taught bigotry. Now, in their backsliding, they have undermined not only glbt students and families but reversed the curricular representation of other minority groups.

Censorship wars at the local level are ongoing. (See appendix J.) Even those objections that appear reasonable at a glance are still essentially back-to-basics arguments that concede no connection between lessening bigotry and curricular content. When school boards attempt to compromise, the result can be ethically

---

### BOX 6.18  LITTLE VISION, LESS COURAGE

"The Board has a responsibility to balance the rights of all students. The language we approved does that. . . . The language is a reasonable accommodation among the demands of competing groups. We have a responsibility to make sure that homosexual students and all students go to school and are not harassed." [She] also said that the Board has a responsibility to parents not to undermine the "traditional rules" that they teach their children at home.

Massachusetts Board of Education vice-chair Roberta Schaefer, in Laura Kiritsy, "Anger Mounts over Ed. Board's Actions on Gay Issues," *Bay Windows* [Mass.], May 6, 1999.

obtuse. A case in point: Fairfax County, Virginia's progressive Family Life curriculum was adopted in 1995 only after the school board agreed to add the disclaimer, "Homosexual behavior is highly controversial in our society with some people viewing it as normal and others viewing it as contrary to normal." Would the same kind of language have been adopted to please opponents of racial intermarriage?

The mere placing of gay-related books in school libraries brings out the censors. Bette Greene's *The Drowning of Stephan Jones*, based on the actual hate-crime murder of a gay teen in Maine, was pulled from eight libraries in South Carolina middle and high schools in 2002. A parent had complained of its alleged vulgarities, although one is hard-pressed to find anything obscene in the book other than the hatred of Stephan's attackers, who forced him over a bridge railing. Irate parents have tried to remove Greene's book and others, like the series *Lives of Notable Gay Men and Lesbians*, and the autobiographical collection *Two Teenagers in Twenty*, from school libraries from Portland to Eau Claire to Anaheim.

## Question 21: What do the courts have to say about school censorship?

Most courts are inclined to favor parental or civic authority over teachers' rights of expression or students' freedom to learn, particularly when possible school disruption, subversion, or sexually offensive speech can be cited. Still, in one important 1996 AIDS education case, the Supreme Court has let stand crucial language of a lower court decision. "Although the program may offend the religious sensibilities of the plaintiffs, mere exposure at public schools to offensive programs does not amount to a violation of free exercise. . . . Parents have no right to tailor public school programs to meet their individual religious or moral preferences."

Other legal precedents are an ambiguous hodgepodge. The courts have held that schools can make sex education a graduation requirement, but they have also said that states can forbid it. School boards and administrators appear to have an absolute right to monitor and censor what students read or are otherwise exposed to in schools. The standard of most courts on library books and curricula is that both may be governed by the social, political, and moral views of the school board. A teacher may be fired for using an unapproved book, regardless of its merit or suitability.

At the same time, the U.S. Supreme Court has made clear that although particular books may be banned for justifiable cause, school officials cannot ban them merely for the thoughts contained in them. Thus, the removal of the gay-positive novel *Annie on My Mind* from school libraries in a Kansas town was overruled on the grounds that local school boards cannot eliminate books just because they disagree with their ideas. But, in a startling 1998 reversal of a lower court decision, a circuit court upheld a parent's suit against a North Carolina teacher for choosing that her students perform the play *Independence*, a drama that includes a lesbian daughter and an unmarried mother.

## Question 22: Isn't it appropriate for parents to have a say in curriculum?

Parent participation on curriculum committees is acceptable. Parents should be invited to take part in many aspects of school life: discipline, policy making, hiring, food services, and so on. But no parent has the right to veto curricular decisions by education professionals and school boards or to prevent children from participating in approved curricular activities.

Besides lobbying for censorship, the most popular parent-involvement strategy for sabotaging gay curricula is "parent notification." Proposals are often identically worded from one community to another, evidence of a coordinated campaign. Parents want to be informed in advance of any lessons involving sexuality, sexual or physical abuse, alcohol or drug use, marriage, divorce, family life, death, grief, self-esteem, and emotional health. They require that no such content be taught without advance permission from parents of all students in the class. This burdensome "opt-in" policy would discourage teachers from presenting any potentially controversial subject matter.

Failing the adoption of an "opt-in" requirement, opponents often substitute an "opt-out" plan that would give them the right to pull their children out of class during objectionable instruction. Although there is evidence that few parents in liberal communities opt out of classes on homosexuality (4 percent) and even fewer opt out of general sex education (2 percent), parent notification squabbles are ubiquitous. (See box 6.19.) Some administrators and parents have used parent notification as a wedge to prevent gsa formation or to intimidate potential members.

It is hard for legislators to vote against parents' rights language, especially when it calls for something as harmless or even desirable as parents' receiving information about their children's school activities and lessons. Even in progressive states, the struggle to defeat such mandates appears futile. Massachusetts held the line against a dangerously broad opt-in bill only through passage of a pared down opt-out bill, giving both the general public and parents the right to preview curricula and remove their children from "courses, course units, assemblies, and other instructional activities that focus on human sexuality or sex education." California has an opt-in requirement for presentations by outside speakers on STDs, AIDS, human sexuality, or family life and an opt-out provision for any instruction in health, family life education, and sex education that conflicts with a family's religious beliefs or moral convictions. Instruction on human sexuality in Michigan must be offered as an elective, with parental notice of content, opportunity for review of materials, and the right to opt out.

Although public officials and school leaders under conservative siege may see opt-out as a lifeline, they should consider where such a course could ultimately

## BOX 6.19   OPTING FOR INTOLERANCE

- Over one thousand young people, approximately 30 percent of Connecticut's Ledyard High School's student body, stayed home to avoid a Diversity Day of some fifty different workshops. Parents actually complained that notices sent them via their children and placed in the newspaper were insufficient notification.
- Students at Modesto (Calif.) High School were allowed to sit in a study hall and work on an alternative assignment if their parents chose for them to opt out of the school's "Day of Respect."
- Ithaca (New York) High School parents who opted their children out of seeing the play *Josh Keenan Comes Out to the World* were furious that the students' alternative assignment included an antihomophobia lesson from Teaching Tolerance.
- Chapel Hill, North Carolina, parents were not allowed to remove their high school junior daughter from her American Literature class, but they could exempt her from reading gay and lesbian selections in a multicultural curriculum.

lead. Would creationists be allowed to pull children from biology classes—or historical revisionists permitted to remove children from forums on the Holocaust—or white supremacists given the right to excuse children from classes that portray blackness as good or even morally neutral? Enshrining parental rights could turn students into shifting masses of ideological pawns or virtual dropouts from comprehensive diversity education. (See box 6.20.)

## BOX 6.20   THE ULTIMATE OPT OUT THREAT

"Schools are being used for the sexualization of our children," said [a First Educators' Alliance member].... "It's overstepping parental rights." [She] said [opt out is] not enough. "Not if they are going to introduce (homosexuality) into the core curriculum.... They would have to opt out of every classroom."

Jane Futcher, "Novato: Diversity's Battleground," *Marin* [Calif.] *Independent Journal*, August 20, 2002.

*Question 23: What is the impact of parental notification requirements on classroom practice?*

These laws have a chilling effect on good pedagogy. Not many teachers want to be the next John T. Scopes. Under a parent notification rule, most would hesitate to plan and present a comprehensive curriculum unit on homosexualities and heterosexism. Some might even shrink from responding spontaneously to a student's explicit question about gay people or a homophobic remark. Indeed, there is some question over what constitutes "curriculum" in the eyes of the legislature and courts, and therefore over what needs to be cleared with parents—a sustained unit, an ad hoc aside, repeated asides over time, a plea for tolerance in the midst of a fracas? These gray areas are sources of fear for educators. That may be just the result the censors want.

*Question 24: How can reformers best respond to the opposition?*

Dialogue is as appropriate and necessary among adults who differ as it is among students. Some extreme opponents of antihomophobia education are less concerned about homosexuality than about amassing money and power. Being reasonable is not important to them, but we can still put our trust in a respectful continuing exchange with others. (See box 6.21.) Ironically, many conservatives who used to attack "values education" are now calling for "character and civic education." The devil will be in trying to agree which values best inform good character and citizenship. Despite U.S. Education Secretary Roderick Paige's expressed preference for schools that impart "Christian values," school policy and curricula can be sensitive to a range of views and still promote the safety, growth, understanding, and autonomy of every student.

---

### BOX 6.21   STRATEGIC GROUND RULES

- Ask people to speak for themselves, rather than for "the community."
- Admit that reasonable people differ on what community values should be or even appear to be.
- Remember that sometimes community norms contradict a family's or a church's values.
- Acknowledge that even the highest courts cannot always agree on what the Constitution and the law require.
- Solicit genuine feelings and discourage political posturing.
- Whenever possible, stress the values that reformers and opponents share.

Opponents often equate multiculturalism, feminism, and tolerance for homosexuality with moral relativism—but they are mistaken. Because race, ethnicity, religious belief, gender, and sexual orientation are morally neutral human differences, acceptance of such diversity is a core principle of justice. Nearly 90 percent of Americans endorse teaching about cultural pluralism in schools and we who want glbt issues to be included should ally ourselves with all proponents of curricular equity. It is useful to remember that prior to organizing against gay rights, some of the same prominent figures campaigned against civil rights for people of color. Recall also that although unabashed cultural and religious conservatives are likely to be outspoken, they are not the only ones who need to be persuaded of glbt equality. For some liberals, homosexuality is more acceptable in the abstract than in reality.

American pluralism's great challenge is to balance what separates and what unites individuals of many colors, faiths, cultures, incomes, gender expressions, degrees of physical capacity, sexualities, and political views. But if this nation's youth learn to probe differences respectfully, to find commonalities where they exist, and, above all, to be comfortable with both heterogeneity and ambiguity, they will have developed a capacity to live and work together that sets an example for a diverse world. (See box 6.22.)

Some teachers might prefer just to act quietly behind classroom doors, doing the right thing as they often do, assuming no critic will notice. Such a course might be sufficient for interrupting name-calling and harassment. But when it comes to

---

**BOX 6.22   THE DEEP IMPACT OF GAY-POSITIVE CURRICULA**

"I always knew that it was mean when people said words like 'fag', but I never knew why. After [this] class, I now know that hate and hateful words are hurtful, not only to the people who they are said to, but also to the whole school."

8th-grade male public school student, Acton, Mass., 2002.

"Before my teacher taught me about homophobia and hate towards gay people, I never knew why it was important to stand up for equality. Everyone has the right to be who they are and should not have to go through life hiding such an important piece of their identity.... [N]ow I plan on joining the GSA when I get to high school next year."

8th-grade female public school student, Acton, Mass., 2002.

implementing real curricula, this approach courts disaster. Progressive educators need allies to avoid isolation, exhaustion, and defeat in this work. There is too much resistance to go it alone. Better that like-minded teachers bring their initiative and courage together in a team effort with parents and community people to lobby administrators and school boards. They should use political leverage of course, but also employ research findings and policy recommendations of scholars and professional organizations like the NEA and APA. GLBT youth and their peer allies must also be heard and respected.

(For further reading, see appendix R.)

# 7

# Changing the Curriculum

*Question 1: Why should the topic of homosexuality be included in the curriculum?*

The humanistic reason for teaching students about homosexuality is to increase understanding of diversity, to lessen antigay bigotry, and to foster the healthy development of all youth. But there are other pedagogically sound reasons as well. Chief among them is that issues of sexuality—both its norms and its variations—rivet adolescents. (See box 7.1.) Over 80 percent of teens consider human sexuality and sexual relationships equally or more important than other subjects taught in school. Anyone concerned about teaching to students' interests should welcome the inclusion of accurate unsensationalized lessons on all aspects of sexuality. They provide a necessary balance to the entertainment media's exploitation of sex to sell products.

However it arises, sexual curiosity is an important part of an adolescent's intellectual and emotional development. Even younger children who are not ready for detailed explanations would benefit from the teachable moments that our sexualized popular culture provides.

Finally, a complete and honest curriculum is more alive and powerful than a censored one. Students are put off by instruction that ignores the world they live in. But do not assume that a curriculum has to be trendy or shallow to be appealing. Genuine nuanced lessons can encourage students to think critically and deeply about their own experiences and the lives of others.

*Question 2: But isn't teaching about homosexuality only about sex?*

A common misconception is that homosexuality is about nothing but sex. Yet, for most people, gay and straight, sexuality is about more than erotic

## BOX 7.1   STUDENTS' QUESTIONS
## ABOUT HOMOSEXUALITY: A BROAD ARRAY

Basic Info: Labels

- If you say you are "unidentified" or you like both boys and girls wouldn't that make you bisexual?
- What is a transgender?

Personal Identity Development

- Were you against or afraid of gay or lesbian people before you realized you were gay, lesbian, or bisexual?
- When exactly did you start to figure out what sex you were attracted to—what age?
- Do you want kids?
- Do you feel like you would have an easier or better life if you were straight?

Friends and Family

- How do you tell your parents that you're lesbian or gay?
- Have you lost any of your best friends or someone you care about because of your sexuality?
- Do your friends that are straight still hang out with you even though they know you might be attracted to them?

Homophobia

- Do you think that a lot of kids at [our high school] discriminate against gays?
- What's the worst experience you've had about coming out at school?
- Do you [experience] any problems outside of school?
- Do you feel as though being called a bad name is like calling someone of a certain race a racist name?
- Yo, what do you think about Eminem's lyrics?

GSAs

- What exactly do you do in [the gsa]?
- What have you learned about yourself since you started going to [the gsa]?

Fayerweather Street School and Cambridge Rindge and Latin High School, 7th-, 8th-, and 9th-grade students' anonymous questions to gsa student panel from Cambridge Rindge and Latin, Cambridge, Mass., 2001–2002.

practices. It is about how one experiences the world as a sexual being. It can be about attraction and romance, disappointment and pain, growth and enlightenment. In other words, it is about the heart and mind as well as the genitalia.

Nevertheless, there *is* a place for clinical descriptions of sex in sexuality education. Wherever it is appropriate to discuss the mechanics of heterosexual erotic practices it is important also to pay attention to nonheterosexual ones. But a comprehensive sexuality curriculum for all students would not only teach the mechanics of sex—it would also study the meanings of sex in individual, cultural, and political contexts.

Teaching about "homosexualities" also requires more than giving students information about particular kinds of people. It should also show them how same-gender attraction became a part of human identity historically. (See chapter 1.) In learning how societies invent identity types, students can think about how these labels influence their own understanding of the past and the present. They can ask, "Who does this culture say I am and you are; on what basis does it make those assessments; and why should I believe them?" Such questions connect sexuality to a variety of other equity issues involving racial, gender, class, and other categories. Some students might even come to doubt the capacity of the labels *straight*, *gay*, *lesbian*, and *bisexual* to describe themselves in any important or useful way.

## Question 3: Does that mean that studying homosexuality will make students gay?

The common notion that introducing homosexuality into the curriculum will turn children gay has been widely used to block reforms. And the usual response to that charge is that because sexual orientation is hardwired from birth nothing can change it one way or the other. Some go on to say that education and counseling can help some closeted glbt students accept the identities that might otherwise remain a source of pain for them.

However, both defenses ignore adolescents' natural sexual explorations and the fluidity of sexual desire and behavior. When parents and schools signal an acceptance of all sexualities, young people are freed of heterosexist constraints that inhibit the expression of their sexualities in all their complexity. Therefore, it is true that school programs can reconfigure the sexual order with the result that fewer students identify as "straight."

## Question 4: Aren't the media already covering homosexuality enough to relieve the schools of responsibility in this controversial area?

Media coverage of this topic is actually a primary reason for schools to teach about it. Educators can correct or fill out the picture of homosexuality that students get from most movies, television, magazines, and popular music. GLBT images in mainstream media are often skewed toward exaggeration, controversy, and stereotype. A 1999 kiss between two female stars on *Ally McBeal* generated the show's largest audience to that time. The first romantic kisses between males on network TV brought viewers to the WB Network's *Dawson's Creek* and *Felicity* in 2000. Bravo aired a weeklong documentary, *Gay Weddings*, in 2002. Heterosexual titillation or the "yuck factor" likely explain their voyeuristic appeal. Affirming messages for minorities are ancillary where ratings are at stake.

Gay caricatures range from the self-involved "Jack" on TV's *Will and Grace* to the oversexed lesbian basketball player in the 2002 film *Juwanna Mann*. Gay characters are often confused and in crisis or serve as jesters or neutered foils for their straight peers. Some are promiscuous, loveless, diseased, suffering, or frivolous, as in Showtime's *Queer as Folk*. Departure from the formula is exceptional (e.g., HBO's *Six Feet Under*).

MTV's *Real World* does arguably less harm, demonstrating that actual gay twenty-somethings can be as banal as straight ones. Although MTV does much better in specials like *True Life: I'm Coming Out* (2002) from its Stop the Hate campaign, their emphasis is on crisis and victimization. So too, HBO's *The Laramie Project*, the TV rendering of Moises Kaufman's play about the Matthew Shepard murder. Even news and public affairs programming can be sensationalized, if not demeaning.

As shallow a medium as television is overall, gays and lesbians still await their reflections in fully fleshed main characters who are given more to embody or contend with than their sexuality. After the cancellation of public television's *My So-Called Life* in the mid-1990s, there has been no portrayal of an unconflicted gay teen as a central figure.

GLBT youth who are isolated from gay culture and need positive dignified messages from the media are often out of luck, but the schools can help by providing alternative images and stories. *Queer Eye for the Straight Guy* needs a counter-narrative.

*Question 5: Is it primarily for gay students that we include these topics?*

Gay students do of course benefit from any curriculum or program that lessens homophobia and gives them safety and dignity. (See box 7.2.) However, all multicultural education should be undertaken both to protect the oppressed and to free majority students from what educator J. A. Banks calls "their own cultural boundaries." Studying homosexuality makes all students wiser and more completely human.

A frequently unacknowledged benefit for nongay students concerns their own sexual development. One of the penalties of their socialization is that many

## BOX 7.2    INTERVENTION—WHO NEEDS IT?

[She] remembers the moment that changed her high school career. Junior year ... Everyday Living class. The teacher and students were discussing a serious topic: sexual assault. "Why" asked the teacher, "would a man rape another man?" "Because they're fags," a student blurted out. Several teens snickered. The teacher and everyone else ignored it. The discussion continued. But [she] grimaced. It wasn't the first time she'd heard such gay bashing. The hallways echoed with "That's so gay!" "You fag!" and similar epithets each passing period. As if being gay or perceived as gay was the worst thing ever; as if gay students had no feelings; as if they had no rights. "How would I feel if I were gay?" [she] thought. How, she wondered, did her brother, who is gay, feel upon hearing such hateful words?

Kristi Wright, "Teen's Efforts Spark Tolerance at High School," *Omaha* [Neb.] *World-Herald*, August 26, 2001.

heterosexuals lose their spontaneous relational voice as they reach adolescence. Young boys are taught to banish all emotion except anger and to hide empathy and vulnerability in their quest for masculinity. Young men's sexuality becomes suspect if they express their true feelings to other men, communicate honestly with women, or heed the uncensored voices of their female partners. (See box 7.3.)

Many boys become obsessed with ridding themselves of any emotion or behavior that appears feminine. They are a source of shame that James Gilligan of Harvard Medical School has called "the primary or ultimate cause of all violence, whether toward others or toward the self." Where only proven athletes and thugs are immune, the male flight from homosexual suspicion can become a sprint toward risky bravado and away from schoolwork. Adolescent boys' aversion to affective and effective communication, seen as female or effeminate, is a factor in their lower verbal test scores in particular.

Adolescent girls, too, are raised to abandon authentic same-gender relations. They often cut ties with female confidantes to compete with them in pursuit of men, some of whom abuse them for uttering their true feelings. Sexism and heterosexism enforce these regulations. Young women's heterosexuality may become suspect if they are strong in self-expression, honest in their assessment of gender injustice, or proficient in conventionally male pursuits.

Few teachers and counselors recognize how a heterosexist curriculum contributes to young men's and women's feeling obliged to abandon same-gender closeness and honest relationality. Although many educators understand the

## BOX 7.3    A STRAIGHT CASUALTY

Dear Beth:

I'm a healthy, athletic 17-year-old high school guy. I know I'm a heterosexual, but for about the last year I've been thinking a lot about my best friend, another male my age. We both have girlfriends. It's hard to explain, but I feel some kind of love for him, but I don't think it's gay. This situation is making me feel real uncomfortable hanging with him. And I know he figures something's up. He keeps on asking me what's wrong. I don't have sexual thoughts about him—it's more like this strong loving feeling. Like I want to hug him or hold him. I don't feel this way about any other guy I know. Is it possible for heterosexual guys to love each other but not be gay? I guess I just don't understand this. What should I do about it? Should I tell him? Thanks a lot for your suggestions.

—CONFUSED AND WORRIED

Globe staff, "Ask Beth," *Boston Globe*, January 25, 2001.

importance of stopping gay and lesbian suicide and bashing, few see how anti-homophobia education might lessen heterosexual self-destruction and violence. (See box 7.4.) Studying the range of human sexual feeling and gender expression can help relieve straight-identified students from the pressures of narrow, inflexible sexuality and gender roles. (See box 7.5.)

Presenting homosexuality without embarrassment or condemnation evidences a teacher's acceptance of sexuality in general and that signal may facilitate better communication with all students. Young people of various orientations often approach openly gay and lesbian teachers to discuss personal and relationship

## BOX 7.4    THE GENDER-BONUS

Masculinity would be something every male possesses, not a test every boy must take. Gay men would be free to follow their hearts without sacrificing prestige—and so would straights. After all, macho is a wound for everyone. It isn't just about boys bonding and dads passing their cojones along to their sons. It's also about boys brutalizing each other to establish a hierarchy based on fear of the feminine, and fathers injuring their sons for failing to make the grade.

Richard Goldstein, "The Myth of Gay Macho," *Village Voice*, June 26, 2002.

## BOX 7.5   WHAT STRAIGHT STUDENTS GET FROM GAY CURRICULA

I think most importantly these are issues that go undiscussed. For kids to get their questions out and answered is crucial because education combats hate from the start. I think a big lesson learned was that many kids start hating (homophobia, racism, anti-Semitism, etc.) early on because they are ignorant on what they are actually claiming to hate, they may just turn to hatred because they don't have anything to live for, or because of a parent or relative preaching hate. If it were up to me all schools would have a mandatory class teaching about issues such as homophobia and other important issues taught in Leadership and Diversity. I know my own views have been broadened...."

11th-grade student, Newton South High School, Newton, Mass., 2002.

issues that they would not broach with anyone else. The students explain that they confide in them because the out teachers seem more open and less judgmental of people's departures from the norm than others are.

*Question 6: Where does one begin to include homosexuality in the curriculum?*

Teachers should not underestimate the importance of simply mentioning glbt people when discussing diversity. For students just to hear the words in an unembarrassed and accepting tone contradicts the notion that the topic is forbidden or shameful. Of course teachers must also challenge homophobic name-calling and other harassment whenever it occurs.

But students should not merely be admonished or punished for using words like *faggot* or *lezzie*. They should also be told who is being hurt by such language and why it is wrong to defame glbt people. In this way a rule against homophobic name-calling can be the germ of a curriculum when enforcement leads to a discussion of tolerance. (See chapter 5, box 5.4.)

Teachers can adopt other simple strategies for making the subject a part of the classroom landscape. (See box 7.6.)

*Question 7: Are these strategies sufficient for most schools?*

These steps are a good start, but realistically not enough. Posters can contribute to a safer environment, one-time speakers can answer a few questions, and teachers can plead for understanding. But effective antihomophobia education

---

**BOX 7.6   TOWARD A CURRICULUM**

Things to Do in the Classroom

- Put up a "Safe-Zone for GLBT People" sticker.
- Put up a poster of faces of glbt youth of all backgrounds.
- Put up a poster of famous glbt people of all backgrounds.
- Spend a few minutes addressing a few stereotypes and misconceptions.
- Invite guest speakers from the glbt community to talk about their lives and answer a few student questions.
- Celebrate Gay Pride Day, the National Day of Silence, or National Coming Out Day.

---

demands serious study and substantive discussion within the disciplines of the school.

Stereotypes, defamation, and omissions must be corrected with appropriate books, fact sheets, lectures, group activities, and a sincere and thorough dialogue. (See box 7.7.) To make the study of any group a sideshow, separate from valued academic endeavors, sends a message that such add-on lessons are not really "school" and that what students learn at such times will not be on the tests that count. Such marginalization reflects the sociopolitical reality that schools exist to transmit dominant cultural content and values rather than to stimulate critical thinking and imagination.

---

**BOX 7.7   WHAT SHOULD STUDENTS LEARN?**

A curriculum should help students:

- understand the nature of sexual identity and same-gender attraction, and how they have been expressed in various times and cultures;
- understand the significance of past and current research and theories about the "causes" of homosexuality;
- analyze how the homo/bisexuality of a historical figure, author, artist, etc., influenced or might have influenced his or her life and work;
- know something about the history of the gay/lesbian community in the United States and current issues in gay life;
- appreciate the diversity and different experiences of gays and lesbians in this country and around the world.

---

When scholarship on homosexuality was slim, good curriculum was scarce. To-day, however, the growth of gay studies provides rich source material that can be adapted and integrated into appropriate school curricula.

*Question 8: Is there a need for separate courses in gay literature or history?*

Such courses could be offered as electives, but one has to wonder who would en-roll. Historically, at least at their inception, specific minority studies have mostly attracted corresponding minority students. In the case of gay electives, moreover, glbt and questioning adolescents might fear to be seen in a class on homosexual-ity or worry about the course title appearing on their transcripts. And what would induce homophobic students—who clearly need to be taught such subjects—to cross the threshold?

To maximize its impact, gay content should be incorporated into existing courses or new, broadly conceived and titled ones.

*Question 9: Why isn't it enough just to mention sexual orientation in the context of diversity without going into details that could bring controversy?*

Some educators try to avoid political repercussions by briefly referring to homo-sexuality in general antiprejudice exercises and ending it there. Although such an approach may seem safe it is likely not to work. It may be interpreted as a token gesture and pass without impact or, more likely, it will provoke a dramatic student response. Since classroom reference to homosexuality is extraordinary in most schools, students will probably demand to know why it has been included. Some may resent any suggestion that gays and lesbians are a legitimate minority group. Superficial or glib responses to such questions and concerns would be inadequate.

*Question 10: How does a teacher answer the objection to gays being included in the curriculum with other minorities?*

Even without adding sexuality to the discussion, gender, race, class, ethnicity, and religion are difficult identity topics to navigate. Sometimes it seems impossible for people to communicate across differences or just recognize their own positions. Including homosexuality in the mix can be explosive, even beyond religious and political considerations.

It takes time to build the trust required for self-exposure and honest dialogue on all aspects of identity. The perception that one is ranking oppressions or in-appropriately analogizing among them can make the discussion run amok. Yet it is imperative in our curricula to link racism, sexism, anti-Semitism, and the like with homophobia and heterosexism. The temporary discomforts that arise are a small price to pay, if they lead to empathy and understanding.

At the same time we need to teach that categorical understanding of human beings is always imperfect. No one's life experience can be completely known. The oppressions we might "compare and contrast" as classroom generalizations are experienced by complex persons whose intertwined identity components influence each other. To study only one aspect of a stigmatized individual's identity would negate the significance of the others and give students the false impression that they can really know race, gender, class, or sexuality out of their multifaceted human contexts. (See chapter 2.) The best lessons on diversity would elaborate on this interconnectedness of any individual's identities.

There are a number of good sources of multicultural curricula (see appendix K), but as a rule they take a serial approach, examining differences as discrete and cumulative, rather than as interdependent components of a personal identity matrix.

*Question 11: What usually happens when a teacher raises gay and lesbian issues in a classroom?*

When a teacher broaches this topic some students respond with intellectual curiosity, but others react less positively. They may:

- become embarrassed and uncomfortable;
- become hostile;
- question the teacher's sexuality;
- make homophobic accusations against other students in the class or against other students and staff within the school;
- report the class activity to administrators and/or parents.

To prevent or minimize negative outcomes, the teacher should be noncombative and relaxed about the topic, avoiding defensiveness on the one hand or disapproval on the other. Students can often sense teacher discomfort with subject matter and sometimes act out. The teacher should not signal "controversial topic today." (See box 7.8.) They also should guard against tokenism and a patronizing attitude, such as sometimes prevails when a minority is given its moment of attention.

The subject has to be germane. Lessons should be presented as thoughtful responses to student needs. For example, the teacher could say, "Last week's discussion about Elton John brought out some strong opinions about gay people. I've gathered some material together on this subject that I think will help us sort out our feelings about gays and lesbians. Today we are going to read a short story about a boy who thought he was gay at a young age and what he did about it."

When a sensitive topic is introduced, some students will be silent. Class discussions might stimulate their thinking, but the preferable direct

## BOX 7.8   CREATING A SAFE ENVIRONMENT

Responding uncritically and with unconditional positive regard toward students provides an atmosphere of respect and open exchange. Modeling honest acceptance of questions and respectful responses creates a safe arena for students to reflect on important personal questions that otherwise would not be asked. What kind of personal interactions do you have with students (combative, superior, accepting, concerned)? Do teens find you to be respectful of their concerns and questions? Are you a good listener? Can you answer difficult questions, maintain a non-judgmental demeanor, and show that you value each student? What are your facial expressions and body language when students ask difficult questions? Are students welcome to express a diversity of views and opinions? Do they know how important their well being is to you?

Mike U. Smith and Mary Ann Drake, "Suicide & Homosexual Teens: What Can Biology Teachers Do to Help?" *American Biology Teacher*, March 2001.

engagement of each student may be more likely in one-on-one conversations with a peer or an adult. Cooperative work in pairs and guided discussion in varied settings can help break down barriers and get everyone actively involved.

*Question 12: What is the best answer to "Why do we have to learn about this?"*

The short response might be, "Because our community is made up of all kinds of people and it will help us all to get along, even if we don't think we like one another." Or, "We spend a lot of time in this class figuring out how straight people operate in this world. We can spend some trying to understand the same things about gays and lesbians who are becoming a more visible minority group." A more thoughtful answer is to explain that the often ignored history of glbt people can teach us new things about stigma, identity, subcultures, and survival—lessons that have relevance to other groups of people as well.

Educators can also concede to conformity-minded young people that heterosexuality is the norm and that heterosexism is not identical to every other oppression.

*Question 13: What does the teacher do when his or her own sexuality is questioned?*

Whatever answer is ultimately given, a critical question for the teacher to ask at the start is, "Would my being gay or lesbian influence how you feel about me or

**BOX 7.9   THE INEVITABLE QUESTION FOR THE TEACHER WITHOUT OBVIOUS HETEROSEXUAL BONA FIDES**

A suggested scenario:

*Student:* Are you gay, Ms. Jones?

*Ms. Jones:* What would you think if I said yes? Would you think I wasn't as good a teacher? Would you like me less than you used to? (Pause for thirty seconds.) Well, actually no, I'm not gay, but I wanted you to think about it for a few minutes. Where do we get our ideas about gay people? I used to have some prejudices about gays and lesbians myself until I got to know some. I had/have a [relative, friend] who is gay and a wonderful person, so I began to change my views. What do you think about that?

what you think about homosexuality?" If the teacher says he or she is not gay but still cares very much about gay people and wants to know more about them, that teacher provides a role model of caring and eagerness to learn. (See box 7.9.)

If the teacher comes out, students discover that people they like, respect, and learn from may be glbt. Disclosure can occur in the context of antigay taunting or as part of a formal curriculum. (See box 7.10.) Further personal information

**BOX 7.10   HOW IT WORKS**

Towards the end of this course, his social studies teacher came out to the [7th-grade] class as a lesbian, consciously personalizing the issues with her students. The students showed a great deal of respect towards her for her courage and honesty, which prompted honest discussions about homophobia and how words such as "fag" and "queer" are hurtful and offensive. Noah was touched by how seriously his teacher took the material, to the extent that she was living it with them. He felt closer to her, and was sad and dismayed that some other students were still so immature that they could like and respect this teacher yet still use hurtful words, including these same ones, to put other kids down. It caused him to consider how he, as a bystander, would respond to put downs, even those not addressed to him.

Beryl M. [parent], "Voices: Parents," *Facing History and Ourselves Website* (www.facing.org/facing/fhao2.nsf/fcb1c2b4c2c0c3c88525696d00535d9b/876d8000 5011c786852568c5004b817f?OpenDocument) (April 2002).

(e.g., whether he or she has a partner) may be shared when appropriate. Of course describing one's erotic practices is no more acceptable for a gay teacher to do than for a heterosexual one. (See chapter 4.)

Declining to answer the identity question might provoke speculation. Student uncertainty could be good if it helps them see that one can't always identify sexual orientation by means of superficial stereotypical behaviors. In fact, a straight teacher might use this strategy for a time, and then, after revealing his or her sexuality, conduct a discussion of the origins and consequences of students' preconceptions.

On the other hand, if a homosexual teacher declines to answer, students may interpret reticence as shame or fear. Teachers who stay in the closet while teaching tolerance may undermine their own goals. They may also send a harmful message to glbt and questioning youth that the school's professed safety is not real.

*Question 14: What does a teacher do when students begin conjecturing or making homophobic remarks about other students in the class or school?*

The teacher should discourage such behavior as invasive and inappropriate. As productive as it might be for glbt students to stand up openly for themselves, teachers should not force such a moment. Even those students who might have come out in other settings have a right to privacy where they want it.

Unfortunately, students who ask questions about or make positive remarks concerning homosexuality are often derided as gay. Teachers, therefore, need a tactic for stopping speculation about another student's sexuality during class discussions. The teacher could say, "I have no interest in guessing if any student or teacher is gay in this school. I do assume by statistical probability that there are gay people in our community." (*Warning*: Saying that there is likely to be a gay person in the *class itself* invites neck craning and finger pointing.) "It's fine to have questions about sexual desires and behaviors. Many of us will spend our lifetime getting to understand our own sexual identity better. But let's not put anybody's private life up for public examination. If none of us knows enough accurate information about homosexuality, we can invite speakers to our class and do other research as well."

When students volunteer that they or people dear to them are glbt, the class has a rare opportunity for a discussion marked by immediacy and the expression of nonhypothetical feelings and perceptions. The brave students who have come out about their own or a loved one's homosexuality need both peer and adult support, but teachers should avoid sermonizing. Students trying to understand difference must talk to each other. The teacher's ideal function is to reiterate and make concise what each "side" is saying and, above all, to keep emphasizing all people's membership in the school or district "community." (See chapter 5.)

When students and teachers who are open about their own or a relative's homosexuality are not available, classes must rely on guest speakers, biography, fiction, film, or third-person accounts and observations. (See appendix B.)

*Question 15: What if students ask about the sexuality of another staff member?*

Educators may respond as suggested above regarding questions about other students. Otherwise, they may say, "I don't discuss other teachers' sexuality. If you want to talk to Ms./Mr. Smith directly, why don't you do that." Be aware that students might go directly to that staff member and misrepresent what you suggested. If the colleague knows in advance what your response to such questions will be, your words are less likely to be misconstrued.

*Question 16: How can community building help?*

Most students want to be accepted and liked by their peers. The norm of the class should be a communitarian one, encouraged and supported by the teacher. To reduce classroom homophobia, one must stress the membership of glbt people or people with glbt loved ones in the classroom community. That is best, although rarely, done by those class members themselves.

Teachers should understand that arguing abstractly for the rights and worth of those who are strangers to the group will not be effective with most students. Teenagers learn first how to be considerate of those around them for whom they already have a predisposition to care. Such feelings can be nurtured in school settings that emphasize community. The inclusion in that community of any stigmatized minority will take some work and not a little conflict.

The more class governance and decision making are shared between teacher and students, the more likely the communitarian model will prevail. Group debate and democratic process create community membership and responsibility. Teachers can and do use the power of their position to govern class behavior, but attitudes are not necessarily changed that way. Witness what often happens when the teacher is absent.

*Question 17: What about negative reactions outside the classroom to lessons on homosexuality?*

Speak with administrators and colleagues in advance about the nature of your classroom activities on the subject of homosexuality. Some parents may become upset. They need to be told of the value of education for diversity. And they need to know that a majority of parents want such instruction. (See box 7.11.) When a critical mass of your school staff agrees on the need for preventing homophobic

## BOX 7.11    MOST PARENTS WANT GAY LESSONS...BUT WHO IS LISTENING?

The Kaiser [Family Foundation] report polled 1,501 sets of parents and students, as well as teachers and principals.... The survey uncovered a gap between what parents say they want and what schools deliver.... [T]hree out of four [parents] want their children to learn about homosexuality and sexual orientation in the classroom.

Diana Jean Schemo, "Survey Finds Parents Favor More Detailed Sex Education," *New York Times* on the Web (www.nytimes.com) (October 4, 2000).

name-calling and violence, you have leverage. It always pays to have your professional allies lined up before the controversy begins.

Conservative, religiously orthodox, or homophobic parents may take some comfort in the notion that the staff's first objective is that people are treated fairly in the school. If some students or parents are unhappy with teaching that all people are equal and deserving of respect, they can continue to believe whatever they want. As long as their beliefs don't lead to behaviors intended to harm or diminish others, they are not a priority.

But, of course, beliefs still are *one* concern of the school. The principles of liberty, equality, and justice for all depend upon a belief system that may be in conflict with certain religious and political tenets. Let the intellectual contest between bigotry and tolerance thrive. Teachers should be confident that most students, given a respectful school environment and an accurate, substantive diversity curriculum, will emerge from this conflict embracing human differences. (See chapter 5.)

It is also important to take the time to choose curricula carefully. There is too much at stake to settle for poorly crafted or age-inappropriate materials. (See box 7.12.)

*Question 18: Is this not more propaganda than education?*

Many conservatives claim that blocking gay content in education would maintain schools as "sexuality-free" or neutral spaces. They are being disingenuous. Classrooms and school lessons have always been both sexualized and heterosexist. Most students, at least from preadolescence, are active players in the cultural dramas of sex and gender, egged on by sex-saturated mass media. School curricula do their part in reinforcing a prescribed heterosexual norm in arguably every subject area. At the same time heterosexist notions and homophobic behaviors

---

**BOX 7.12    IFFY CHOICES FOR YOUNGSTERS WITHOUT A SENSE OF IRONY (AND THEIR PARENTS)**

[9th-grade students] were asked questions such as: "If you have never slept with a person of the same sex, is it possible that all you need is a good gay lover?" [A school district spokesman] said [the school] was given only a "general description" of the program beforehand and only three of the six handouts received by students.

Amy Brunjes and Dana Loustalot Duncan, "Dwyer Teaches Tolerance of Gays," *Jupiter* [Fla.] *Courier*, May 26, 2001.

---

are rarely challenged in schools. The reform recommendations in this book are aimed at correcting these existing problems of sexuality bias and bigotry. Doing nothing is not neutral.

*Question 19: Which academic disciplines most often incorporate gay content?*

Homosexuality, if it is brought up at all, is discussed most commonly in the health class, frequently in connection with HIV/AIDS. Even so, the amount of HIV/AIDS education deemed "highly sensitive" to the needs of glbt youth is miniscule. Prevention is still taught with a heterosexual slant. Safer sex information for all should be part of a comprehensive health curriculum, but when students hear about glbt people *only* in this context, they could conclude that homosexuality is mainly about pathology. That is not the way to reduce homophobia or help glbt students develop a positive identity.

Moreover, confining homosexuality to health curricula reduces gays and lesbians to the physical domain. The study of straight sexuality in the health class is at least balanced by a more holistic study of male-female relationships in history, literature, and other subjects.

Even when the goal is sex education, the curriculum must be about more than plumbing. To be credible and effective, it must address pleasure, spirituality, and power in every kind of sexual relationship.

*Question 20: Could a family life class provide a more complete picture of gay life?*

A family life curriculum can explore how gays and lesbians create alternative families. Students can learn about same-gender household arrangements, spousal

## BOX 7.13  "WHICH OF YOU IS THE HUSBAND?"

This persistent question posed to gay and lesbian couples has to do with power. It can be the entry way to discussions of gender roles in relationships, regarding, for example:

- Career decisions
- Breadwinning
- Childcare
- Child rearing
- Budgeting
- Sexual relations
- Household chores
- Conflict resolution

relationships, child rearing, extended biological and adopted family, work-sharing, and financial planning. Gay youth could learn some of the skills they might need and all students would find a new context for examining gender roles. (See box 7.13.) They would likely expand their notions of such relationship variables as sharing, commitment, communication, and conflict resolution.

For example, a well-devised curriculum would provide insights into the nonviolence, volunteerism, and tolerance that make gay men good community members, debunking the common stereotypes of them as antifamily, promiscuous, immature, and self-absorbed. It would also examine the growing phenomenon of lesbians successfully raising children. (See chapter 4.)

*Question 21: What areas in social studies present opportunities for inclusion?*

History, political science, sociology, anthropology, and psychology are natural places for gay and lesbian curricula. Topics might include:

- how same-gender sexuality has been understood and judged in different cultures and periods;
- the evolution of modern Western glbt identities;
- important "homosexual" people in history;
- current gay issues, including civil rights, medicine, activism, and politics.

Although lists of prominent glbt historical figures make a nice display, they don't become a curriculum until the "poster people" are studied. For instance, students could simply be told that gay mathematician Alan Turing helped break the Nazi war codes and start the computer industry, but the *indispensable* human rights lesson lies in the study of his arrest for homosexual activity, his forced hormone therapy, and his suicide. To that end, they might read or see the play/video *Breaking the Code*, based on Turing's life. As another example, they could examine why what would later be called "gay liberation" was an integral part of Emma Goldman's radical agenda in the 1920s.

The documentary film *Out of the Past* documents the historical progression of homosexuality from sin to sickness to community through the lives of Michael Wigglesworth, Sarah Orne Jewett, and Barbara Gittings. (See appendix L.) Bayard Rustin, another of the film's subjects, personifies the convergence of multiple identities in a social justice warrior. A gay, African American leftist who triumphed over sexual, racial, and political obstacles, Rustin organized the 1964 March on Washington for Civil Rights.

The list of figures inviting study is easily expanded to: T. E. Lawrence, Dag Hammerskjold, Margaret Fuller, Susan B. Anthony, Katharine Lee Bates (lyricist of "America the Beautiful"), Irish patriot Sir Roger Casement, Sweden's Queen Christina, leaders in medicine and public health like Sara Josephine Baker, domestic partners Ethel Collins Dunham and Martha May Eliot, and many others.

## Question 22: Aren't these lists of famous homosexuals far-fetched?

The sexuality of historical figures, especially of the pre-twentieth century, is sometimes hard to categorize. As much as gay people, like other minorities, want to take pride in the lives of great forebears, teachers need to be as accurate as they can be.

For example, although he shared a bed with another man for three years, Abraham Lincoln was less likely gay than was James Buchanan, whose sexuality was openly questioned during his presidency. Both men may exemplify nineteenth-century intimate and effusive male bonding more than homosexuality. Good student research on such questions is more important than the conclusive verdicts. (See box 7.14.)

## Question 23: How can modern gay history be included?

U.S. history and sociology classes could study gay liberation in comparison to other civil rights struggles. One might begin with the 1969 Stonewall Riots in New York, the raucous eruption of drag queens and street youth that has been called the spark of the modern gay movement. It offers colorful firsthand accounts that engage students. It can also provide an entry point to a more complete

**BOX 7.14   WAS ELEANOR ROOSEVELT A LESBIAN?**

People like Eleanor Roosevelt illustrate the limitations of sexuality labels, especially to describe people from another era. One can never know all the details of her female relationships (some with lesbians), although scholar Blanche Wiesen-Cook has ably documented her intimacies with both Associated Press reporter Lorena Hickok and her bodyguard, Earl Miller. One might more accurately call her bisexual. But the teaching point is not to pinpoint her sexual orientation, but to see these ties as a significant factor in her life and a likely influence on her political activist views.

history, including its antecedents. (See box 7.15.) An overview of same-gender sexuality from the colonial period through the pre-Stonewall years could focus on urbanization, the ascendancy of science, the impact of the world wars, and Nazi victimization.

Compelling topics in the thirty years after Stonewall include: the gay movement's shift from sexual freedom to civil rights, de-listing homosexuality as a mental illness, the role and image of women and transgender people in the liberation struggle, and the effect of HIV/AIDS on the glbt community and its politics. (See appendix M.) Moreover, the growing literature on regional U.S. history (e.g., George Chauncey's *Gay New York*, James T. Sears's *Lonely Hunters: An Oral History of Lesbian and Gay Southern Life 1948–1968*, and the History Project's *Improper Bostonians*) can bring gay history literally home to students. Lastly, the

**BOX 7.15   STONEWALL: QUESTIONS
FOR FURTHER STUDY**

- Who were these rioters?
- Why were they at the Stonewall Inn?
- Had there always been glbt people in New York?
- What is the significance of this event historically—was it a turning point in our national awareness?
- How does the riot compare with the other homosexual protests, both before and after Stonewall?
- How was Stonewall influenced by the tactics and language of the Black Civil Rights Movement and the Women's Movement?
- How is the campaign for gay rights similar to and different from these other civil rights struggles?

ongoing public discourse on gay marriage and gays in the military, Boy Scouts, and Big Brothers are appropriate to current events discussions and debates.

### Question 24: Isn't the study of gays in the Holocaust disrespectful to Jews?

Supporting a monument to gay persecution, Holocaust historian Daniel Goldhagen observed, "There is no hierarchy among victims." The gay and lesbian experience under the Nazis points to universal features of bigotry and provides a lens to examine prejudice and dehumanization in the world today. The historic similarities between anti-Semitism and homophobia are in fact remarkable. Students could learn about the German antigay laws, the destruction of the work of the Jewish gay historian Magnus Hirschfeld, treatment of gays and lesbians in the camps, the experience of the survivors, and the issues of memorials and reparations. (See appendix N.)

### Question 25: What can be done in language arts and literature?

GLBT life is treated in fiction and biography, prose and poetry. Students can study the details of such literature in which homosexuality is explicit or clearly implied. They could also investigate other work by glbt writers to see how their sexualities might have influenced their perspective, that is, to see whether writing by a homosexual author can still be considered gay writing even when it has no apparent gay content.

Some glbt writers like Whitman, Gide, James, Hansberry, and Baldwin are already part of school syllabi. Others whose sexualities are uncertain or harder to classify also make for interesting analysis, such as Marlowe, Goethe, Byron, Dickinson, Hopkins, and Hughes.

World and immigrant literature can enhance students' appreciation of the international scope of "homosexualities." (See chapter 2.) Likewise, gay content in English as a second language and bilingual materials creates opportunities to broach the issue of sexual diversity with students from other cultures.

### Question 26: What is the point of raising an author's sexuality when it is ambiguous or irrelevant?

Sexuality, like gender or race, is often an important factor in a writer's life and hence an influence on his or her work. It is crucial to understanding many heterosexual authors—and not just the salient ones like Nin or Hemingway. Yet when teachers want to explore homosexuality (apparent or speculative), they often encounter a double standard concerning its relevance and appropriateness.

Asking whether particular authors experienced same-gender attractions, what these feelings may have signified to them, and how both are reflected in their work can be illuminating. For example, Thoreau's possible homosexuality helps us analyze the romanticism of his poem "Sympathy" ("Lately, alas, I knew a gentle boy") and provides a fascinating perspective on *Walden*.

There is much to mine as well in Langston Hughes's eleven-line poem, "Café: 3 a.m.," about undercover police officers arresting "fairies" in the 1950s. (See appendix O.) Besides raising the provocative issue of Hughes's own sexuality, the poem can serve as an introduction to other Harlem Renaissance figures who were openly gay and lesbian, like Bessie Smith, Gladys Bentley, Ma Rainey, Countee Cullen, Bruce Nugent, and Wallace Thurman.

Many have studied Willa Cather's "Paul's Case" without reference to the sexuality of either the title character or the author. No one can really understand that short story without a gay lens. Although we don't have to know every detail about Cather's women companions, the story resonates quite differently if we know about Cather's early condemnation of Oscar Wilde and her own masquerade—as a man!

*Billy Budd*, the "Handsome Sailor," can be read as a tale of repressed homoerotic desire. Moreover, Ishmael and Queequeg's relationship in *Moby-Dick* is cast in a new light when students learn about Melville's views of sexuality in the South Seas islands and his passionate relationship with Hawthorne.

Homosexual possibilities arise in Shakespeare, too. (See box 7.16.) Although critics may challenge such interpretations, they would be hard pressed to censor the "classics."

*Question 27: Are there any gay films suitable for the language arts curriculum?*

Many commercial and independent films deal with homosexuality in a way that would be acceptable in many communities. Where motion picture ratings dictate, parents will have to sign off beforehand. Teachers should bring the same standard of judgment to film as they do to literature, since it takes more than a gay theme to make a movie worthwhile. There should be both preparation and follow-up activities (discussion, writing, etc.) to teach both critical viewing skills and content. (See appendix P.)

*Question 28: Is there any literature appropriate to the middle schools?*

Some early books weren't well written, didn't have gay or lesbian main characters, omitted females and minorities, and were negative about the gay experience. Happily, there are numbers of good young adult fiction titles today from Jacqueline Woodson's *From the Notebooks of Melanin Sun* and Nancy Garden's

### BOX 7.16   A SMALL SAMPLE OF WHAT'S "GAY" IN HIGH SCHOOL SHAKESPEARE

- All female parts in Shakespeare's time were played by male actors who, in the comedies, sometimes tease the audience about this gender reversal.
- Male actors sometimes played women who cross-dress as men, e.g., in *Twelfth Night*, Count Orsino keeps calling his lover Cesario until "he" changes from his male disguise into women's clothes.
- There is a close relationship between Antonio and Sebastian in *Twelfth Night*.
- Hermia and Helena have an intense friendship in A *Midsummer Night's Dream*.
- Iago is jealous of Othello's marriage; and also has a physical attachment to Cassius.
- The bisexual authorial voice of the sonnets is clear; the first 126 written to a fair younger male patron (believed to be Henry Wriothesley, 3rd Earl of Southampton, of whom a portrait in drag was recently discovered) and the last 28 to a dark lady.

*Holly's Secret* to Alex Sanchez' *Rainbow Boys*. There are also nonfiction anthologies like Clifford Chase's *Queer 13: Lesbian and Gay Writers Recall Seventh Grade*. An annotated bibliography can help teachers and librarians choose the right books for their students. (See box 7.17.)

*Question 29: How can writing classes incorporate gay issues?*

Teachers should consider topics for student writing, such as opinion pieces about civil rights questions, research on historical figures, fiction with gay characters, and first-person exercises in the voice of a gay person.

Although closeted or questioning students might fear disclosure, personal writing can be a vital means of self-expression for glbt youth who have the courage to attempt it. Teachers must let students know that they are receptive to sexuality topics. To maximize respectfulness, they can divide classes into small private writing groups. Furthermore, students can designate some of their writing as "teacher's eyes only."

Even with these provisions, some student writers will be indirect about their sexuality issues. When sensitive teachers catch on, they can be gently supportive in written comments, private conferences, and discrete public comments.

**BOX 7.17   CHOOSING YOUNG ADULT TITLES: SOME GUIDANCE**

- Frances Ann Day, *Lesbian and Gay Voices: An Annotated Bibliography and Guide to Literature for Children and Young Adults* (Westport, Conn.: Greenwood, 2000).
- Donovan R. Walling, "Gay- and Lesbian-Themed Novels for Classroom Reading," *Journal of Gay and Lesbian Issues in Education* 1, no. 2 (2003).
- Rose Casement, "Breaking The Silence: The Stories of Gay and Lesbian People in Children's Literature," *New Advocate* 15, no. 3 (Summer 2002): 205–13.
- GLSEN Booklink <www.glsen.org/templates/booklink/index.html>
- GLSEN/Boston, *Annotated Bibliography, 2000 K–8 Edition for Students and Educators* (2000 high school edition also available), <www.glsenboston.org/resources/bibliography.html>

*Question 30: Can classes in the fine and performing arts broach sexuality issues?*

Many works of painting, sculpture, photography, and film are related to sexual imagination, relationships, and desire. Art history classes can find expressions of homoeroticism from Michelangelo and Caravaggio to Beardsley, Kahlo, Johns, Rauschenberg, Warhol, Hockney, and Duane Michaels.

Similar observations can be made in music appreciation, in both classical idiom (e.g., Handel, Tchaikovsky, Chopin, Ravel, Copeland, Bernstein, Britten, and Virgil Thompson) and popular (e.g., Billy Strayhorn, Bessie Smith, Elton John, KD Lang, and Melissa Etheridge). Dance students may study Diaghilev, Nijinsky, Michael Bennet, and Alvin Ailey.

Young people can also express themselves through graphic art and photography, either abstractly or realistically, perhaps inspired by Adam Mastoon's *The Shared Heart* (New York: HarperCollins, 1997), which presents glbt adolescent lives in photos and text.

Drama and dance classes can bring the subject to life with rehearsed performance, improvisation, and role-playing. Students could perform scenes from full-length plays and screenplays like *The Children's Hour, The Sign in Sidney Brustein's Window, Torchsong Trilogy, As Is, The Normal Heart, The Color Purple, Falsettos, Fifth of July, The Laramie Project,* and so on. Original work and spontaneous pieces evoke a particularly personal voice, for example, *Building Houses on the Moon,* a play by Jeffrey Solomon (212-688-1292 or jeff.solo@onebox.com).

> **BOX 7.18   THEATER AS ANTIHOMOPHOBIA CURRICULUM**
>
> The advanced drama class ... will perform "Scare Crow" today at a state high school drama competition ... The play is based on the life and death of [Matthew] Shepard, a gay college student who was brutally beaten and left to die on a fence in Wyoming. Drama teacher James Warren wrote the play ... "I really didn't know that much about Matthew until I called up some articles on the Internet," Warren said. "But his story touched me a great deal."
>
> Michele Sager, "Students' 'Scare Crow' Goes to Drama Contest," *Tampa Tribune*, November 3, 2001.

Public art is also a significant opportunity. Students can reduce homophobia in their schools and communities through music, dramatic performance, posters, and art installations. (See box 7.18.)

*Question 31: Are the sciences totally divorced from gay and lesbian topics?*

Although math, physics, and chemistry seem far removed from sexuality, there are still ways to make connections, albeit mostly tangential ones. First, the biographies of scientists are often part of the curriculum, especially in the early grades and general science courses. Students could learn that da Vinci, Francis Bacon, Florence Nightingale, John Maynard Keynes, Margaret Mead, Harry Stack Sullivan, and perhaps George Washington Carver were gay or bisexual.

Some hypothetical problems in math and science could be given a gay twist, just to remind students not to assume a heterosexual context. For example, "Sally and Mary are going to Ikea to buy wall-to-wall carpeting for their bedroom ..." or "The Harvey Milk Club softball team wants to inflate a balloon for their float in gay pride parade...."

More gay content is called for in biology, biochemistry, and psychobiology, where students explore the connections among body, mind, and behavior. Teachers could present the changing scientific understandings of same-gender desire from Plato to modern genetic theories. The influence of culture and politics on scientific research could be examined historically—for example, how has "science" been used over time to understand and explain poverty, crime, feminism, and homosexuality? Are there similarities among the "scientific" theories that have been used in different periods to discriminate against the Irish, Jews, blacks, women, homosexuals, and so on?

## BOX 7.19   AN AGENDA FOR REDUCING SEXISM AND HOMOPHOBIA IN PHYSICAL EDUCATION AND SPORTS

1. Eliminate gender segregation in physical education.
2. Explore motivations for physical fitness, performance, and competition.
3. Stress the importance of teamwork.
4. Understand the meaning of winning.
5. Introduce and value cooperative games.
6. Discuss and challenge the social dictates of masculinity and femininity.
7. Clarify the differences among and relative acceptability of competitiveness, aggression, and violence, on and off the field.
8. Interrupt gender, sexuality-based, and other insults.
9. Punish athletes seriously for sexist and homophobic remarks or actions.

*Question 32: Aren't physical education and sports a difficult arena for sexuality issues?*

Like drill sergeants, male coaches and players often use homophobic insults to encourage solidarity, morale, performance, and aggression. Sexist and homophobic taunts can also be used to rattle and demean opposing teams. No jock wants to be called a sissy. Females, on the other hand, are sometimes lesbian-baited for their skill and dedication to sport. (See chapter 1.) Lesbian athletes may shrink from excellence or even quit the team. Off the field, girls are forced (sometimes by coaches) to rev up their femininity to avoid suspicion.

These practices must be reversed through thoughtful reform of physical education and sports curricula. (See box 7.19.)

*Question 33: Can any glbt subject be raised in the elementary school curriculum?*

The best way to introduce gays and lesbians in preschool and the lower grades is in connection with bullying and name-calling based on gender role or sexuality and with family diversity. As they advance in school, children can be taught, at increasing levels of intellectual and moral sophistication, why it is wrong to discriminate against people who are different but not "bad." Teachers should remove classroom images—posters, book illustrations, visitors, and the like—that may contribute to gender/sexuality stereotyping.

In the early grades teachers should introduce nontraditional families and relationships in terms that children can understand and in multicultural contexts. They can use peer show and tell, picture collages of family groupings, stories from books, teacher storytelling, videos, and class visitors. (See appendix Q.) The last option had a spectacular success in 2002, for example, when the Park Day School, a K-6 school in Oakland, California, hosted forty-five speakers on glbt issues in one day!

These strategies support children who already suffer from gender stereotyping and homophobia as well as those who will later discover their own or a loved one's homosexuality.

When some young children express discomfort or disapproval, teachers should empathize, but also urge them to respect others, regardless of whom they love.

In the middle grades, children can begin to study the diversity within the glbt community, the roots of heterosexism, and the contributions of glbt people to our culture.

*Question 34: How can teachers answer the charge that homosexuality is an inappropriate topic for elementary schools?*

The students in any classroom represent a range of sexual knowledge and maturity that cannot be predicted by grade level. Many adults want to believe that a child's sexual imagination and experience begin at puberty, but most know that sexual interest and pleasure, however uninformed, begin earlier, particularly in an era of sexually explicit media.

Educators should respond to children's natural inquisitiveness by answering simply and providing a positive human context for sexuality. Teachers shouldn't worry that every sexual question will bring on a barrage of more. A few words often suffice as an answer, especially with young students.

Youngsters with gay parents, relatives, or family friends are likely to be better informed about homosexuality, but others might know something too. Teachers should not pretend gay people do not exist or imply through silence or embarrassment that homosexuality is shameful.

Some critics fear the impact such topics have on students' developing sexualities. It is natural for children and adolescents to wonder what their own same-gender feelings and activities mean. They need to understand that many people have them and that some folks develop into gays, lesbians, or bisexuals, that others become heterosexuals, and that some don't like to label themselves at all. When teachers do not signal that the heterosexual outcome is better than the others, some parents become distraught. They fear that children have not been properly informed, inoculated, or adequately intimidated.

Teachers must select defensible materials and thus may have to compromise with "community standards." One questionably appropriate sentence in an otherwise suitable book or handout can incite valid objections. Practical judgment dictates matching the level of explicitness to acceptable heterosexual curricula. Even then, most censors will not be satisfied. (See chapter 6.)

Teachers should be ready to defend their choices on the basis of curricular quality and pedagogical soundness. Discretion sometimes favors excerpts over whole works.

*Question 35: Is there really a double standard between gay and heterosexual curricular content?*

Consider that the heterosexual relationships in Shakespeare, Austen, George Eliot, Hardy, Fitzgerald, and Hemingway have been hallmarks of literature syllabi for decades. Moreover, no one would claim that a discussion of Thomas Jefferson and Sally Hemmings, or Abraham Lincoln and Mary Todd, or Eleanor and Franklin Roosevelt had no place in an American history class.

Yet when it comes to homosexual figures, historical and fictitious, their sexual orientation, if named at all, is never supposed to be fleshed out. Their loves and sexual behavior are omitted as either unimaginable or unspeakable. This hesitancy or silence merely confirms a common assumption that homosexuality is only about sex acts. Even those who see nothing wrong with gays as part of Human Relations Week can become distraught over homosexuals in the "real curriculum."

Any curriculum should contain the same level of analysis of same-gender relationships as of heterosexual ones. As there are likely to be many student questions about the topic in the middle and higher grades, all teachers, not just sex education specialists, should be prepared to respond to serious questions and to discourage disrespectful prurience and other insults.

*Question 36: Does gay inclusion really mean propaganda?*

Tolerance education should not be cheerleading. In fact, multicultural curricula are weakened when only the positive aspects of minority communities or individuals are presented. Accuracy and credibility require the inclusion of both role models and flawed characters and of both heroic moments and morally dubious episodes.

Gay people are not uniformly brave, generous, or inspirational. For example, the Nazi Ernst Roehm, the pathetic Roy Cohn, the violent "Birdman of Alcatraz," the ridiculous J. Edgar Hoover, the agonized Dr. Tom Dooley, and the recently assassinated Dutch reactionary Pim Fortuyn provide some counterpoint to a

## BOX 7.20  HITLER: THE LETHAL BUTCH

Adolf Hitler's homosexuality has been demonstrated beyond question.... But the crucial role within the Nazi movement of the most vicious and lawless types of homosexuality ... is even more important.... The Butches were openly and deliberately lawless. They defied criminal statutes.... They were anti-Semitic, militaristic and gratuitously brutal. Their sexual ideal was the man-boy relationship.... They considered these pederastic activities morally superior to sex with women, whom they despised as useful only for breeding.... When will today's liberal supporters of homosexuality ... recognize how deliberate defiance of traditional sexual morality can lead to that deliberate defiance of all traditional morality, which defined the Holocaust!

Nathaniel S. Lehrman, "Was Hitler's Homosexuality Nazism's Best-Kept Secret?" *Insight Magazine (Washington Times)*, February 25, 2002.

mostly noble main story. Exaggerated or false accounts of gay villainy, on the other hand, are a homophobic ploy. Recent "scholarship" on Nazism has been viciously distorted in this way. (See box 7.20.)

Some gay people behave badly because of internalized homophobia—a lesson in itself—but do so merely because all humans are fallible. Rather than deferring to stereotype, we must learn that each case merits its own analysis. In literature, the same care should be taken in explicating deadly perversity in *Billy Budd*, or the suicide in *Paul's Case*, as is given to the troubling aspects of *The Merchant of Venice* or *Black Boy*.

An overall affirming curriculum that portrays glbt people "warts and all" is both inspiration and warning to students of every sexual orientation. Moreover, truthful, nuanced curricula are imperative both as good scholarship and as the best defense against charges of "lifestyle promotion."

*Question 37: So some critics are right to advocate balance?*

Unfortunately, the kind of thoughtful accuracy recommended above is not the "balance" most critics of gay curricula have in mind. Many cultural conservatives just want schools to reinforce their own religiously based views of homosexuality, which they call a "deadly lifestyle." (See box 7.21.) Their demands to present "the other side" must be rejected as strongly as schools would refuse to balance their tolerance curriculum with anti-Semitic or racist tracts.

---

**BOX 7.21    AN INDELICATE BALANCE**

#4. DEMAND FAIRNESS. If you cannot stop a pro-homosexuality event in your child's school, or pro-"gay" tolerance sessions for the school's teachers, a fallback strategy is to demand that both sides of the homosexuality issue be presented. It is hard for school administrators to say that they are not promoting homosexuality if they refuse to allow teachers or students to hear the other side of the issue.

From Peter LaBarbera, "Top 10 Strategies Used by Homosexual Activists in Schools," FRC (Family Research Council) Insight Paper, November 23, 1999. [IS99F4HS.]

---

*Question 38: What role can school libraries play?*

The library is a vital student resource, particularly in schools that forbid or limit classroom instruction on gay subjects. Although some librarians encounter censorship, they generally have greater discretion in obtaining gay-related materials than teachers or counselors do.

Access and privacy concerns are central. Some students may be fearful about asking for help with this topic. Their worry may be greater in libraries that employ students as assistants. Special sensitivity and procedures are required. (See box 7.22.)

---

**BOX 7.22    GLBT LIBRARY RESOURCES:**
**MAXIMIZING ACCESSIBILITY**

- Provide private alcoves.
- Scatter gay and lesbian fiction and nonfiction throughout the collection.
- Include a range of multicultural glbt titles.
- Lend materials on an honor system.
- Put some materials in other parts of the school such as a guidance library or student resource center with open borrowing.
- Don't leave a title on a phone message or send notices on postcards.
- Replace vandalized or stolen materials quickly.
- Note: gay philanthropy may be available for purchasing or donating books and other materials.

*Question 39: Are there any subject area textbooks that already incorporate gay topics?*

Not to any meaningful degree. The gay and lesbian civil rights movement is virtually ignored in high school history texts, but AIDS sometimes is mentioned. It would be an achievement for gays to catch up with women and people of color in marginal notes and supplementary boxes. Even health texts lack substantive information. Textbook publishers understand that courageous decisions on these matters would hurt sales in most states, particularly the large states (Texas, California, and Florida) with centralized adoption committees. Just a few historically valid sentences written for a school's most mature and able students can provoke strong objection. (See appendix J.)

*Question 40: Do teachers need training to incorporate gay topics into their teaching?*

If glbt issues are to be successfully integrated in school curricula, there is no question that teachers must master both content and methodology. They should begin by examining their own attitudes toward the subject and assessing their knowledge base. Since most do not study glbt topics in college or professional schools, they must learn new material and methods to catch up with this branch of multicultural inclusion. They do not have to know everything and should welcome mutual exploration of the subject with their students, but they should know where to look for reliable answers.

Of course they need strategies to respond to student or parent discomfort and opposition. They should be prepared to answer or effectively rebuff attacks on their own sexuality, politics, motives, and morality.

*Question 41: What should be done about preservice and veteran teachers who resist professional development to prepare them for glbt curricular inclusion?*

Every teacher must be able to recognize and challenge heterosexist behaviors. To that end, antiharassment training is not optional. Some content mastery can also be required in a number of disciplines.

On the other hand, real curricular reform cannot be mandated from above. Students inevitably sense teacher discomfort with or opposition to such projects and disgruntled educators always find ways to undermine the changes. When high stakes tests and other graduation standards include a component on glbt and other diversity topics, reformers will have a big stick. During the probable long wait for that era, the carrot will have to do.

All teachers should be prepared for inclusion of glbt issues. Those who are not amenable to classroom implementation should not be forced. Others should start small, if necessary, and build support through peer persuasion, model teaching, sharing of lesson plans, and so on.

(For further reading, see appendix R.)

# Appendices

## APPENDIX A   SAFE HAVENS

### Denominations

- Metropolitan Community Church (gay founded, Protestant) (www.ufmcc.com)
- Unitarian Universalist
- United Church of Christ
- Some Episcopal, Presbyterian, Lutheran, and Methodist congregations
- Reform and Conservative Jewish

### Organizations

- Affirmation (Mormon) (www.affirmation.org)
- Al Fatiha (Muslim) (www.al-fatiha.net)
- Am Tikva (Jewish) (www.amtikva.org)
- Brethren/Mennonite Council for Lesbian and Gay Concerns (www.webcom.com/bmc)
- Dignity (Catholic) (www.dignityusa.org)
- Evangelicals Concerned (www.ecwr.org)
- Friends for Lesbian and Gay Concerns (Quaker) (www.quaker.org/flgc/)
- Gay Men's Buddhist Sangha (www.gaysangha.org)
- Integrity (Protestant) (www.integrityusa.org)
- Office of BGLT Concerns (Unitarian Universalist) (www.uua.org/obgltc)
- Seventh-Day Adventist Kinship International (www.sdakinship.org)

## APPENDIX B   RESOURCES FOR GLBT ADOLESCENTS

### Nonfiction Books

- Ellen Bass and Kate Kaufman. *Free Your Mind: The Book for Gay, Lesbian and Bisexual Youth and Their Allies*. New York: HarperCollins, 1996.
- *Bisexual Resource Guide*. Cambridge, Mass.: Bisexual Resource Center, 1999.
- Marion Dane Bauer, ed. *Am I Blue? Coming Out from the Silence*. New York: HarperTrophy, 1995.
- Clifford Chase, ed. *Queer 13: Lesbian and Gay Writers Recall Seventh Grade*. New York: Rob Weisbach Books, 1998.
- Mary L. Gray. *In Your Face—Stories from the Lives of Queer Youth*. Binghamton, N.Y.: Haworth Press, 1999.
- Ann Heron, ed. *Two Teenagers in 20: Writings by Gay and Lesbian Youth*. Los Angeles: Alyson Publications, 1995.
- Michael J. S. Maher. *Being Gay and Lesbian in a Catholic High School: Beyond the Uniform*. Binghamton, N.Y.: Harrington Park Press, 2001.
- Eric Marcus. *What If Someone I Know Is Gay? Answers to Questions about Gay and Lesbian People*. New York: Price Stern Sloan, 2000.
- Kirk Read. *How I Learned to Snap: A Small Town Coming of Age and Coming Out Story*. Athens, Ga.: Hill Street Press, 2001.
- Amy Sonnie, ed. *Revolutionary Voices: A Multicultural Queer Youth Anthology*. Los Angeles: Alyson Publications, 2000.

### Magazines

- *Curve* <www.curvemag.com>—lesbian (older teen to adult)
- *Joey* <www.joeymag.com>—teen male
- *QvMagazine* <www.qvmagazine.com>—for English-speaking gay Latinos (older teen to adult)
- *XY* <www.xy.com>—teen male

### Films

- *As If It Matters*—six stories beneath the surface—created for youth by nine GLBT and straight ally youth. Deals with homophobia, cultural acceptance, body image, relationships, and labels. (22 min.) (GSA Network, 160 14th St., San Francisco, CA 94103)
- *I Just Want to Say*—tennis champion Martina Navratilova hosts a discussion of the antigay climate faced by youth in schools. (1998, 15 min.) (1-800-247-6553)

- *I Know Who I Am . . . Do You?*—documentary featuring Black and Latino Gay and Lesbian youth successfully reaching their goals despite issues of discrimination (1998, 10 min.) (1-800-247-6553)
- *In Other Words*—explores the impact of homophobia on a group of young people who speak courageously about their fears, concerns, anger, and pain. (National Film Board of Canada) (2001, 25 min.) (1-800-247-6553)
- *In the Life: Educational Special Edition—Gay and Lesbian Youth*—eight separate stories, focusing on issues confronting gay and lesbian youth. (2000, 85 min.) (1-800-247-6553)
- *Just Call Me Kade*—portrait of a 14-year-old transgendered youth who gets support from family and friends throughout his transition. (2001, 26 min.)
- *One of Them*—discussion-starter drama for high school students that follows the story of a teenager who learns her best friend is gay. (National Film Board of Canada) (2001, 25 min.) (1-800-247-6553)
- *Out for a Change: Addressing Homophobia in Women's Sports*—exposes the impact of homophobia on all women athletes. (28 min.) (www.Unlearning Homophobia.com)
- *Out! Making Schools Safe for Gay Teens*—a two-video program for educators and teens that promotes safer schools. (1999, 42 min. for educators and 26 min. for students) (1-800-247-6553)
- *Outside the Lines: The World of the Gay Athlete*—the journeys of two students struggling to compete as openly gay athletes in climates that are alternately hostile and welcoming. (2000, 17 min.) (1-800-247-6553)
- *Prom Fight: The Marc Hall Story*—wanting to bring his boyfriend to the prom, a young Canadian gay man gets community support. (2002, 60 min.)
- *SPEAK UP! Improving the Lives of Gay, Lesbian, Bisexual, & Transgendered Youth*—how glbt students and allies have made schools safer and more welcoming. (2002, 30 min.) (Media Education Foundation: 1-800-897-0089)
- *Straight from the Heart*—parents' journeys to a new understanding of their lesbian and gay children. (1994, 24 min.) (www.UnlearningHomophobia.com)
- *Youth Out Loud! Addressing Lesbian, Gay, Bisexual and Transgender Youth Issues in Our Schools*—chronicles the activism of several high school students working for change from local school district policies to state and federal laws. (2000, 46 min.) (1-800-247-6553)

## Telephone Numbers and Internet Sites

- GAPA—Gay Asian Pacific Alliance <www.gapa.org>
- Gay Christians Teen Resources <www.gaychristians.org/teens.htm>
- Gay, Lesbian, Bisexual and Transgender Helpline: 617-267-9001 (toll-free 888-340-4528) and Peer Listening Line: 617-267-2535 (toll-free 800-399-PEER)

- GLBT Youth of Color <www.youthresource.com/community/yoc/index.cfm>
- Hetrick-Martin Institute—New York City glbt youth shelter and wellness center <www.hmi.org>
- Keshet—Jewish youth (keshetyouth@yahoogroups.com)
- Lavender Youth Recreation and Information Center, San Francisco <www.lyric.talkline.info@tlg.net>
- LLEGO—The National Latino/a GLBT Organization <www.llego.org>
- Mermaids—Family support group for children and teenagers with gender identity issues <mermaids.freeuk.com>
- National Coalition for Gay, Lesbian, Bisexual & Transgender Youth <www.outproud.org>
- Oasis Magazine—for queer and questioning youth <www.oasismag.com>
- P.E.R.S.O.N. Project <www.youth.org/loco/PERSONProject>
- Sexual Minority Youth Assistance League, Washington, D.C. <www.smyal.org>
- trans*topia—Transgender youth resource area of Advocates for Youth (see <www.youthresource.com>)
- Trevor Project—24-hour national toll-free suicide hotline for gay and questioning youth (1-800-850-8078)
- Trikone—GLBT South Asians <www.trikone.org>
- White Ribbon Campaign—Japanese Resources <www.wrcjp.org/yourself.html>

## Online Communities

- Gay Teen Meeting Place <http://gayteenmeeting.tripod.com>
- WEBRINGS—Youth Resource, connecting with other glbt youth across the Internet <www.youthresource.com/community/webrings/index.cfm>
- Young Gay America <www.younggayamerica.com>
- Youth Guardian Services <www.youth-guard.org>
- Youth Zone <http://content.gay.com/people/youth_zone>

## Health Resources

- Coalition for Positive Sexuality—teen safer sex ed <www.positive.org>
- The National Clearinghouse for Alcohol and Drug Information, "A Provider's Introduction to Substance Abuse Treatment for Lesbian, Gay, Bisexual, and Transgender Individuals" (free, call 1-800-729-6686, order #BKD392)
- "Reflections on Body Image and Queer Identity" <www.youthresource.com/ourlives/bodyimage/index.cfm>
- Sex, Etc.—by and for teens <www.sxetc.org>

- Smoking cessation information for glbt youth, from Tobacco Education for Gay and Lesbian Youth (TEGLY), Boston, Mass. (Dan Aguillar: 617-585-7548), and from the National Youth Advocacy Coalition Tobacco Control and Prevention Youth Advisory Council (202-319-7596) <www.nyacyouth.org>
- YouthHIV—for youth living with HIV/AIDS <www.youthhiv.org>

## APPENDIX C    RESOURCES FOR FAMILIES

PFLAG (Parents, Friends, and Families of Lesbians and Gays: www.pflag.org), a national and local organization working to foster acceptance, reconciliation, and pride within families.

### Films

- *All God's Children*—sexual orientation analyzed by African American politicians, religious leaders, academics, family members, and activists (1996, 26 min.). Includes a classroom study guide. <www.UnlearningHomophobia. com> or 1-800-343-5540
- *De Colores*—a bilingual documentary about how Latino families are replacing homophobia with love and tolerance. (28 min.) <www.Unlearning Homophobia.com>
- *I Exist*—lives of lesbian and gay people of Middle Eastern cultures living in the United States. (56 min.) <www.UnlearningHomophobia.com>

### Books

- *Beloved Daughter*—letters from Chinese mothers, fathers, brothers, and sisters to their lesbian/bisexual daughters/sisters. (Contact: maplbn@labrys.org or MAPLBN, c/o Hanna Lu, 3103 Shelter Creek Lane, San Bruno, CA 94066)
- *Coming Out, Coming Home: Asian and Pacific Islander Family Stories*—API-PFLAG Family Project, PO Box 640233, San Francisco, CA 94164, 415-921-8850 (voicemail box #2) or e-mail apipflag@aol.com
- *Conversaciones: Relatos por Padres y Madres de Hijas Lesbianas y Hijos Gay*—Spanish-language coming out book for families of lesbians and gay men. Mariana Romo-Carmona, ed. (San Francisco: Cleis Press, 2001)
- Rinna Riesenfeld, *Papa, Mama, soy gay* (Mexico: Editorial Grijalbo, 2000)—A Spanish-language guide for parents.

### Support Groups—African American

- Family Reunion—sponsor: PFLAG Detroit, 313-527-7955 <pflagdetroit@cs.com>
- For Those We Love—sponsor: Metro-D.C. PFLAG, 202-638-3852 <forthosewelove@aol.com>
- Obsidian—Columbus, Ohio, 614-463-1183

## Support Groups—Catholic

- Catholic Parents Network, St. Francis Chapel and City Ministry Center, 58 Weybosset St., Providence, RI 02903, 401-331-6510, ext. 137

# APPENDIX D   RESOURCES FOR GAY FAMILIES AND THEIR SCHOOLS

## Organizations and Websites

- Alternative Family Institute—nonprofit counseling agency for glbt individuals, couples, and families. <www.altfamily.org>
- Children Of Lesbians And Gays Everywhere (COLAGE)—for children of glbt parents. 2300 Market St. #165, San Francisco, CA 94114. <*www.colage.org*> 202-583-8029
- Family Pride Canada <http://familypride.uwo.ca>
- Family Pride Coalition—for glbt parents and families. <www.familypride.org>
- Human Rights Campaign FamilyNet <www.hrc.org/familynet/index.asp>
- In the Family—online magazine for glbt families. <www.inthefamily.com>
- TransFamily of Cleveland—global resources for transgendered individuals and families. <www.transfamily.org>

## Print

- Gay Parenting Magazine <*www.gayparentmag.com/*>

# APPENDIX E   LEGAL RESOURCES

*A Guide to Effective Statewide Laws/Policies: Preventing Discrimination against GLBT Students in K-12 Schools*, by Lambda Legal Defense and Education Fund and GLSEN. Contact: David Buckel, 212-809-8585, ext. 212

# APPENDIX F   GSA RESOURCES

"Courtyard" (GSA Network Web Newsletter), Massachusetts Governor's Commission on GLBT Youth <www.state.ma.us/gcgly/newslet>

Gay-Straight Alliance Network, Carolyn Laub, Executive Director, 160 14th Street, San Francisco, CA 94103, 415-552-4229, carolyn@gsanetwork.org <www.gsanetwork.org>

GLSEN Student Organizing Department, 121 West 27th St., Suite 804, New York, NY 10001, 212-727-0135 <www.glsen.org>
See: GSA activities in "Jump-Start" kits, gsa journal ideas, etc.

## APPENDIX G    WHAT ONE TEACHER CAN DO—A CHECKLIST

1. Inform yourself about gay/lesbian/bisexual people and about homophobia.
   *LOW RISK*
   - Learn about gay/lesbian history, culture and current concerns by reading books, journals, and periodicals.
   *SOME RISK*
   - Attend gay/lesbian film series or lectures.
   - Attend a meeting of a gay/lesbian organization.
   - Attend an "allies" meeting (e.g., PFLAG).
   - Have conversations with openly gay/lesbian people.
   *GREATER RISK*
   - Engage heterosexual people, including your family and friends, in discussions of homosexuality/homophobia.
2. Create a safe and equitable classroom.
   *LOW RISK*
   - Change your assumption that everyone is heterosexual unless they tell you otherwise.
   - Use inclusive language that *implicitly* allows for gay/lesbian possibilities (e.g., "parent" rather than "mother" or "father"; "spouse" rather than "wife" or "husband"; "date" rather than "boyfriend" or "girlfriend").
   *SOME RISK*
   - Challenge homophobic language and name-calling.
   - Put up gay/lesbian-friendly posters, pictures or signs.
   - If you are heterosexual, don't be quick to inform others of your heterosexuality. Ask what they might think if you told them you were gay or lesbian.
   *GREATER RISK*
   - Be clear about your willingness to support gay/lesbian students.
   - Use language that *explicitly* allows for gay/lesbian possibilities (e.g., "Emily Dickinson and her boy- or girl-friend").
   - Invite gay/lesbian speakers to your classroom.
   - Use gay/lesbian curriculum.
   - If you are gay/lesbian/bisexual, come out to your students.
3. Create a safe and equitable school.
   *LOW RISK*
   - Be a role model of acceptance.

*SOME RISK*
- Challenge name-calling and harassment.
- Work to establish policies protecting gay/lesbian students from harassment, violence, and discrimination.
- Call for the inclusion of gays, lesbians, and bisexuals in diversity presentations.
- Work to form a gay/straight alliance and/or support group for gay/lesbian students.
- Call for faculty and staff training in gay/lesbian youth issues (including crisis intervention and violence prevention).
- Call for counseling services for gay/lesbian/bisexual youth and their parents.

*GREATER RISK*
- Invite gay/lesbian/bisexual and transgender speakers to your school.
- Join a gay/straight alliance.
- Call for and develop a gay/lesbian/bisexual awareness day.
- Work with the PTA and other community-based support groups regarding the educational and health needs of gay/lesbian students.
- Solicit the cooperation of gay/lesbian/bisexual alumni/ae in motivating the school to meet the needs of students who have succeeded them.
- Call for faculty training in gay/lesbian studies.
- Encourage colleagues to develop and use gay/lesbian curriculum.
- If you are gay/lesbian/bisexual, come out to the school community.

## APPENDIX H    AB 537 RECOMMENDATIONS

- Ensure that all school personnel are informed of the provisions of AB 537 and that all district and site personnel are trained in the law's requirements.
- Develop and provide guidelines for students about their rights and responsibilities related to AB 537. Support student participation in preventing harassment, violence, and discrimination on the basis of actual or perceived sexual orientation and gender identity.
- Ensure that exemplary educational resources used to eliminate discrimination, harassment, and hate-motivated violence based on actual or perceived sexual orientation and gender identity are identified and developed for use in California schools.
- Integrate methods to monitor compliance with AB 537 into existing educational compliance systems and develop additional systems to support compliance.
- Seek resources to develop a public information campaign to promote awareness of AB 537 and educate school board members, district administrators, certified and classified staff members, parents/guardians, community

members, students, and businesses regarding the purpose, protections, and benefits of AB 537.

- Create a permanent advisory committee to review policy, legal compliance, training, resources, and data issues, and to provide suggestions on revisions incorporating AB 537 requirements, issues, and concerns into curricular standards.
- Request the legislature to appropriate additional resources for civil rights compliance and training related to AB 537 and for a full-time staff position to assist school districts with AB 537 compliance requirements.
- Acknowledge lesbian, gay, bisexual, and transgender historical figures and related events, concepts, and issues in the revisions of content standards and curriculum frameworks, when appropriate. Identify and expand the available lesbian, gay, bisexual, and transgender resources for school library materials.
- Propose legislative or budget language to fund research of promising programs preventing discrimination, harassment, and violence based on actual or perceived sexual orientation and gender identity and to fund replication of effective models.
- Modify existing data gathering systems to provide information on the prevalence in schools of threats, harassment, or violence against students based on sexual orientation or gender identity.
- Charge the permanent advisory committee with developing further recommendations that specifically protect the rights of transgender students in California public schools.
- Recommend that the California State Board of Education revise its policy on Hate-Motivated Violence [to incorporate the provisions of AB 537].

## APPENDIX I   REDUCING ANTIGAY BIAS—PART OF THE MISSION

- Educators for Social Responsibility <www.esrnational.org>
- Facing History and Ourselves <www.facinghistory.org>
- National Center for Hate Crimes Prevention <www.edc.org/HHD/hatecrime/id1.htm>
- National Conference for Community and Justice (NCCJ), formerly the National Conference of Christians and Jews <www.nccj.org>
- Phi Delta Kappa Educational Foundation <www.pdkintl.org>
- Seeking Educational Equity and Diversity (S.E.E.D.) of the Center for Research on Women (www.wcwonline.org/seed)
- Sex Education and Information Council of the U.S. <www.siecus.org>

- Teaching Tolerance of the Southern Poverty Law Center <www.tolerance
.org>
- A World of Difference of the Anti-Defamation League of B'nai Brith
<www.adl.org/awod/awod _ institute.html>

## APPENDIX J   ATTACKS ON THE FREEDOM TO LEARN

- A conflict rages between PFLAG, who wants to donate gay-themed books
to Fairfax County high school libraries, and a right-wing group, that claims
there are already too many such books on the shelves.
- Collier County, Florida, school officials removed an advanced placement
European history textbook after a teacher objected to nine passages about
homosexuality in its 1,063-pages—particularly "graphic descriptions of alternative and aberrant sexual practices during the Renaissance." Publisher
Houghton Mifflin replaced the books with older editions.
- In Acushnet, Mass., the superintendent and the Ford Middle School principal assured the school committee that their Holocaust curriculum would
no longer mention gays in its discussion of tolerance for minority groups but
would still include Jews, other ethnic minorities, African Americans and the
physically and mentally disabled. A right-wing newsletter article had criticized gay inclusion in the curriculum.
- School board trustees in Surrey, B.C., banned for classroom use three books—
Asha's Mums; Belinda's Bouquet; and One Dad, Two Dads, Brown Dad, Blue
Dads—on the grounds that many parents, particularly religious parents,
did not want their five- and six-year-old children to learn about homosexuality.
- A California parent demanded Sesame Street not be shown in a kindergarten class because the cohabiting characters Bert and Ernie would promote
homosexuality.
- Miss America's AIDS awareness campaign was banned from some schools,
including all those in North Carolina, for using the words heterosexual and
homosexual.

## APPENDIX K   INCLUSIVE TOLERANCE CURRICULA

- "Close the Book on Hate" and other programs from the "World of Difference"
of the B'Nai Brith Anti-Defamation League
- Curricula from the Facing History and Ourselves Project
- "GLBT Rights: A Human Rights Perspective" from Amnesty International's
OutFront Project
- The S.E.E.D. Program (Seeking Educational Equity and Diversity) from the
Wellesley Center for Research on Women

- "The Shadow of Hate," "A Place at the Table," "Us and Them," and other materials from the Teaching Tolerance Project of the Southern Poverty Law Center

## APPENDIX L   SIN, SICKNESS, CELEBRATION: A CLASSROOM GUIDE FOR OUT OF THE PAST

The activities below are adapted from the video, *Out of the Past: The Struggle for Gay and Lesbian Rights in America*, dir. Jeff Dupre, Unipix Films, 1997 <www.glsen.org>.

### Michael Wigglesworth

- What exact sin did Wigglesworth confess in his diary?
- What effect might that secret sin have had on his worldview?
- What lines in his poetry hint at sexual sinning?
- Is Christian Original Sin related to sex?

### Activity: (Role-play) "Michael Wigglesworth and His Counselor"

A high school guidance counselor from 1999 is transported to seventeenth-century Cambridge, Massachusetts. He or she has a session with a tormented young Wigglesworth, who has clearly not been performing well in his studies at the Boston Latin School.

### Sarah Orne Jewett

- Why was passionate or romantic friendship between women not viewed as a threat to society before the late nineteenth century?
- How did a new branch of science help to justify the view that these women were dangerous and/or monstrous?
- Were lesbians the only women to be pathologized?
- What influence did Fields have on Jewett's life and work?

### Activity: Write a Letter

Write a letter from Annie Fields to the publisher who has just advised against including all of Jewett's letters in a posthumous book of her correspondence.

## Barbara Gittings

- How did Gittings and her associates promote the message "gay is good" at both the popular and the scientific levels?
- What other social movement inspired gays and lesbians and what tactics did gay liberation borrow from it?
- What were some of the "treatments" that were being used to cure homosexuality?
- In what ways did Gittings's work prepare the way for Kelli Peterson's campaign in Utah in the 1990s?

### *Activity: Research*

Half of the class will go to the library or the web to find out a little bit more about Gittings's organization, The Daughters of Bilitis. The other half will research its male predecessor and counterpart, The Mattachine Society. Take notes and be ready to report back to the class about what you found.

### Closing Debate

Premise: "In the year 2001 Michael Wigglesworth, Sarah Orne Jewett, and Barbara Gittings would not encounter the problems or attitudes that they faced in the seventeenth, nineteenth, or mid-twentieth centuries."

## APPENDIX M   GAY HISTORY RESOURCES

- Kevin Jennings. *Becoming Visible: A Reader in Gay and Lesbian History for High School and College Students*. Boston: Alyson Publications, 1994. The first gay/lesbian history anthology for high school students explores a number of cultures over 2000 years.
- L.A. Gay & Lesbian Center's Safe Haven Project (323-993-7671 or safehavenproject@laglc.org). Lessons from 1–5 class periods on: civil rights, the Holocaust, Manifest Destiny, and witch hunts.
- Neil Miller. *Out of the Past: Gay and Lesbian History from 1869 to the Present*. New York: Random House, 1995.
- *Out of the Past: The Struggle for Gay and Lesbian Rights in America*, video, dir. Jeff Dupre, Unipix Films, 1997. www.glsen.org
- Ntanya Lee and Alex Robertson Textor. *Transforming the Nation: Lesbian, Gay, Bisexual and Transgendered U.S. Histories, 1945–1995*. New York: School Voices Press, 1998. Presents issues of race and sexuality by decade.
- People About Changing Education (PACE, 115 West 28th St., #3-R, New York, NY 10001. 212-643-7867). *Struggle for Equality: The Lesbian and*

*Gay Community.* Stories and case studies with some New York focus to relate modern gay history to the quests for equality of women and people of
color.

## APPENDIX N    GAYS AND LESBIANS IN
## THE HOLOCAUST: RESOURCES

- *Aimeé and Jaguar*, dir. Max Färberböck, 1999.
- Gad Beck. *An Underground Life: Memoirs of a Gay Jew in Nazi Berlin.*
  Madison: University of Wisconsin Press, 1999.
- *Facing History and Ourselves: Holocaust and Human Behavior: Resource Book.*
  Brookline, Mass.: Facing History and Ourselves National Foundation, 1994.
- Heinz Heger. *The Men with the Pink Triangle: The True Life-and-Death Story
  of Homosexuals in the Nazi Death Camps.* Los Angeles: Alyson Publications,
  1980.
- *Paragraph 175*, dir. Rob Epstein and Jeffrey Friedman, 2000. Documentary.
- Lutz Van Dijk. *Damned Strong Love: The True Story of Willi G. and Stefan K.*
  New York: Henry Holt, 1995.

## APPENDIX O    STUDY QUESTIONS FOR LANGSTON
## HUGHES'S POEM, "CAFÉ: 3 A.M."

- What is a vice squad? How might they be dressed? Why might they be in a
  café at 3 A.M.?
- What are "fairies?" What other names have been used to denote such people?
- Was homosexuality a crime in the United States when Langston Hughes
  wrote this poem in 1951? Is it still?
- Give some examples of so-called degenerate kinds of people. Why would ho-
  mosexuals be considered degenerate?
- Why do you think the detectives' eyes are weary? Why sadistic? Is that a
  contradiction?
- How could the detectives know who is homosexual? Could they be wrong
  sometimes? What is entrapment?
- What three opinions about homosexuality are expressed in the second stanza?
  Is there any reason today for people to agree with one of these views?
- How is the last stanza an example of irony? Does this irony relate to question 5? Can someone be both homosexual and a police officer? How does the
  last line of the poem reinforce this irony?
- Find evidence in the poem of Hughes's own attitude toward the detectives'
  activities and toward homosexuality.

## Suggestion for Writing

Assume you are a police officer who has just arrested several people in a café for being homosexual. Write an entry in your personal diary.

## APPENDIX P    FILMS FOR HIGH SCHOOL AUDIENCES

- *Beautiful Thing*, dir. Hettie Macdonald, 1996. Two English boys fall in love, despite poverty and family violence.
- *Better Than Chocolate*, dir. Anne Wheeler, 1999. Visiting mom discovers daughter's lesbian life and is won over in sit-com style.
- *Boys Don't Cry*, dir. Kimberly Pierce, 1999. Based on the actual murder of a working-class, transgendered adolescent.
- *The Edge of 17*, dir. David Moreton, 1999. Ohio high school boy's coming out story is sensitive and authentic.
- *Get Real*, dir. Simon Shore, 1999. British high school boy falls in love with closeted classmate.
- *The Incredibly True Adventures of Two Girls in Love*, dir. Maria Maggenti, 1995. Romance of two high school seniors of different classes and races.
- *Ma Vie en Rose*, dir. Alain Berliner, 1997. Young Belgian boy's cross-dressing leads to parental acceptance.
- *The Truth about Jane*, Lifetime Network Movie and Starlight Signature Series, 2000. Adolescent lesbian and her family come to love one another.
- *Wild Reeds*, dir. André Téchiné, 1995. The evolving relationships and sexualities of three French adolescents, gay and straight, at the end of the Algerian war.

For further titles, see Don Lort, *Coming of Age Movie & Video Guide*, v. 1, 1997, and Brandon Lacey, *Coming of Age Movie & Video Guide*, v. 2, 2001 <http://companionpress.com>.

## APPENDIX Q    SOME RESOURCES FOR ELEMENTARY SCHOOLS

### For Ages 4–8

- Bobbie Combs. *A B C, A Family Alphabet Book*. Ridley Park, Penn.: Two Lives Publishing, 2001.
- Bobbie Combs. *1 2 3, A Family Counting Book*. Ridley Park, Penn.: Two Lives Publishing, 2001.
- Tomie De Paola. *Oliver Button Is a Sissy*. New York: Harcourt, 1979.

- Barbara Lynn Edmonds. *Mama Eat Ant, Yuck!* Eugene, Oreg.: Barby's House Books, 2000.
- Rosamund Elwin. *Asha's Mums.* London: Women's Press, 2000.
- Harvey Fierstein. *The Sissy Duckling.* New York: Simon and Schuster, 2002.
- Sol Gordon. *All Families Are Different.* Amherst, N.Y.: Prometheus Books, 2000.
- Eric Hoffman. *Best Best Colors.* St. Paul, Minn.: Redleaf Press, 1999 (in English and Spanish).

## For Ages 9–12

- Lois Abramchik. *Is Your Family Like Mine?* Brooklyn, N.Y.: Open Heart Open Mind, 1996.
- Leslea Newman. *Gloria Goes to Gay Pride.* Boston: Alyson Publications, 1991.
- Performance book: Norma Bowles and Mark E. Rosenthal, eds. *Cootie Shots: Theatrical Inoculations against Bigotry for Children, Parents and Teachers.* New York: Theatre Communications Group, 2001. Plays, songs, poems, and interactive performance pieces.
- Photo book: Gigi Kaeser. "Love Makes a Family: Living in Lesbian and Gay Families." Amherst: University of Massachusetts Press, 1999. Portraits of thirty families with accompanying texts. Two editions: grades K–6 and older student–adult.

## Films

- *Both My Moms Are Named Judy, Children of Lesbians and Gays Speak Out*—interviews with children (ages 7–11) who have lesbian and gay parents. (Lesbian and Gay Parents Association, 1994, 11 min.) (800-247-6553)
- *Oliver Button Is a Star*—animation, news stories, classroom footage, songs, and interviews celebrate men and women who break gender stereotypes. (PBS, Dan Hunt, producer, 2001, 60 min.) (www.oliverbuttonisastar.com)
- *Our House*—children of five diverse families encounter varied reactions to their parents' sexual orientation. (Sugar Pictures, 1999, 56 min.) (800-723-5522)
- *Sticks and Stones*—kids with same-sex parents discuss peers' name-calling. (National Film Board of Canada, 27 min.) (Grades 3–7) (800-542-2164)
- *That's a Family*—gay and lesbian families in the context of other family differences. (Women's Educational Media, 2000, 30 min.) (415-641-4616)

## For Teachers and Parents

- Jean M. Baker. *How Homophobia Hurts Children: Nurturing Diversity at Home, at School, and in the Community.* Binghamton, N.Y.: Harrington Park Press, 2002.
- *Preventing Prejudice: Lesbian Gay Bisexual Transgender Lesson Plan Guide for Elementary School.* Women's Educational Media <www.womedia.org> (415-641-4616)
- *"What Does Gay Mean?" How to Talk with Kids about Sexual Orientation and Prejudice.* National Mental Health Association <www.nmha.org/whatdoes gaymean> (800-969-6642).

## APPENDIX R   SUGGESTIONS FOR FURTHER READING

### Chapter 1: Homophobia and Heterosexism

- Warren J. Blumenfeld, ed. *Homophobia: How We All Pay the Price.* Boston: Beacon Press, 1992.
- John D'Emilio. *Sexual Politics, Sexual Communities: The Making of a Homosexual Minority in the United States 1940–1970.* Chicago: University of Chicago Press, 1983.
- Lilian Faderman. *Odd Girls and Twilight Lovers: A History of Lesbian Life in Twentieth Century America.* New York: Penguin Books, 1991.
- Byrne R. S. Fone. *Homophobia: A History.* New York: Metropolitan Books, 2000.
- Pat Griffin. *Strong Women, Deep Closets: Lesbians and Homophobia in Sport.* Champaign, Ill.: Human Kinetics Publishers, 1998.
- David M. Halperin. *One Hundred Years of Homosexuality.* New York: Routledge, 1990.
- Gregory M. Herek, ed. *Stigma and Sexual Orientation: Understanding Prejudice against Lesbians, Gay Men, and Bisexuals.* Thousand Oaks, Calif.: Sage Publications, 1998.
- Michael S. Kimmel. *The Gendered Society.* New York: Oxford University Press, 2000.
- M. E. Kite. "When Perceptions Meet Reality: Individual Differences in Reactions to Lesbians and Gay Men." In Beverly Greene and Gregory M. Herek, eds., *Vol 1. Lesbian and Gay Psychology: Theory, Research, and Clinical Applications.* Thousand Oaks, Calif.: Sage Publications, 1994.
- Richard D. Mohr. "Gay Basics: Some Questions, Facts, and Values." In Robert M. Baird and Stuart E. Rosenbaum, eds., *Bigotry Prejudice and Hatred: Definitions, Causes and Solutions.* Buffalo: Prometheus Books, 1992, 167–82.
- Richard Mohr. "The Thing of It Is: Some Problems with Models for the Social Construction of Homosexuality." In Richard D. Mohr, *Gay Ideas: Outing and Other Controversies.* Boston: Beacon Press, 1992, 221–42.

- D. J. Parrott, H. E. Adams, and A. Zeichner. "Homophobia: Personality and Attitudinal Correlates." *Personality and Individual Differences* 32, no. 7 (2002): 1269–78.
- David Plummer. *One of the Boys: Masculinity, Homophobia, and Modern Manhood*. New York: Harrington Park Press, 1999.
- Victor J. Seidler. "Reason, Desire and Male Sexuality." In Pat Caplan, ed., *The Cultural Construction of Sexuality*. New York: Tavistock Publications, 1987.

## Chapter 2: Homosexualities

- Gary David Comstock. *A Whosoever Church*. Louisville, Ky.: Westminster John Knox Press, 2001.
- Anthony R. D'Augelli and Charlotte J. Patterson. *Lesbian, Gay, and Bisexual Identities and Youth: Psychological Perspectives*. New York: Oxford University Press, 2001.
- Peter Drucker, ed. *Different Rainbows: Same-Sex Sexualities and Popular Movements in the Third Word*. London: Millivres Books, 2001.
- F. J. Floyd and T. S. Stein. "Sexual Orientation Identity Formation among Gay, Lesbian, and Bisexual Youths: Multiple Patterns of Milestone Experiences." *Journal of Research on Adolescence* 12, no. 2 (2002): 167–91.
- Beverly Greene, ed. *Ethnic and Cultural Diversity among Lesbians and Gay Men*. Thousand Oaks, Calif.: Sage Publications, 1997.
- B. Heinz, L. Gu, A. Inuzuka, and R. Zender. "Under the Rainbow Flag: Webbing Global Gay Identities." *International Journal of Sexuality and Gender Studies* 7, nos. 2–3 (2002): 107–24.
- Kevin Kumashiro. *Troubling Intersections of Race and Sexuality*. Lanham, Md.: Rowman & Littlefield Publishers, 2001.
- Kevin K. Kumashiro, ed. *Restoried Selves: Autobiographies of Queer Asian-Pacific American Activists*. New York: Harrington Park Press, 2003.
- Russell Leong, ed. *Asian American Sexualities: Dimensions of the Gay and Lesbian Experience*. New York: Routledge, 1996.
- Michael J. S. Maher Jr. *Being Gay and Lesbian in a Catholic High School: Beyond the Uniform*. New York: Harrington Park Press, 2001.
- Stephen O. Murray and Will Roscoe, eds. *Boy-Wives and Female-Husbands: Studies of African Homosexualities*. New York: St. Martin's, 2001.
- Stephen O. Murray and Will Roscoe. *Islamic Homosexualities: Culture, History, and Literature*. New York: New York University Press, 1997.
- Paula C. Rodriguez Rust, ed. *Bisexuality in the United States: A Social Science Reader*. New York: Columbia University Press, 1999.
- Ritch C. Savin-Williams. "Sexual Identity Trajectories among Sexual-Minority Youths: Gender Comparisons." *Archives of Sexual Behavior* 29, no. 6 (2000): 607–27.

- S. A. Thompson, M. Bryson, and S. de Castell. "Prospects for Identity Formation for Lesbian, Gay, or Bisexual Persons with Developmental Disabilities." *International Journal of Disability, Development and Education* 48, no. 1 (2001): 53–65.
- Ruth Vanita and Saleem Kidwai, eds. *Same-Sex Love in India: Readings from Literature and History.* New York: St. Martin's Press, 2000.
- Nicola Yelland, ed. *Gender in Early Childhood.* New York: Routledge, 1998.

## Chapter 3: Counseling GLBT Students and Their Families

- S. M. Blake, R. Ledsky, T. Lehman, C. Goodenow, R. Sawyer, and T. Hack. "Preventing Sexual Risk Behaviors among Gay, Lesbian, and Bisexual Adolescents: The Benefits of Gay-Sensitive HIV Instruction in Schools." *American Journal of Public Health* 91 (2001): 940–46.
- D. E. Bontempo and A. R. D'Augelli. "Effects of At-School Victimization and Sexual Orientation on Lesbian, Gay, or Bisexual Youths' Health Risk Behavior." *Journal of Adolescent Health* 30, no. 5 (2002): 364–74.
- D. J. Carragher and I. Rivers. "Trying to Hide: A Cross-National Study of Growing Up for Non-Identified Gay and Bisexual Male Youth." *Clinical Child Psychology and Psychiatry* 7, no. 3 (2002): 457–74. Bryan N. Cochran, Angela J. Stewart, Joshua A. Ginzler, and Ana Mari Cauce. "Challenges Faced by Homeless Sexual Minorities: Comparison of Gay, Lesbian, Bisexual, and Transgender Homeless Adolescents with Their Heterosexual Counterparts." *American Journal of Public Health* 92 (2002): 773–77.
- A. R. D'Augelli. "Mental Health Problems among Lesbian, Gay, and Bisexual Youths Ages 14 to 21." *Clinical Child Psychology and Psychiatry* 7, no. 3 (2002): 433–56.
- A. R. D'Augelli, S. L. Hershberger, and N. W. Pilkington. "Suicidality Patterns and Sexual Orientation-Related Factors among Lesbian, Gay, and Bisexual Youths." *Suicide and Life-Threatening Behavior* 31, no. 3 (2001): 250–64.
- A. R. D'Augelli, N. W. Pilkington, and S. L. Hershberger. "Incidence and Mental Health Impact of Sexual Orientation Victimization of Lesbian, Gay, and Bisexual Youths in High School." *School Psychology Quarterly* 17, no. 2 (2002): 148–67.
- Naomi Freedner, Lorraine H. Freed, Y. Wendy Yang, and S. Bryn Austin. "Dating Violence among Gay, Lesbian, and Bisexual Adolescents: Results from a Community Survey." *Journal of Adolescent Health* 31, no. 6 (2002): 469–74.
- Gilbert Herdt and Bruce Koff. *Something to Tell You: The Road Families Travel when a Child Is Gay.* New York: Columbia University Press, 2000.
- S. Bayley Imich and K. Farley. "Equalities and Gay and Lesbian Young People: Implications for Educational Psychologists." *Educational Psychology in Practice* 17, no. 4 (2001): 375–84.

- Gerald P. Mallon. *Let's Get This Straight: A Gay-and Lesbian-Affirming Approach to Child Welfare.* New York: Columbia University Press, 1999.
- Gerald P. Mallon. *Social Services with Transgendered Youth.* New York: Harrington Park Press, 2000.
- Corrine Muñoz-Plaza, Sandra Crouse Quinn, and Kathleen A. Rounds. "Lesbian, Gay, Bisexual and Transgender Students: Perceived Social Support in the High School Environment." *The High School Journal* 85, no. 4 (2002): 52–63.
- J. S. Peterson and H. Rischar. "Gifted and Gay: A Study of the Adolescent Experience." *Gifted Child Quarterly* 44, no. 4 (2000): 231–46.
- Margaret Rosario, Joyce Hunter, Shira Maguen, Marya Gwadz, and Raymond Smith. "The Coming-Out Process and Its Adaptational and Health-Related Associations among Gay, Lesbian, and Bisexual Youths: Stipulation and Exploration of a Model." *American Journal of Community Psychology* 29, no. 1 (2001): 133–60.
- Stephen T. Russell. "Queer in America: Citizenship for Sexual Minority Youth." *Applied Developmental Science* 6, no. 1 (2002): 258–63.
- S. T. Russell, B. T. Franz, and A. K. Driscoll. "Same-Sex Romantic Attraction and Experiences of Violence in Adolescence." *American Journal of Public Health* 91 (2001): 903–6.
- Stephen T. Russell and Nikki Sigler Andrews. "Adolescent Sexuality and Positive Youth Development." In Daniel F. Perkins, Lynne M. Borden, Joanne G. Keith, and Francisco A. Villarruel, eds., *Community Youth Development: Programs, Polices, and Practices.* Thousand Oaks, Calif.: Sage Publications, 2003.
- Caitlin Ryan and Donna Futterman. *Lesbian and Gay Youth: Care and Counseling.* New York: Columbia University Press, 1998.

## Chapter 4: Gay Teachers and Gay Families

- N. Anderssen, C. Amlie, and E. A. Ytterøy. "Outcomes for Children with Lesbian or Gay Parents: A Review of Studies from 1978 to 2000." *Scandinavian Journal of Psychology* 43, no. 4 (2002): 335–51.
- Virginia Casper, Steven B. Schultz, and Elaine Wickens. *Gay Parents/Straight Schools: Building Communication and Trust.* New York: Teachers College Press, 1999.
- Mark French. "In Defense of Gay and Lesbian Educators." *Principal* 81, no. 4 (2002): 66.
- Karen M. Harbeck. *Coming Out of the Classroom Closet: Gay and Lesbian Students, Teachers and Curricula.* New York: Harrington Park Press, 1992.
- Noelle Howey and Ellen Samuels, eds. *Out of the Ordinary: Essays on Growing Up with Gay, Lesbian, and Transgender Parents.* New York: St. Martin's Press, 2000.

- G. R. Janson and F. J. Steigerwald. "Family Counseling and Ethical Challenges with Gay, Lesbian, Bisexual, and Transgendered (GLBT) Clients: More Questions Than Answers." *The Family Journal: Counseling and Therapy for Couples and Families* 10, no. 4 (2002): 415–18.
- Kevin Jennings, ed. *One Teacher in 10*. Boston: Alyson Publications, 1994.
- Rita M. Kissen. *The Last Closet: the Real Lives of Lesbian and Gay Teachers*. Portsmouth, N.H.: Heinemann, 1996.
- Linda Leonard Lamme and Laurel A. Lamme. "Welcoming Children from Gay Families into Our Schools." *Educational Leadership* 59, no. 4 (December 2001/January 2002): 65–69.
- G. B. Lewis and H. E. Taylor. "Public Opinion toward Gay and Lesbian Teachers: Insights for All Public Employees." *Review of Public Personnel Administration* 21, no. 2 (2001): 133–51.
- E. F. Litton. "Voices of Courage and Hope: Gay and Lesbian Catholic Elementary School Teachers." *International Journal of Sexuality and Gender Studies* 6, no. 3 (2001): 193–205.
- Charlotte J. Patterson and Anthony R. D'Augelli, eds. *Lesbian, Gay, and Bisexual Identities in Families: Psychological Perspectives*. New York: Oxford University Press, 1998.
- James T. Sears. "Responding to the Sexual Diversity of Faculty and Students: Sexual Praxis and the Critically Reflective Administrator." In Coleen A. Capper, ed., *Educational Administration in a Pluralistic Society*. New York: State University of New York Press, 1993, 110–72.
- Fiona L. Tasker and Susan Golombok. *Growing Up in a Lesbian Family: Effects on Child Development*. New York: Guilford Press, 1997.

## Chapter 5: Effective School Reforms

- Jean M. Baker. *How Homophobia Hurts Children: Nurturing Diversity at Home, at School, and in the Community*. New York: Harrington Park Press, 2002.
- Colleen A. Capper. "Administrator Practice and Preparation for Social Reconstructionist Schooling." In Colleen A. Capper, ed., *Educational Administration in a Pluralistic Society*. Albany: State University of New York Press, 1993, 288–315.
- S. J. Ellis. "Moral Reasoning and Homosexuality: The Acceptability of Arguments about Lesbian and Gay Issues." *Journal of Moral Education* 31, no. 4 (2002): 455–67.
- P. Griffin and M. Ouellett. *Going beyond Gay-Straight Alliances to Make Schools Safe for Lesbian, Gay, Bisexual, and Transgender Students*. Amherst, Mass.: Institute for Gay and Lesbian Strategic Studies, 2002.
- Rita Kissen, ed. *Getting Ready for Benjamin: Preparing Teachers for Sexual Diversity in the Classroom*. Lanham, Md.: Rowman & Littlefield, 2002.

- Kevin K. Kumashiro. *Troubling Education: Queer Activism and Antioppressive Pedagogy*. New York: RoutledgeFalmer, 2002.
- C. Lee. "The Impact of Belonging to a High School Gay/Straight Alliance." *The High School Journal* 85, no. 3 (2002): 13–26.
- William J. Letts IV and James T. Sears, eds. *Queering Elementary Education: Advancing the Dialogue about Sexualities and Schooling*. Lanham, Md.: Rowman & Littlefield, 1999.
- J. Nicole Little. "Embracing Gay, Lesbian, Bisexual, and Transgendered Youth in School-Based Settings." *Child and Youth Care Forum* 30, no. 2 (2001): 99–110.
- Corrine Mufioz-Plaza, Sandra C. Quinn, and Kathleen A. Rounds. "Lesbian, Gay, Bisexual, and Transgender Students: Perceived Social Support in the High School." *The High School Journal* 85, no. 4 (2002): 52–63.
- Jeff Perrotti and Kim Westheimer. *When the Drama Club Is Not Enough: Lessons from the Safe Schools Program for Gay and Lesbian Students*. Boston: Beacon Press, 2001.
- K. H. Robinson and T. Ferfolja. " 'What Are We Doing This For?' Dealing with Lesbian and Gay Issues in Teacher Education." *British Journal of Sociology of Education* 22, no. 1 (2001): 121–33.
- Eric Rofes. "Rethinking Anti-Gay Harassment in Schools." *Democracy and Education* 13, no. 3 (2000): 52–59.
- Jonathan G. Silin. *Sex, Death, and the Education of Children: Our Passion for Ignorance in the Age of AIDS*. New York: Teachers College Press, 1995.
- S. Talburt and S. Steinberg, eds. *Thinking Queer: Sexuality, Culture, and Education*. New York: Peter Lang, 2000.
- Gerald Unks, ed. *The Gay Teen: Educational Practice and Theory for Lesbian, Gay, and Bisexual Adolescents*. New York: Routledge, 1995.
- J. Zine. " 'Negotiating Equity': The Dynamics of Minority Community Engagement in Constructing Inclusive Educational Policy." *Cambridge Journal of Education* 31, no. 2 (2001): 239–69.

## Chapter 6: Progress and Resistance

- S. Birden, L. L. Gaither, and S. Laird. "The Struggle over the Text: Compulsory Heterosexuality and Educational Policy." *Educational Policy* 14, no. 5 (2000): 638–63.
- Debbie Epstein, ed. *Challenging Lesbian and Gay Inequalities in Education*. Philadelphia: Open University Press, 1994.
- Debbie Epstein and Richard Johnson. *Schooling Sexualities*. Briston, Penn.: Open University Press, 1998.
- Debbie Epstein, Sandra O'Flynn, and David Telford. *Silenced Sexualities in Schools and Universities*. Stoke-on-Trent: Trentham Books Ltd., 2002.

- Didi Herman. *The Antigay Agenda: Orthodox Vision and the Christian Right.* Chicago: University of Chicago Press, 1997.
- Janice M. Irvine. *Talk about Sex: The Battle over Sex Education in the United States.* Berkeley: University of California Press, 2002.
- National PTA. "Respecting Differences Resource Guide." <www.pta.org/parentinvolvement/helpchild/respectdiff/index.asp>

## Chapter 7: Changing the Curriculum

- Christina Allan. "Poets of Comrades: Addressing Sexual Orientation in the English Classroom." *English Journal* 88, no. 6 (1999): 97–101.
- E. Atkinson. "Education for Diversity in a Multisexual Society: Negotiating the Contradictions of Contemporary Discourse." *Sex Education* 2, no. 2 (2002): 119–32.
- William J. Broz. "Defending Am I Blue." *Journal of Adolescent & Adult Literacy* 45, no. 5 (2002): 340–50.
- William J. Broz. "Hope and Irony: Annie on My Mind." *English Journal* 90, no. 6 (2001): 47.
- Betsy J. Cahill and Rachel Theilheimer. " 'Can Tommy and Sam Get Married?' Questions about Gender, Sexuality, and Young Children." *Young Children* 54, no. 1 (1999): 27–31.
- Anthony Consiglio. "Gender Identity and Narrative Truth: An Autobiographical Approach to Bias." *English Journal* 88, no. 3 (1999): 71–77.
- N. Douglas, S. Kemp, P. Aggleton, and I. Warwick. "The Role of External Professionals in Education about Sexual Orientation: Towards Good Practice." *Sex Education* 1, no. 2 (2001): 149–62.
- Greg Hamilton. "Reading Jack." *English Education* 30, no. 1 (1998): 24–43.
- Deborah Jean Kinder. "To Follow Your Heart: Coming Out through Literacy." *English Journal* 88, no. 2 (1998): 63–69.
- L. Lampela. "Lesbian and Gay Artists in the Curriculum: A Survey of Art Teachers' Knowledge and Attitudes." *Studies in Art Education* 42, no. 2 (2001): 146–62.
- J. E. Petrovic. "Promoting Democracy and Overcoming Heterosexism: And Never the Twain Shall Meet?" *Sex Education* 2, no. 2 (2002): 145–54.
- Jenifer Jasinski Schneider. "No Blood, Guns, or Gays Allowed! The Silencing of the Elementary Writer." *Language Arts* 78, no. 5 (2001): 415–25.
- Nancy Schniedewind. "Embracing the Rainbow: An Integrated Approach to Diversity Education." *Multicultural Perspectives* 3, no. 1 (2001): 23–27.
- James T. Sears. "Centering Culture: Teaching for Critical Sexual Literacy Using the Sexual Diversity Wheel." *Journal of Moral Education* 26, no. 3 (1997): 273–83.
- James T. Sears. "School Administrators as Public Intellectuals: Developing a Sexuality Curriculum in a Multicultural Society." In Sandra Tonnsen, ed.,

*What Principals Should Know About: A Primer on School Subjects*. Champaign, Ill.: Charles Thomas, 2000, 138–46.

- S. Sharpe. " 'It's Just Really Hard to Come to Terms With': Young People's Views on Homosexuality." *Sex Education* 2, no. 3 (2002): 263–77.
- Mikki Shaw. "What's Hate Got to Do with It? Using Film to Address Hate Crimes in the School Community." *English Journal* 87, no. 2 (1998): 44–50.
- *Social Education and Sexual Identity*. Special section of *Theory and Research in Social Education* 30, no. 2 (2002): 178–319.

# Index

# About the Author

**Arthur Lipkin,** an associate editor of the *Journal of Gay and Lesbian Issues in Education*, is a former instructor at the Harvard Graduate School of Education. He directed the Safe Colleges Program of the Massachusetts Governor's Commission on Gay and Lesbian Youth and taught in the Cambridge public schools for twenty years. He is also the author of *Understanding Homosexuality, Changing Schools* (1999).